Western Riding

WESTERN RIDING

by

Charlene Strickland

A STOREY PUBLISHING BOOK

STOREY

Storey Communications, Inc.
Schoolhouse Road
Pownal, Vermont 05261

*The mission of Storey Communications is to serve our customers
by publishing practical information that encourages personal independence
in harmony with the environment.*

Edited by Kathleen Bond Borie and Elizabeth McHale
Cover and text design by Cynthia McFarland
Text production by Cynthia McFarland and Susan Bernier
Production and editorial assistance by Meredith Maker
Front cover photograph by Jeff Barnes, National Barrel Horse Association
Back cover photographs by Jeff Kirkbride Photography (top), Louise Whitney (center),
    and Jeff Vanuga (bottom)
Drawings by Elayne Sears
Photographs by Charlene Strickland unless otherwise credited
Indexed by Northwind Editorial Services

Printed in the United States by R.R. Donnelley
First Printing, June 1995

Library of Congress Cataloging-in-Publication Data

Strickland, Charlene.
     Western riding / Charlene Strickland.
          p.   cm.
     "A Storey Publishing book."
     Includes index.
     ISBN 0-88266-890-0
     1. Western riding.   I. Title.
SF309.3.S83   1995
798.2—dc20   95-2150
                  CIP

CONTENTS

1

Introduction to Western Riding

Partners — horse and rider — can share the freedom and adventure of the Old West. Whether it's a Pinto, golden Palomino, or Appaloosa, a sturdy horse can transport the equestrian into a uniquely American sport.

Seated in a Western saddle, you can mosey along a desert path, lope across a mountain meadow, or gallop your horse pell-mell down a hill in pursuit of a wily steer. Choose your level of excitement; when you grab the horn and swing up into the saddle, you relive the nostalgia of riding the range.

Like the West itself, riding perpetuates the traditions of a romantic past, yet it is a contemporary recreation. The horse keeps the sport vibrant and real, not artificial or pretentious.

You can pursue many types of Western riding. Even today, you can roam the same country that the frontiersmen and pioneers traveled. You can escape into the plain, down-in-the-dirt action that is as rustic as the lives of Jesse James and Billy the Kid were. If you just want to ponder the solitary pleasures of the trail, you can listen to the creak of saddle leather and the steps of your horse. If competition is in your blood, you can choose your arena — from the trail to horse shows to cattle-roping events. Whatever you choose, all trace their origins to the legendary American cowboy.

With the help of his horse, the cowboy continually tested his competence in handling livestock.

THE LEGEND OF THE COWBOY

Around the world, equestrians admire the cowboy as a heroic figure. He lived a rigorous lifestyle. His life was clear-cut, clean, pastoral, close to the rhythms of nature. When you think of a cowboy, you envision a set of values: independence, simplicity, courage, toughness, and grace.

The cowhand practiced these values on horseback. With his equine partner, he deftly performed physical tasks with skill. He proved himself genuinely competent at horsemanship and handling livestock — driving cattle, cutting calves, and roping steers.

That mystique continues to stir the imagination. The figure of the lean, weathered cowboy perpetuates the thrills of the American frontier. When you sit on a stock horse, you can re-enact those long, dusty days of cattle work, or display equestrian elegance in the precision of exact movements. You can share a rapture, the sense of freely riding a horse through a landscape.

Western riding gives you an escape. On a typical weekday, you wrestle with machines of all types — a toaster, a car, a microwave, a computer, a cash register. Machines force you to conform to their rules.

Dealing with a horse puts you in charge. Horses aren't robotic, and you would never treat them with a blasé attitude. Horses are delightful, unpredictable creatures that are capable of more emotional connection than you'd expect from a beast of burden.

Western riding also exposes you to risk. The cowboy accepted risk as part of his daily life, and his courage survives today in rodeo contestants. Rodeo cowboys set the style for today's Western ethic. In rodeo, athletes compete without the protective devices so prevalent in other sports. Rodeo seems to fly in the face of a society obsessed with safety precautions and the threat of litigation.

When you ride Western, you're making a statement. You choose an alternative to a lifestyle of peace and boredom. Risk appeals to you. You seek the vigor of days past and the companionship of the cowboy's most important buddy, the horse.

Anyone can emulate the cowboy's back-to-basics approach to horsemanship. Few, however, can claim to be cowboys, earning a living by working on a ranch. But, for the price of admission, you can associate with authentic cowhands on professional dude ranches. There you can rub elbows with real cowboys and cowgirls who make their living on ranches. It's a unique opportunity to learn

Western riding nurtures a proud free spirit and relies on the trust between man and horse.

the traditions of Western horsemanship from genuine horsemen. On dude ranches, cowboys and cowgirls are the mentors who communicate the traditions of Western horsemanship.

TRADITION

Western riding developed from the same foundation as other riding disciplines. European masters studied the classical principles of equitation in the sixteenth century, and their contemporaries conquered the Americas.

Spanish conquerors founded Western horsemanship in their seat and saddlery, which also influenced the military riding traditions of the world's cavalry forces. European horsemen studied horsemanship so they could wage war. Spain, France, and Italy developed similar schools of riding, all using saddles with a high pommel and cantle and long stirrups. This Moorish design held the warrior in place during long marches and the dangers of battle.

The Spanish riding style used a deep, balanced seat, similar to that practiced today at Vienna's Spanish Riding School. Riders relied on the powerful curb bit to keep the horse collected, and they used spurs with large rowels to cue the horse.

On dude ranches, cowboys and cowgirls communicate the traditions of Western horsemanship.

The goal in Western riding is graceful, unified movement at any speed.

(A rowel is a small wheel with points, attached to the shank of a spur.)

As Spain expanded its military frontiers in North America, Spaniards spread their culture throughout the American West. The vaqueros followed the traditions of the Old World, using Spanish methods of handling livestock on the vast ranches.

The vaquero evolved into the cowboy, who remained a man of the horse. Other riders also adapted European ways, riding styles, and saddlery to their needs. On the vast spaces of the frontier, horsemanship was a critical skill. The horse was necessary to the Westerner's work of expanding the frontier and establishing cattle ranches.

The horse extended man's mobility and gave individual freedom. As Easterners moved West, through the Great Plains toward the Great American Desert, they relied on equine power to traverse geographical barriers. Horses were used in exploration, hunting, cattle drives, war, and all types of commerce. Horsemen and their horses built the West.

HORSEMANSHIP TODAY

Western riding has progressed a long way since early cattle drives. Today the masters blend the ways of the West with classic equitation and aim for a smooth horse that performs without resistance.

The archetypal cowboy was supremely comfortable on a horse. Like all expert horsemen, he demonstrated an elite skill. Today's horseman maintains that proud, free spirit and nurtures the trust between himself and his horse.

The wise horseman conserves his mount's energy. He moves in a low-key manner, quietly telling his horse what to do. He knows when to take command, such as telling his horse to gallop to head off a determined steer. He also senses when to let the horse choose its moves, such as when walking slowly on a treacherous mountain trail.

Horse and rider move in harmony, as closely attuned as a dressage pair. Yet unlike the dressage rider who controls his horse with constant contact with reins, the Western rider can make his horse do his bidding on a loose rein.

Ten-year-old Ashley Tootle winning the National Barrel Horse Association Youth Championship.

Sport	Description	Appeal
TRAIL RIDING	Riding horse along a path Can be informal, or organized for a group	Slow-paced Pleasant
DISTANCE RIDING	Riding a marked trail, judged by (1) horse's condition at finish, (2) time, and (3) horsemanship	Competitive situation Allows you to prove your horsemanship in preparing the horse and conquering the course
SHOW RIDING	Prepares horse and rider to compete in association's events	Show off horse and horsemanship Dress up Win prizes
HALTER CLASSES	Show horse of any age in breed shows	Exhibit your animal Win prizes
REINING	Ride a pattern at speed	Follow a precise pattern Win prizes
CUTTING	Sort through a herd of cattle, separate a cow, and prevent it from rejoining the herd	Thrill of riding a horse with cow sense Win prizes
ROPING	Run after a calf or steer, and rope it	Enjoy the teamwork as your horse positions you so you can rope the cow easily Win prizes
TEAM PENNING	You and 2 other riders separate 3 steers from a herd and chase them into a pen	Enjoy the teamwork of your horse and your fellow riders

Horsewoman Terry Berg has compared the Western horse to his English counterpart. "People think because you use a bigger bit, you're cruel. But all you have to do is ride a horse that gives lightly when all you've done is barely pick up the reins. You may not even take the slack out of the reins. Your hand comes up slightly, and the horse responds. There's nothing like it — it's fabulous."

With the effective touch of the rein, the horse obeys every command. He immediately adjusts speed or direction or impulsion at the rider's slightest cue.

The movement is graceful, unified, and coordinated at any speed. The rider doesn't display emotion as he communicates his wishes. The horse responds to gentle handling, accelerating with quiet excitement and returning to a calm state.

Riding is a skill, and horsemanship is a special relationship between two partners. The horse teaches the rider, and the rider teaches the horse. When they become attuned, they reach the ultimate — the horse becomes an extension of the horseman.

In past centuries and cultures, this talent was passed down through generations. A horseman was born into it, and he naturally absorbed knowledge from mentors both human and equine. Chances are, you didn't grow up riding horses every day, sitting in front of Dad's saddle or piloting your own pony. Even if you were not "born in the saddle," you can consciously study to gain physical skill and the horseman's mental attitude. Today you can gain this expertise, whether or not you live in the West.

This handbook introduces you to all facets of Western riding. It communicates the excitement of casual trail rides, the challenge of show-ring maneuvers, and the fast-paced action of working stock. The information in this book assumes you're an amateur, seeking a leisure activity as well as the sport's physical and spiritual pleasures.

Western disciplines vary, and most riders specialize. Few horses and riders sucessfully cross over into different areas, although you and your horse may enjoy the variety of other activities.

This book will guide you from preparation to performance of each Western riding discipline. You'll learn the basics as well as how to refine your horsemanship skills.

Authorities across the United States, from Florida to California, have contributed their advice and offered strategies for success. Champions in every discipline, judges, and proficient riders have shared their philosophies and methods. You'll find that occasionally these experts' opinions conflict, but this is the equestrian tradition — every horseman has an opinion about the "right way."

If you're new to the sport, expect months of practicing before you really know how to ride a horse and years more before you're worthy of the term *horseman.*

But first, begin by picking your partner — the Western horse.

2

Meet the Western Horse

The horse that carries you across pastures, around the show ring, or up mountainous trails reflects the characteristics of his ancestors — the horses that built the West. Sure, you can cinch up a Western saddle on an Thoroughbred, or even a European Warmblood, but these horses are not Western horses.

The Western, or stock, horse was bred to handle livestock. Horses and cattle were essential to life. Ranchers raised cattle as a source of food and sign of prosperity, and they needed stock horses to work the cattle.

The horses of the West had to outrun cattle and let the cowboy drive, rope, or drag a cow. Spanish horses, bred for the ranches and bullrings of Iberia, also worked cattle in the West. The first cowboys, the vaqueros, sought mounts with the speed and strength to handle the wild range cattle they chased across the plains.

Horses of the West also served as beasts of burden. They carried riders long distances, pulled wagons and coaches, and packed supplies and goods across the terrain. The Western horse symbolized power.

The horse made America, and the geography of the West influenced the type of horse that thrived. The Spanish conquerors of the sixteenth century brought the Barb horse to the New World. Originally from the Barbary region of North Africa, the Barb and Arabian breeds accompanied the Moors to conquer Spain. Iberian horsemen developed the Spanish Barb, horses that helped the nation conquer others around the world. These graceful horses displayed spirit and a proud carriage. The

The Spanish Barb displays sure-footedness and proud carriage. The horse's endurance and strong build make him reliable on long rides.

The Spanish Mustang preserves pure Spanish blood and is energetic and alert.

Barb influenced breeds across Europe, and even horses of the English colonists originated from Spanish blood.

The Spanish horse was an important commodity in North America. This animal was short-backed, with shorter legs than the modern Western horse. He was sure-footed and could carry his rider through the stress of battle. A durable animal, he could withstand extreme conditions. Spanish horses showed all colors, including spotted horses, buckskins, and Palominos.

Introduced to the American West around 1600, Spanish horses flourished. Their descendants were smaller, short-legged, chunky animals, fitted to enduring hard work. Ranchers and some Native Americans practiced selective breeding, but many horses ran wild. Natural selection altered these wild animals, and those that survived were adapted to tough conditions.

The horse's endurance and strong build made it reliable on long rides. The horse worked cattle on trail drives, traveling 10 to 15 miles per day. When pressed, a rider could push his horse to cover 40, 80, or as much as 100 miles a day.

A rider afoot was in great danger, so the horse was a crucial partner and the cowboy's most valued tool. On a tough mount, the cowboy was safe from wild longhorns and could control livestock.

Riders chose certain horses to handle stock. The cow horse had to have the spirit to "chouse" (round up) cattle and the speed to overtake a galloping cow. Once the horse caught up to a cow, steer, or bull, he had to display the courage to control the animal. Cowboys quickly learned that horses of Spanish heritage demonstrated more "cow sense" than animals of English descent.

Westerners favored a horse built for short bursts of speed. Its close-coupled body, heavy shoulders, powerful loin and hindquarters, and dropped-off croup gave it the conformation to dig into the ground at the takeoff. Short cannon bones and muscled forearms and stifles supported the horse's weight and made the horse look stout, and good withers held a stock saddle in place.

The stock horse weighed from 1,000 to 1,100 pounds. He was able to run, stop, and turn quickly.

With his small size and short legs, he was sure-footed on uneven terrain and had good action to move over rocks. He carried his short neck low, which allowed him to watch his footing and increase his efficient movement by reducing wind resistance.

Bred to work, the Western horse was tough, physically and mentally. He could go long distances, and he withstood strenuous, demanding work for 8 to 12 hours a day.

THE WESTERN HORSE TODAY

Western horses inherited the stamina and agility of their Spanish progenitors. Spanish blood was crossed with horses from the East, adding the influence of the English Thoroughbred. From the horses of the nineteenth century, horsemen developed specific breeds.

Among the breeds, contemporary horses for Western riding are of three basic types: the reliable trail horse, the agile ranch horse, and the pretty show horse. Each breed may include animals of all types.

The Quarter Horse type dominates. Blending the hardy Spanish cow horse with the fast, graceful Thoroughbred, the early Quarter Horse displayed heavy muscle on the forearm, shoulder, loin, hip, and gaskin. He had a small head, broad chest, deep body, and short coupling.

The Quarter Horse earned a reputation as a horse built for speed that could run and work. Some Quarter Horses worked all week and raced on the weekend. They had the stamina to travel long days and were "good keepers." The breed's calm disposition and responsive attitude helped make this horse the world's most popular breed. Its versatility has influenced Western sports, and "America's Horse" continues to win major titles in racing, rodeo contests, cutting, reining, Western pleasure, and cattle events.

Except for the Spanish Barb and Mustang, horses of other breeds strongly resemble Quarter Horses. The color breeds incorporated Quarter Horse sires and dams, and most still register animals of Quarter Horse breeding.

CHOOSING YOUR FIRST HORSE

Acquiring a new horse can mean the realization of a life-long dream. But as you search for the perfect match, keep in mind what you expect of your horse in its personality, performance, and appearance.

First and foremost, the type of horse you choose depends on the type of riding you plan to do. If you're just starting out, you want to pick the right partner for your riding career. Take the time to define your goals and shop wisely.

Try to rate a candidate objectively, without falling in love with a horse that might not fit your needs. If you're focusing on a certain riding discipline, pick a horse that matches that style. Don't choose one that's unfit for the type of riding you plan to do and then try to make him succeed.

In fact, Terry Berg advises to "go with what the horse is built to do. Just because you want him to

If you're new to riding, you'll benefit by taking lessons from a qualified instructor.

BREED COMPARISONS

Breed	Physical Characteristics	Colors	Attributes	Association
QUARTER HORSE	Powerful loins and croup Sloping croup Stocky legs 15 hands 900–1,200 lbs.	Bay, brown, black, gray, palomino, dun [AQHA limits the extent of white markings. If horse has too much white for AQHA registration, he's a "cropout" and can be registered with APHA.]	Speed Calm disposition Agility Sure-footedness Rugged constitution	American Quarter Horse Association
SPANISH BARB	Clean, well-defined head Deep, strong neck, chest, and body Average to short back Rounded croup and hip Proud carriage 14.2 hands 850–1,000 lbs.	All colors except gray or white	Stamina Agility Intelligence	Spanish Barb Breeders Association
SPANISH MUSTANG	Sturdy, wiry, smooth body with long, smooth muscling Deep heart girth Short back Strong legs and feet Convex facial profile Arched neck Full mane and tail 13.2–15 hands 750–1,000 lbs.	Bay, chestnut, black, Appaloosa, dun, grulla, pinto, Medicine Hat, War Bonnet	Descendant of the Spanish horse, preserves pure Spanish blood Toughness, energy, endurance Naturally gaited Alert, even disposition	Spanish Mustang Registry

Appaloosa

Paint

Breed	Color/Coat Pattern	Bloodlines	Association
APPALOOSA	Blanket, spots, blanket with spots, roan, roan blanket, roan blanket with spots Mottled skin White sclera Vertical stripes on hooves	One parent registered with ApHC Other parent may be AQHA, Thoroughbred, Arabian	Appaloosa Horse Club (ApHC)
PAINT	Overo Tobiano Tovero No Appaloosa coat patterns	Both parents registered with APHA (or the former American Paint Quarter Horse Association or American Paint Stock Horse Association), AQHA, or Thoroughbred	American Paint Horse Association (APHA)
PINTO	Overo Tobiano Coat pattern meets specific color requirements White and colored markings are ideally 50–50 proportions No Appaloosa coat patterns	Parents registered with PtHA or approved outcross (AQHA, APHA, Thoroughbred, Standardbred)	Pinto Horse Association (PtHA)
PALOMINO	Golden coat with mane and tail a minimum of 85% white hairs No dun factor markings or body spots	Parents registered with PHBA or one PHBA parent and other AQHA, Thoroughbred, Morgan, Arabian, Part-Arabian	Palomino Horse Breeders Association (PHBA)
BUCKSKIN	Buckskin, dun, red dun, grulla, brindle dun Dun factor markings: dorsal stripe, leg barring/mottling, shoulder stripe, rib barring, neck stripe/patches, face mask/cobwebbing, ear frames/barring, manemane/tail frosting	Any stock horse meeting color requirements	American Buckskin Horse Association (ABHA) International Buck-skin Horse Association (IBHA)

Pinto

Palomino

Buckskin

be a Western Pleasure horse doesn't mean that's what he should do. A horse that isn't a natural mover for pleasure may be a good reining or roping horse."

Don't be afraid to enlist help to find your equine partner, ideally a mentor who can advise you. On your own, you can make a lot of mistakes. An authority can help steer you in the right direction and avoid frustrations. For example, you may envision buying a mare and raising a champion foal, but this challenges even the professionals. Don't even consider a stallion, which is a horse only for the expert horseman. A gelding is the most realistic choice for a first horse.

Be sure you find a qualified expert to advise you. A 4-H horse leader or college horsemanship instructor are ideal choices. You can also hire a professional to help you find and start with a new horse (be sure to check the horseman's credentials thoroughly). Hiring a trainer is like contracting for any other service. You make a list of local candidates who might meet your needs and then inquire about their qualifications. Talk to riders you know, breed and show officials, tack shops, feed stores, breeders, or even other trainers. No doubt you'll hear a range of opinions and individual viewpoints.

When you're ready to meet the trainer, introduce yourself and explain your goals. You're hiring her to perform a service, so you conduct an interview. Find out if this person wants you as a prospective customer and if your personalities mesh.

If you are new to horseback riding, you would benefit from taking riding lessons from an instructor. This professional can also help you find your own horse. You would learn the basics and gain confidence by riding school (lesson) horses, which have the temperament to tolerate beginners. You could spend several months or even a year developing horsemanship skills before you buy your own horse.

When you try out a horse, let the horse tell you about himself. Your friendship begins with these first impressions, so allow the animal to express his attributes through his body language. Observe how he reacts to all handling, on the ground and under

saddle, and make a list of positive and negative points.

The horse's personality is key. To move in accord, the two of you must avoid personality clashes. Most people look for a tranquil companion, one that meets the description of "gentle." If you're an aggressive rider, you might prefer an amenable yet courageous partner. However, if you're more timid and indecisive, you might enjoy a bolder animal that takes more initiative.

Investigate the horse's background as much as possible while he's in a familiar environment. Get used to handling and riding him while his owner or trainer is present. Under saddle, test the candidate on gymnastic movements to see how athletic he is, and simulate as many situations as you can while you test the horse.

Your mentor can help you rate the horse's previous schooling, disposition, and ability to excel in the type of riding you plan. You can ask about the horse's history of training and performance. Talk to a previous trainer if you can. You want to find out how the horse succeeded in his previous work. If the seller advertised the horse as a reining prospect, you may discover the horse competed in Western Pleasure. Why is he no longer showing as a pleasure horse?

You won't be able to observe every behavior before you buy, so interview the seller. For example, how does the horse react to the farrier and the veterinarian? Will he accept all types of grooming, including bathing and clipping?

Also investigate the horse's diet. You'll want to continue the same type and amount of feed when you bring the horse to your barn. Does he receive any special supplements or medications? Does he have any unusual eating or drinking habits?

Examine the tack used on the horse. To ease the transition, plan to use similar, if not identical, equipment when you take the horse home. You might be able to purchase or borrow his familiar tack. If not, test your saddle and bridle on the horse to verify that they fit correctly.

With a registered horse, examine the registration papers. Read the description of color and markings and confirm that it matches the animal.

You may prefer riding a tough, durable mule. Mules are intelligent, curious, and sure-footed.

PONY OR MULE?

You don't have to choose the conventional horse. You may prefer riding a horse sized to you, or a tough, durable mule: a horse mule (a gelded male) or a molly mule (mare).

The mule reflects its horse parent, so you have the choice of Quarter Horse, Paint, or Appaloosa mules. Distance riders often prefer a mule with a purebred or part-Arabian dam.

MULE CHARACTERISTICS

Mule Fact	Mule Fable
Long ears Smaller, narrower feet Low withers Shorter hip and smaller, peaked hindquarters Longer back	Ugly
Intelligent and curious Level-headed Stays sound, has good sense of self-preservation Requires consistent, patient training and handling Needs time to adapt to change Develops close equine friendships Has a sense of humor	Stubborn Balky Nasty temperament
Great endurance Heat tolerance Long-lived	
Agile Sure-footed Steady mover Slow speed	Short-strided Rough gaits
Holds grudges Won't tolerate injustice Can aim kicks	Cunning and mean Always kicks
Resistant to water founder	Will never founder

Mule riders consider themselves superior to those mounted on mere horses. A mule is the offspring of a jack sire (male donkey) and a mare dam, and differs from a horse in several ways.

Many young riders start out with horses, but a pony may be more fun. Western ponies are scaled-down horses, which meet the same requirements as a riding horse. Despite his short stature, a pony can perform as well as a horse. He can turn fast and run hard. Some critics dislike the pony's gait, which may appear short-strided if compared to a horse. The Quarter Pony has Quarter Horse characteristics, and the Pony of the Americas looks similar to an Appaloosa.

AN OBJECTIVE EYE BEFORE YOU BUY

You evaluate a performance horse by matching his potential with the sport you choose. Set aside your feelings about a particular horse, and take a close, objective look at him.

You want to see the horse in his natural, unprepared state. For this, you might stop by the barn without an appointment, or an hour ahead of a scheduled time. Yes, this might be impolite, but you want to see the horse before the seller prepares him for your visit. Lameness may be undetectable after the owner exercised the horse, but soreness can show up when you first take the horse from his stall or corral.

Either you or your mentor can perform this observation. If you feel confident about doing this by yourself, use the checklist on pages 17–18 to study the horse. You should be able to recognize the basic signs of a healthy animal, as you're looking for deviations from the normal.

Don't worry about what the seller thinks, or let her intimidate you. You should have the right to investigate the horse carefully before deciding to purchase. You'll also learn more about the horse when you examine him thoroughly.

Observe the horse in his stall. First look at the surroundings. Is the floor marked from the horse weaving or stallwalking? Does the door show signs of cribbing? And when you query the owner, does the person quickly make excuses about this horse not being in his usual stall?

Don't expect every seller to lie, but suspect anything that you hear. You're planning to make a major investment in money, time, and emotion, and you want to purchase an honestly presented animal. (Here's another reason for consulting a previous handler or owner and enlisting the aid of a mentor. An experienced horseman can see through feeble excuses.)

After looking at the animal in the stall, lead him outside to check his gait. Ask the seller or your advisor to hold the lead rope while you check the animal's conformation from the front, back, and each side. Don't ignore the off side, which many people don't really see. Many colic surgeries are performed on the horse's right side, and you could miss the resulting scar. Even with successful surgery, a horse could be prone to colic for the rest of his life.

Find out about the animal's medical history. Is he current with shots and worming? Has he suffered from frequent attacks of colic or any other serious conditions? Ask to see the Coggins certificate and other official medical records, preferably from the horse's regular veterinarian. Also ask if the horse is HYPP negative (free of hyperkalemic periodic paralysis). This cell disruption affects thousands of Quarter Horses tracing to the stallion Impressive, and it has spread to horses of other breeds with Quarter Horse ancestry.

While the seller is present, don't criticize the horse. Ask questions, and note any deviations you see. Discuss them with your mentor later, and decide if you plan to buy the horse. If so, you may decide to have your veterinarian perform a formal, professional examination. This could include radiographs and even ultrasound, depending on the horse's value and planned work.

Don't expect to locate a perfect horse, because there aren't any. Weigh the evidence and learn to recognize the obvious faults that will limit a horse's useful life. You're on your way to finding your equine partner, and you'll avoid needless medical bills while saving yourself some heartbreak.

Consider a horse's resale value. Arizona Quarter Horse trainer Casey Hinton has rated these characteristics as important: "Prettiness, bloodlines, conformation, and performance make up the value of a horse. He can be a great mover with good conformation and still win a lot, but not be pretty. The value is higher if he's pretty. You can always sell one that's pretty."

Horses at auction.

KATHY KADASH

Where to Search for Your Horse

By choosing a professional or experienced amateur as your mentor, you've enlisted the aid of an insider who knows the market. A trainer will have especially established a wide range of contacts. She'll be able to research the background of horses in your price range. She knows whom to trust, and she can represent you well by asking those tough questions.

A trainer will want to find you the right horse so you'll remain a customer. She'll also verify that the seller represents the horse fairly, and that any registration papers are in order. It's worth paying a commission or finder's fee for the peace of mind.

A trainer can charge a fee of 5 to 10 percent. Usually the seller pays this, so the trainer quotes you a price that includes the fee.

You can also buy a horse through advertisements, sales, or horse dealers. Here you definitely want to bring your mentor along, because every seller has a reason for selling his or her horse. You don't want to end up with someone else's problem!

A horse auction offers a variety of animals for comparison, but comparison shopping demands an expert's eye. It's easy to get "auction fever," especially when you see good-looking horses going for reasonable prices. The impact of the economy has affected sale prices, and you can find a bargain if you shop carefully.

Attend only a reputable auction, such as one affiliated with a breed association or an established sales agent. Such sales will provide a Coggins certificate and proof of registration. Here you'll register with the sales office as a qualified buyer. With your mentor, sort through the catalog for prospects, inspect them, and try out the likeliest candidates.

The consignor may have determined the horse's reserve – the minimum bid. This may be a sealed bid that the auctioneer announces when bidding stops. If you have the highest bid, and the reserve price is higher, either you raise your bid to meet the reserve or you don't buy the horse.

In order to evaluate a horse you are interested in, you will want to see him moving freely in his natural state.

In today's market, the attractive Western horse displays the elegance of Thoroughbred breeding. He doesn't have to resemble a hunter or a stakes winner, but he should show the influence of a slightly longer-legged ancestor.

THE BALANCED HORSE

A horse's form definitely influences his function. An equine athlete must display natural balance. His skeletal structure determines how every part fits together — proportions and angles.

Horsemen evaluate the animal's balance by comparing these parts and seeing how the horse ties together. Prominent judge Don Burt has said: "The balance of angulation should be symmetrical and match in all parts, regardless of the animal's size. You could have a horse that is 16.2 hands with the parts of a smaller one — a straight, up-and-down shoulder and a long cannon bone. You want to see a shorter cannon and longer shoulder to get the right relationship between the forearm and pastern."

Burt has also emphasized how the angles influence the horse's movement. He described the balanced horse as standing in a trapezoid. "Look at the angles of the shoulder and hip. If they are equal, the horse will be balanced. A short topline and a long underline complete the trapezoid." (See illustration of Don Burt's description on page 22.) He adds that both shoulder and hip angles should match in length as well as slope. A horse with one shorter angle, such as a steep shoulder or dropped-off croup, will be off balance. He'll find it difficult to collect himself, to work off the hindquarters.

"If the horse has too much angle in front, and not enough in back, his parts can't work together," Burt explained. "He starts to tire, usually first in the back. The back has to move forward and back for impulsion. The horse loses his impulsion if the rear has to drive more to push the front. When the angles work together, the horse carries a level topline."

Casey Hinton has advised looking at a horse from the withers, the animal's balance point or

CHECKLIST FOR RATING A HORSE

Component	Detail	Questions to ask yourself
CONFORMATION	Overall balance (see page 22)	Does the horse show breed type? Does he have a short head that shows breed character?
SOUNDNESS AND HEALTH	Eyes	Does the horse seem to have normal vision? Do you see any infection in either eye?
	Nostrils	Do you see any discharge?
	Mouth	Do teeth meet evenly? Does the breath smell abnormally strong? (The horse could have an abscessed tooth.) Are the gums a normal pink? Check the capillary refill by pressing your thumb against the gum, releasing, and watching how quickly the pink color returns (see page 107).
	Neck	Are ventral muscles overly developed? (The horse could be a cribber.)
	Legs	Is the horse lame? Does the horse move evenly on all 4 legs? Do his joints and bones look strong and powerful? Does the horse have any abnormalities – enlargement or scar – on any leg? Feel inside and outside, front and back, of each leg, and look for unusual heat, or splints, or swellings.
	Hooves	Does the pulse feel strong and normal? (Feel it on the posterior digital blood vessels on the pastern.) Are hooves smooth on the surface?
	Back	Feel for smooth vertebrae on back and withers. Does the horse have strong loins? (Press on the loins to see how the horse reacts to your fingers.)
	Tail	Does the horse move his tail normally? (Grasp the tail to see how the horse moves it.)
	Wind	Does the horse breathe abnormally after exercise at the trot or lope?

Component	Detail	Questions to ask yourself
TEMPERAMENT	Attitude under saddle	Does the horse feel light and responsive? Will he put up with your riding skills? Is he calm and level-headed? Does he show any bad habits or potentially dangerous behaviors?
	Manners on the ground	Does the horse have soft eyes and a friendly expression? Do you feel confident handling him? Will he load readily into a trailer?
	Movement	Does the horse move smoothly at all gaits? Does his way of going match the riding you plan to do?
ATHLETIC ABILITY	Moves in balance at all times	Does the horse have light or heavy muscling? Too little or too much can affect his performance. Does the horse move straight? Does the horse react quickly, or does he seem lazy? Does the horse show the courage and heart to perform?
PHYSICAL CONDITION	Muscle tone Strength Endurance	Does the horse's frame appear substantial, rugged, and durable?
	Amount of flesh	Is the horse in good shape, not too fat or too thin? You should be able to just feel the ribs, without them being apparent to the eye.
AFFINITY	Appeal	Is this horse pretty to look at? Is he fun to be around?
	Color	Do you like his color and markings? If a Paint, Pinto, or Appaloosa, does he have "loud" color?
	Size	Is he the right size for you? Average horse size would be 14.3 to 15.2 hands.
	Presence	Does the horse look alert?

center of gravity. "This is where he's going to balance himself. The shoulder comes from the withers, so the horse sets his balance. A higher-withered horse is better, because he balances on his hip. The more a horse can do naturally on his hip than on his front, the better he'll be. The horse that floats backwards as he lopes — lopes from his hip — will always be a good mover."

Hinton has said that the longer the neck, the better the horse's natural balance. He can predict a good mover by observing the structure of the neck and the hip.

To Buy or Lease

Buying a horse is a major decision, and it's much easier to buy one than to sell one. If you're serious about horsemanship, realize that your first horse may not be the animal that becomes your genuine partner. California trainer Gill Swarbrick has said: "When you're learning, the horse has to be a machine. You don't necessarily keep your first horse. You're going to make mistakes, and the only way you learn is through making mistakes. Hopefully the horse has the personality that will hold together even through all the mistakes."

One horse may be perfect to start with, but you may want to move on to a specialist or a different type of horse later. Or, your first horse may not be the horse for you.

If you want your own horse but aren't sure about buying one, consider leasing a horse that you can learn on. Your instructor might have an older horse that she doesn't want to sell, but you can have exclusive use of him for a period of time. You can test your riding skills and develop your goals without the permanent commitment to a particular horse.

When leasing a horse, be sure both parties sign a written agreement. The American Quarter Horse Association (AQHA) uses a Lease Authorization form for its members, which proves to the association the lessee's authority. Both owner and lessee sign the authorization. You should follow up a form like this with an agreement that lists specific responsibilities of both parties.

When you are ready to buy, you will note that prices vary, depending on the horse's age, training, potential, and condition. Here are some average starting prices for a trained horse suitable for an amateur or youth rider:

* Unregistered pleasure horse — $500-2,000
* Registered pleasure horse — $2,000-up
* Registered show horse (Pleasure, Horsemanship) — $3,500-up
* Games horse — $2,000-up
* Cutting or reining horse — $5,000-up

Expect some sort of written agreement at the time of sale. You might receive only a handwritten bill of sale for an unregistered horse. With a registered animal, the seller should complete an official transfer form. Usually the seller sends the original registration papers and the transfer to the association, and the association mails you the papers after recording the transfer.

Don't pay the seller until you see that signed transfer form in your hand. You might choose to have the seller sign, and you submit the paperwork to the association. If you're unsure about this process, telephone the secretary of the association for the official procedure.

And, according to Don Burt, collection plus impulsion results in balance, whether the horse stands still or moves out. When you study a horse for balance, ask a handler to stand the horse square. He should stand with weight on all four legs placed under his body.

Then watch the horse in motion, being led at the walk and trot, or longed at trot and canter. Look for a good mover, a horse that moves in balance. You're going to ride the horse, so look for smooth gaits that will be comfortable for you for hours at a time.

A horse with correct angles should move cleanly. Watch how he changes gait, turns, and stops. You want to see him maintain his own balance, with or without a rider. For a show horse, he should be a "big stopper," or stop immediately with his hindquarters under himself.

CONFORMATION POINTS

Part	Angle	Proportion
OVERALL SYMMETRY		Body in thirds of equal proportion: forehand, barrel, hindquarter Length equals height, so horse can carry weight Parts blend together smoothly Muscling appears smooth, with a combination of Quarter Horse and Thoroughbred appearance
HEAD	Held in a comfortable position	Sized to fit the horse Length related to horse's weight and height
EYES	Placed on the sides of the head about ⅓ the distance from poll to muzzle	Large Same size
EARS	Erect	Short Alert Same size Sized to fit the head
JAW		Prominent, well-defined
MUZZLE		Well-defined, refined chin
NECK		Long, trim neck for flexibility Defined jugular groove Distance of topline (withers to poll) equals twice the bottom line
THROATLATCH		Trim throatlatch Distance from poll to throat measures ½ the length of the head – large enough for an unobstructed airway
SHOULDER	Sloped at 45° for a longer stride Should match angle of hip	Big shoulder Long shoulder for a long neck Distance from point of shoulder to haunch equals length of head
WITHERS		Sharp, prominent Slightly higher than croup for "uphill" appearance that lightens the weight on the forehand
CHEST		Sufficient width between the forelegs Broad chest indicates athletic breathing capacity Prominent V-muscling indicates power
HEART GIRTH		Deep for lung capacity Measurement equals length of head and length of foreleg From the side, ribs look well sprung

Part	Angle	Proportion
FORELEG	Placed straight under the horse Forearm forms 90° angle with shoulder Bones run straight into the hoof Viewed from the front, a plumb line can run from the middle of the hoof to the point of the shoulder Horse does not toe in or out Horse does not camp out or behind Horse is not over or back at the knee	Viewed from the front, all parts of both forelegs match from right to left Cannons short so knees are close to ground Long, well-muscled forearm blends into shoulder
FRONT FEET	Pastern and hoof sloped at 45° Stands square on feet Heels are equal	Round shape Sized for the horse Same size Pastern fairly long Pastern forms one slope, not broken for coon foot or club foot
UNDERLINE	Smooth curve from girth to flank	Long, measured from elbow to stifle
HIP	Slope matches shoulder's slope (measure from the muscle on the hip, just ahead of the flank, to just above the gaskin) Hip and stifle joints meet at 90°	Powerful source for all gaits Higher set tail indicates length of femur is longer than pelvic bone, for a longer stride Viewed from the side, the hindquarters appear square and wide from stifle to stifle
HIND LEG	Viewed from the side, an imaginary line should run down middle of gaskin, hock, hoof From behind, legs don't angle together (cowhocked) or stand too far apart (base wide) Hocks form a 130° angle Hocks aren't too angled (sickle hock) or too straight (post legged)	Cannons short so hocks close to ground Long and strong muscles Stifle blends into hindquarter Prominent muscles in gaskin, but not so heavy that the horse loses flexibility
TOPLINE	Horizontal	Short, not concave (length of back varies; a long-backed horse may still be athletic)
LOIN	Horizontal	Wide and strong to carry rider, flexible enough to bend laterally and longtitudinally so horse gets hind end under himself
HIND FEET	May toe out slightly Heels equal	Oval shape Same size
CROUP	Sloped Top matches or slightly below point of the shoulder, straight across	Long and wide

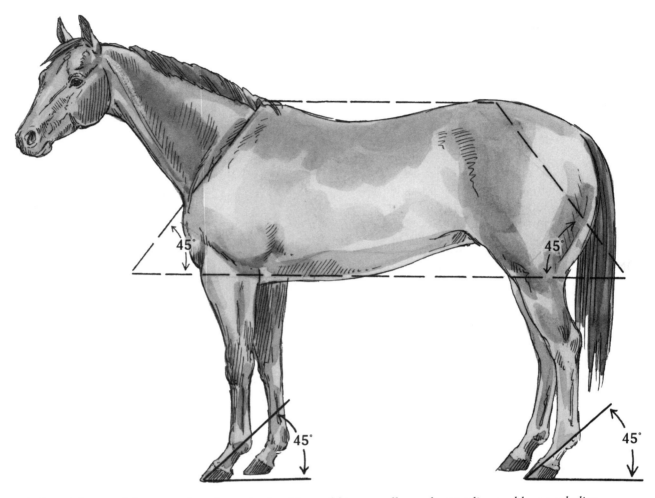

A balanced horse will have equal angles at the shoulder and hip, as well as a short topline and long underline.

From the side, does the horse move true, with pure gaits? Do you see free shoulder movement, with a soft, swinging back? From the front, does he walk straight? From the rear, does the hind end move smoothly? It shouldn't shift or bounce.

"A horse goes as he is designed to go," according to Burt. "You cannot make a horse with bad angles go as balanced as one with good angles."

GETTING ALONG WITH YOUR NEW HORSE

When your new horse moves in, the two of you enter into a new friendship. You'll learn all about his personality, and he'll learn about yours. As you begin to adjust to one another, you'll become acquaintances, and then comrades.

Expect it to take at least six months for you to understand your horse. He may be used to different handling, and both of you need to explore the other's responses. Like teammates in basketball, you'll learn all your horse's moves so you can mesh into a congenial partnership.

Horses are creatures of habit, and they crave regularity. Change upsets many animals. You'll adjust more rapidly to the horse than he will to you, so don't rush the process. Gradually introduce any changes in stabling, diet, or routine.

Moving can stress your new horse. You can ease his anxiety by allowing some time alone to explore his stall or paddock. If possible, keep curious

Gait	Footfalls	Attributes	Faults
WALK	4-beat gait, with no period of suspension 1-2-3-4	Horse moves forward with energy and impulsion, so he covers ground. He flows in a fluid motion, pushing from the hips. He moves flatfooted, places center of hoof on ground. Neck moves flexibly so the horse breathes easily in motion.	Interfering: feet brush or knock each other Hits ground on outside or inside edge of feet, which creates stress on legs
TROT	2-beat gait 1-2	Horse covers ground, definitely moving forward. He trots or jogs smoothly and rhythmically. He trots in cadence, with his opposite feet hitting the ground at the same instant. He can lengthen his stride and keep his impulsion without increasing speed. Topline remains level and the back "round." When turning, the horse rolls his back and drops his head.	Interfering Horse appears rough-gaited, his topline jolting up and down. He raises his head to maintain his balance (a too-high head weakens the back). He trots "strung-out," with too much weight on the forehand. When turning, he hollows his back, raises his head, and bounces.
LOPE	3-beat gait 1-2-3 (emphasis on the first footfall)	Level topline Fluid way of going Horse sweeps forward with his hind legs, lifting the forehand. He lopes effortlessly. His front feet land flat, low to the ground.	Horse pounds the ground. He shows excess action at the knee and hock. His topline rolls. He 4-beats, or seems to trot in front and walk behind (listen to the gait to confirm). He moves in a short, choppy lope. The lope looks lateral.
GALLOP	3- or 4-beat gait, depending on speed		

Walk

Trot

Lope

Gallop

Observe the horse being led or longed. Look for smooth gaits that you will be comfortable riding for hours at a time.

equine neighbors at a safe distance. Duplicate the horse's previous environment as much as you can, and definitely offer familiar feed. You certainly don't want to trigger an immediate attack of colic!

Watch your horse in the stall or paddock, so you can observe his normal actions. This will help you discern any changes due to ill health or injury.

At home, you might notice your new horse acting differently than he did when you observed him before. Expect unusual behavior as he adjusts to his new home, and don't assume that he'll act predictably.

For example, never turn a new horse into a pasture with an already-established herd. Maybe he

lived peaceably with other horses, but the new group requires that he find a place in the pecking order. It's safer to introduce him to one or two others at a time, allowing less hazardous interaction.

You're anxious to start working with your new horse, but let him have some time to adjust before you start handling him. Never just saddle up and set off for a fast ride.

Trainer Gill Swarbrick rides the new horse for a rider, to find out any idiosyncracies. She can then advise the rider how to deal with him, and to predict what he'll do in any situation. "The horse and rider need to get to know one another, and they can't do that in a high-stress situation. At the

Give both yourself and your horse time to establish harmony by getting to know each other face to face, on the ground.

beginning, I say, 'Don't try to *do* anything with the horse. Just go out and walk, trot, lope, but don't do anything intense. If you do and you have a fight and you lose, it's going to be harder.'"

Give yourself and your horse both time to establish harmony. First you'll get to know your horse face to face, on the ground. Chapter 3 will help you begin to handle your horse.

3

Handling Your Horse

You want the Western horse to be your partner. Riding becomes fun when your horse joins with you. As dominant partner, you dictate his actions. You influence the relationship through your first interactions.

By handling the horse on the ground, you learn how he responds to you before you ride him. Watch his expression to anticipate his reactions to you, other horses, and other sights and sounds in the area. The horse learns about you by observing your body language, your movements, and your emotions.

To enjoy your horse, you must be able to contain him. If you don't control the horse, the horse will control you. At all times, you must supervise the horse's actions. You handle the horse gently but firmly; your goal is to contain him without force.

Trainer Pat Parelli has explained how horses look up to a leader. "Horses are natural followers. Your horse sizes you up. He respects you for your leadership qualities."

Establish yourself as a leader by knowing what you want to do with a horse *before* you start an action. Visualizing your goal helps you carry through, and you will communicate your desire to the horse. You act without threatening him. As you move deliberately around your horse, he'll understand and follow your lead. Your confidence — and kindness — will keep you in control.

Gently maneuver the strap over the muzzle, bring the loose end of the crownpiece over the poll, and buckle the two ends.

For a broke horse, some handlers prefer a neck rope rather than a halter and lead rope.

CATCHING THE HORSE

Few riders today actually catch horses with swinging ropes. A more correct description would be to approach and halter the horse while he remains motionless. Most riders use a halter and lead rope.

A halter contains the horse safely, with a lead rope snapped to the halter's center ring. Drape the unbuckled halter, with the lead rope attached, over your arm or shoulder while you approach the horse in the stall, corral, or pasture. Coil the lead so it doesn't drag on the ground or trip you.

If your horse has proven difficult to catch, you may wish to conceal the equipment behind your back. Walk up to him, stopping at his near (left) shoulder. Pet the shoulder and neck as the horse stands quietly, and gradually ease the halter noseband toward the muzzle. Use both hands to spread open the noseband, and hold it low so the horse is less likely to raise his head. A gentle horse will lower his head to allow you to place the halter.

Gently maneuver the straps of the halter over the muzzle. Slide your left hand along the near cheekpiece, toward the ear, and reach under the throat with your right hand. Grasp the loose end of the halter's crownpiece on the offside, and buckle the two ends of the crownpiece before collecting the lead rope.

You might choose to place the lead rope over or around the neck before you slip on the halter. This won't really hold a horse that tries to bolt away from you, but it can convince the animal that you've caught him.

With a broke horse, some handlers prefer using a neck rope instead of a halter and lead rope. The neck rope has a rope or metal loop in place of a snap. You form a non-slip noose using the metal adjuster. Hold the loop in your right hand and approach the horse's near shoulder. Move your hand under his neck and gently lift the loop over his muzzle and ears. Tighten the loop snug around the neck, which can be a few inches behind the poll or mid-neck.

Leading the Horse

With the horse contained, you walk him as you would a dog. You indicate the gait and direction, and the animal moves alongside you as a partner.

Stand on the near side, about one foot away from the horse's shoulder. Place your right hand on the lead rope, six to eight inches from the snap or neck loop, with the rope slack. Hold your arm straight out from your body at a comfortable level.

Gather the rest of the lead rope into coiled loops, and wrap your left hand over — never through — the loops. You can feed out rope if necessary, and if the horse jerks the rope, the coils won't tighten around your fingers or hand. Don't let the end of the lead rope drag on the ground. You or the horse could step on it.

Facing forward, signal the horse to move by striding ahead. The broke horse automatically follows on a slack lead. Rely on your peripheral vision to observe his response. If you look at him, you could distract him.

As you lead the horse through doorways or gates, aim him straight between each side. Don't try to squeeze him through an opening narrower than four feet or he could injure a hip on the post or jamb.

Use caution when the two of you pass a fence, walk down a barn aisle, or pass stable tools. Just when you least expect it, the horse could swish his tail and snag the hairs on a wire fence, get bitten by a stalled horse leaning over the door, or fall over a rake.

The horse should pace his steps to your strides and keep his neck beside your right shoulder. Ideally he maintains a safe distance from your shoulder, hip, and feet.

Don't allow your horse to push forward or lag behind. If you need to turn him, turn him away from you, to the right. Turn the head, and the body will follow.

When you arrive at the hitching rail, stop, which signals the horse to halt. If he doesn't, tug downward on the lead shank and say, "Whoa."

When leading, pace your steps to your horse's stride, keeping his neck beside your right shoulder. Maintain a safe distance from your shoulder, hip, and feet.

Tying the Horse

Tying is another learned behavior; it contains the horse and curbs his instinct to move. You secure your horse's head to ensure that he remains in one place while you prepare for riding. He should stand tied as long as you decide, whether it's a few minutes or several hours. Usually you knot the lead rope or neck rope to a solid object, so the horse won't get loose.

Pick a safe area, where your horse won't contact any potentially dangerous objects. If other horses are tied nearby, be sure that yours cannot contact his neighbors.

You can use a tie rail, sturdy fence, solid post, tree or stout limb, ring on the side of a horse trailer, or cross ties. Whatever you choose, test it for strength. Will it securely hold a horse that fights the lead rope? If you can budge a post or rail by pushing or lifting it, don't tie your horse to it.

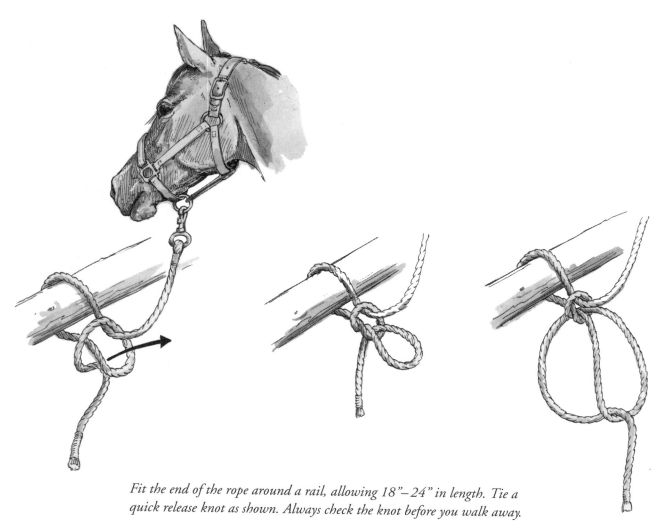

Fit the end of the rope around a rail, allowing 18"–24" in length. Tie a quick release knot as shown. Always check the knot before you walk away.

The cross tie secures the horse with two ropes, one on each side of his head. You can cross tie a horse between two objects — fences, walls of a barn or stall, posts, or trees.

Whether you tie with one rope or two, position the restraint so the horse's head remains in a comfortable position. The rope should not force the head downward or the neck upward, and the knot should remain in place. A rope at the height of the horse's withers is safest, so he won't catch a forefoot over the tie rope.

Fit the end of the rope around a rail or through a tie ring. Allow about 18 to 24 inches in length, and tie a knot that you can jerk loose instantly, as illustrated in the diagram. This knot will untie easily, even if your horse pulls against it and tightens the rope.

Check the knot before you walk away. Don't leave the horse unattended unless you know he's broke to tie and won't fight the rope or try to untie it.

When you untie a knot, all you need to do is loosen it by pulling near the end of the rope. Then untie.

Never tie a horse by the reins. If he spooked and tried to flee, the sudden pressure of the bit could injure his mouth. Fighting the pressure, the horse would likely pull harder and break the reins.

Unfortunately, you'll see riders who do tie their horses by the reins, and nothing ever happens to them. Here's an equine Murphy's Law: If a shortcut works with someone else's horse and you try it one time, you'll have a wreck!

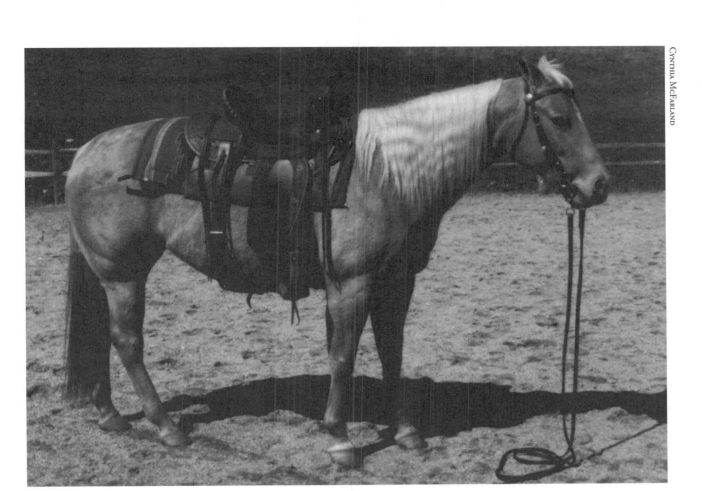

Some horses will "ground tie" and wait for their riders to return.

Some Westerners teach their horses to *ground tie.* Whenever the rider dismounts and drops the reins ahead of the horse, to the ground, the broke horse freezes. He stands in place, waiting for the rider to return.

Those movie cowboys who galloped to the saloon and tossed their reins over the hitching rail were actually ground tying their horses. The "parked" horses were trained to ground tie — the hitching rail was a prop.

Some riders rely on hobbles, which restrain the horse by encircling the two front legs. Hobbles strap the forelegs together at or above the fetlocks. They don't stop a horse from moving, but they restrict his movement.

A hobbled horse will usually stand still. Some might "hop" slowly, or even try to gallop, but they usually won't stray very far.

A short piece of cotton rope forms a simple set of hobbles for a hobble-trained horse. The rope is looped around the off foreleg, twisted a few times, and looped around the near fore. Tie a loose double knot that will not be difficult to unfasten. A cotton rope will not tighten as much as nylon or poly, and it will not burn the skin if the horse pulls against the rope.

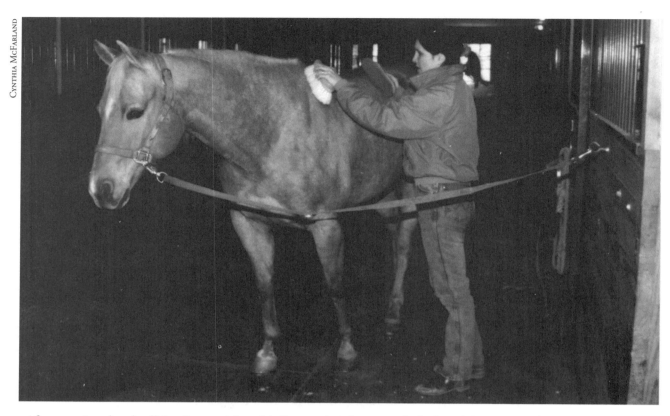

After currying, brush off the dirt particles with firm strokes that go with the lay of the coat.

You'd usually restrain a horse with hobbles while trail riding, to keep your horse in camp. If you have a horse trained to hobbles, you don't need to tie him with a rope to groom him. Simply tie rope or feed-sack hobbles, or buckle manufactured hobbles of leather or braided mohair cinch cord. With rope hobbles, stand at the near foreleg and flip the hobble around the off foreleg. Twist the rope a few turns and wrap the near leg. Tie with a square knot, which will hold in place yet untie easily.

Your horse may be trained to accept a picket rope. Here you attach the horse's halter or neck rope to a long rope, tied to a stake driven into the ground. You can also use a stake-out hobble, in which one strap buckles around a foreleg. A rope snaps to the hobble. The horse can move freely the length of the rope, to graze in a certain area.

Never stake out or hobble a horse unless you are sure the animal is used to these methods. He must accept the restraint. A horse trained to a picket rope knows how to avoid becoming tangled, and knows to stand quietly if he does tangle the rope around his feet.

Groups of trail riders often use the picket line, adopted from the Old West. This is an improvised tie rail made of stretched rope, to which the riders tie their horses overnight or on a long rest stop.

GROOMING THE HORSE

With your horse tied, clean him before you saddle up. Currying massages the skin and coat, while brushing strokes the coat to whisk off dirt and loose hair raised by the curry. You can also clean the coat with a rough-textured cloth, either a folded burlap sack or a cactus cloth.

Start at the horse's neck. Stand so you face toward the horse's rear. With a currycomb or cloth, scrub the coat and skin in a circular or back-and-forth motion. Work against the lay of the coat to raise dirt to the surface. Once you've curried both sides of the horse, including back and belly, use a brush to whisk off dirt particles. Brush with firm strokes over the entire body, including the face.

Brush the mane and forelock flat against neck and forehead. Brush the tail, separating strands with your fingers so you don't pull out tail hairs.

As you groom, observe the condition of coat and skin. If your horse has any abrasions or sores, treat them with medication after you finish brushing the coat.

Touching the horse while grooming helps the two of you bond with each other. Most horses enjoy the touch, especially when you rub the coat with a soft brush or the palm of your hand. Watch the horse's facial expression as you groom. Look for favorite spots, and spend extra time rubbing these areas.

THE BROKE HORSE

The first horse you handle should be a gentle "broke" horse. The broke horse allows you to handle him. He accepts your dominance through all contact.

Through training, the broke horse has learned good habits. Repetition has taught him to respond to any handler. He feels comfortable and he behaves as expected.

You master the animal through your intelligence, as you cannot physically overpower a horse or pony. You reinforce the horse's habitual behaviors by consistent reward and punishment.

Trainer Casey Hinton has said: "The horse is a creature of habit. We teach him the habits, so use the same habits every day."

As you observe horses, you see that they tend to seek the path of least resistance, or a lack of punishment. You reward the horse that leads correctly by not punishing him. You discipline the resistant horse by voice, pressure of the lead rope, or use of a whip. If you allow the horse to do what he wants, you allow him to begin a bad habit. With careless handling, even a broke horse could become rank, behaving dangerously on the ground or under saddle. "Horses are totally subservient to humans," accord-

ing to Art Gaytan, a California trainer. "The horse should do only what you ask, not what he wants."

Casey Hinton: "What motivates a horse is rest, or food. If you use that to your advantage, a horse will do almost anything for those things. Part of training him is training his mind to think that he's surrendering, giving in to you, because he thinks he'll get rest."

Hinton has defined training as "Command, respect, response." And Gaytan has said: "The secret to training horses is three elements: Ask, put on the pressure that equals the horse's resistance, and reward."

A horseman respects his or her horse and expects respect in return. The horse learns that when he responds to a person's command, he displays and receives respect.

Trainer Terry Berg has described this as boundaries that both parties observe. "The horse has his space, and you have your space. A horse is a big enough animal that he can step on your foot, and it

Mutual respect is an important part of the horse and rider relationship.

A Broke Horse

⭐ Has manners, both on the ground and under saddle.
⭐ Gives to the pressure of a strap, rope, hand, or leg.
⭐ Doesn't run away from most threatening sights and sounds.
⭐ Is attentive to you.
⭐ Accepts your dominance and respects you.

hurts. He can do a lot of damage. If he won't move away from you on the ground easily, or back up, or stay out of your space, you're in trouble."

Respect doesn't mean fear. The horseman avoids frightening the horse. The horse avoids threatening the person. According to Berg, "The horse shouldn't come out of his boundary and into the person's boundary. That shows the horse is telling the person where the boundary is. That is a real dangerous point."

You're always training a horse, whenever you interact with him. Horses respond differently, and Oregon trainer Tom Sorensen has explained how you can test an equine personality just by leading the horse. "You can have a horse with a hot mind in a hot body, a hot mind in a cold body, a cold mind in a hot body, or a cold mind in a cold body. All horses ride exactly the way they lead. The horse that's always right there, shoulder to shoulder with you, is very trainable. That's the hot mind in the cold body — the horse that you can turn on and off like a light switch."

The broke horse responds through his training, not by instinct. One strong instinct is to push against pressure. The late Jack Baker, a legendary California horseman, said: "The first time you put a halter on a colt, he's going to pull away from the pressure that you put on him. It comes from self-preservation. The system of teaching him to give to pressure is the most important thing, and just about the only thing, you're going to teach him in his lifetime."

Trainers agree that another powerful instinct is flight, to flee from fright. The horse naturally defends himself by running away. Trainer Monty Roberts said: "The horse is a flight animal. He thinks he should leave when he sees danger."

By learning containment — to stand tied no matter what — the horse overcomes this instinct. But although the broke horse acts predictably most of the time, he may behave differently when in danger. Even a well-trained animal never loses his basic instinct of self-preservation. Any horse will run from danger if he can. This animal can injure you when you try to help him, or even himself as he struggles to flee.

Working around horses is risky, so consider a horse to be potentially volatile. Don't become obsessed about what might happen, but be aware of the animal's inherent nature. An accident can happen at any time. As a horseman, you'll scan the environment for a possible hazard. You won't be able to prevent all accidents, but you can prepare yourself to react if necessary.

EQUINE LANGUAGE

Whenever you handle a horse, you "speak" to him. All your moves speak to the horse in his language.

To enjoy being around horses, you must adapt to their language. You learn to speak it by learning to "be" a horse, instead of thinking like a human.

This speech is the language of respect, of dominance and submission. You act to control the horse, as another horse would. Your horse submits to your actions, and you reward him by "going submissive." You're copying the behavior of two horses, with your horse submitting to the dominant one, you. He wants to follow you, because you've communicated in a language he can understand.

Master horsemen have learned this language, and some of them teach it to their fellow humans. Trainer Monty Roberts has demonstrated how his body language communicates to the horse. His moves encourage the horse's response. "With communication and kindness, I can get him to want to go with me, rather than to go away."

Roberts works the green horse in a round pen. The horse starts out by running in a circle, then gradually comes to the center to stand still. The trainer rewards him by letting him stand still when he cooperates. He becomes submissive, turning his back to the horse. When the horse "argues" with the trainer, the trainer takes command and causes him to return to running the circle.

"He decides to renegotiate a contract, to join up with me," said Roberts. "He talks to me in the language 'Equus,' which is 75 million years old. He joins with me as soon as he knows it's good to be with me."

Roberts has communicated with over 7,000 unbroke horses, speaking to them to gain their confidence and trust. When horse and man can communicate, the horse accepts unfamiliar handling.

In the same vein, trainer Art Gaytan has explained how horses understand a different language. "I never talk to horses in my language, but always in their language. A horse's language is 98 percent through his eyes, and 2 percent through sound."

The horse's eyes and ears work together. A horse turns his head to look, to focus on a sight. His ears also tell where he looks, as he can see in two directions at once. One ear may turn toward you, while the other indicates that the horse also observes another distraction.

Roberts has pointed out how the horse speaks with eyes, ears, and mouth. As the horse watches a human, his inside ear (the one closest to the person) remains fixed on the person. He demonstrates his submissive response by lowering his head.

Trainer Pat Parelli has said: "Body language is universal with all beings. A horse with his head up is defensive. Down, he's relaxed. Licking his lips shows he understands, he's digesting a thought. You look for that final understanding, to see his eyes and ears look a little different, for him to lick his lips."

A horse perceives slight changes in the way you move. He sees your mental attitude through your physical attitude. You don't have to make broad moves to elicit the desired response. You should control and soften your actions.

Gaytan has explained how the horse's eyesight affects its thinking. "What a horse sees with his left eye, he doesn't recognize when he sees it with the right eye. The horse has two separate sides of his brain, and he can't transfer information from one eye [side of the brain] to the other."

For this reason, realize that a horse should become used to objects and movement on both sides. You need to mirror your actions left and right. For example, your horse may be accustomed to you holding a whip on its near side. Move to the off side, and the same whip could spook him. Let him see the whip on both sides so he learns to recognize the object.

Gaytan has noted how horses respond to the handler's movements. "Your motion cues a horse when you lead him. The rope is only to keep the horse from running off, because you can't pull him along."

If you find yourself in a tense situation on the ground, re-establish your dominance with your body language and voice.

Even though horses focus on your body language, you can enhance your control with your voice. Some experts recommend regular conversation, humming, or whistling.

You can soothe a nervous animal or discipline one with your voice. If you sense a horse might kick, a sharp "Quit!" often corrects his misconduct.

If you find yourself in a tense situation on the ground, re-establish your dominance with your body language and voice. Stop your movement, take a breath, and say "whoa" to freeze the action.

You might use the Tellington-Jones Equine Awareness Method (TTEAM), developed by Linda Tellington-Jones. TTEAM can change the horse's personality. The TTouch bodywork reduces his tightness and sensitivity by relaxing him. Specific touches on the head encourage him to lower his head. TTEAM ground exercises help him to overcome fear and listen to your guidance.

SAFE, DEFENSIVE HANDLING

Veterinarians note that most accidents occur during handling — leading, tying, grooming, medicating, and trailer loading. On the ground, you are vulnerable to four common injuries: getting kicked, stepped on, bitten, or shoved. You can protect yourself by expecting that injury. Stand away from any possible danger, let the horse know your location, and tune into his body language.

The typical Western horse or mule weighs 1,000 to 1,400 pounds. Even a pony weighs about 600 pounds. Its very size makes the horse a formidable animal, so apply the 4 A's: Alert and Assertive Avoids Accidents. Here's a checklist of safety guidelines:

1. Avoid standing directly in front of a horse. Every horse will spook. If he strikes or leaps forward, can you jump out of the way quickly? Be alert for any sudden movement. For example, realize that irritating insects can cause him to throw his head, smacking you by accident.

2. Develop "eyes in your feet" whenever you walk near or beside a horse. Keep your two feet at least 12 inches away from all four hooves. While grooming or saddling, stand in a forward-leaning posture. Lean toward the horse instead of standing too close beside him.

3. Always wear protective shoes or boots. A thick rubber, vinyl, or leather boot gives you some cushion against an unexpected stomp. Heed an equine Murphy's Law: The one day you *don't* swap tennis shoes for boots, your horse will plant a hoof right on your toe.

4. Always inspect your equipment's condition. A frayed strap or rope can break if that 1,000-pound horse jerks against it. Metal hardware is the weakest part of your halter and lead rope. Name-brand tack should use better metal parts, which are less likely to break under stress.

On the ground, you are vulnerable to four common injuries: getting kicked, stepped on, bitten or shoved. Always stand away from any possible danger, let the horse know your location, and tune into his body language.

5. Instead of a steady pressure, use a pull and release. Think of the lead rope as a rubber band. Any horse can revert to his instinct to fight pressure. You can't overpower a horse by outpulling him.

If a horse shoves you with his head, shoulder, side, or hip, shove him right back and make him quit or move over with a verbal reprimand, "Get over!"

6. Make your horse respect your space when you're close beside him. If he crowds you when leading or won't stand still when tied, correct him with voice and a slap. "Quit!" or "Stand!" can discourage this movement, which can endanger you and others around your horse.

7. Watch every rope and strap whenever you handle a horse. Many old-time horse trainers are missing finger joints from becoming entangled in a rope. Never wrap a rope around your finger or hand, and keep your feet away from a rope loop or a dangling lead rope.

A horse that becomes entangled in a rope can panic. Always keep a sharp pocket knife in the barn or trailer to cut through the rope in an emergency. You can cut the rope to release a struggling horse. (Stay out of the way, because he could bolt when he feels the pressure released.)

8. Kicking poses the greatest danger. The power of the equine hoof can kill you, and every equine can kick. Avoid a kick by simply staying out of the way. Imagine a semicircle, about four feet out from the horse's hindquarters. When you must enter this zone, move close to the horse's side. If he does kick, you'll receive only a shove, not the full force of the kick.

You can avoid a possible kick by reminding the horse of your presence. Pull down on his tail, or keep contact with your hand, shoulder, or leg.

Some animals cowkick, kicking forward or even sideways with the hind leg. Again, draw an imaginary circle around the kicking zone. Keep yourself out of danger, except when you must handle the hindquarters or belly. Enter the zone assertively, keep body contact, and watch the legs.

Don't underestimate the kicking zone. A short-coupled horse or pony can cowkick you when you bend over to pick up a forefoot. Keep an eye on the hind leg when you clean a front hoof on the same side. Your pony might kick forward at a fly on his belly, striking your head!

Whenever a horse kicks, correct him immediately. This is an attack, so never tolerate kicking. Let him know you won't accept this threat. And it doesn't matter if you weren't the intended target — a kick can kill you whether the horse meant to kick you or another victim.

Feet endanger you even when the horse lies down. Stay out of the way when he rolls and kicks

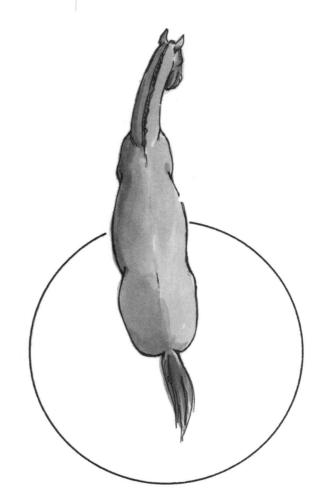

Imagine a semicircle about four feet out from the horse's hindquarters. When you enter that "kicking zone," be assertive, keep body contact, and watch the horse's legs.

all four legs in the air. If he becomes caught in the stall or under a fence, be careful when you help him regain his feet. In his excitement, he can kick you by accident.

When you bend down or squat to groom the horse's feet or lower legs, keep an eye on the opposite foot. He can lift a foot to knock off a fly and hit you by accident.

9. When you groom a horse, watch his expression. Some horses are ticklish on legs or belly,

To feed a horse treats, hold your hand flat with fingers together.

Your Horse Enclosure

In the Old West, few horses lived inside barns. Most ranged in huge pastures or in corrals near the ranch. Today's Western horse can live in a backyard pen, a barn, a field, or ranch land. You can choose among facilities, depending on your preference and circumstances. In his enclosure, the horse needs food, water, and shelter.

Every horse must eat and drink to survive, but the type of shelter depends on the local climate and his needs. A pleasure horse may not require a full-scale barn; a simple roof or three-sided shed will protect him from weather extremes.

The enclosure must contain the horse safely. Barbwire, the fence that changed the West, confines cattle more safely than horses. A horse snagged in barbwire can fight and injure himself severely. Safer fences for Western horses include metal pipe, wood post and rails, and woven wire. Your horse might respect "hot wire," or electric fencing.

Keep your horse safe by horse-proofing your barn and enclosures. Try to anticipate every possible hazard.

The footing should never be slippery; always remove any poisonous plants; and secure the door to the feed room. Check the heights of ceilings and overhangs. Eliminate any electrical hazards, and see that all gates and doors close tightly. Dispose of trash regularly.

Safe fences for horses include metal or woven wire.

or around their ears, and they will warn you by moving away, pawing, or threatening to bite or kick. Handle these areas gently so the horse tolerates your touch. Discipline him whenever he resists handling, with a sharp word or slap. Sternly correct a horse that bites or kicks, and watch closely for a repetition of the threat.

10. Prevent accidental nips by holding your hand flat and fingers together when you feed a treat or touch a horse's nose. Few horses bite out of meanness, but some will nip in play. Those big teeth can break bones, so correct this misbehavior immediately.

Dealing with Misbehavior

Pat Parelli has said: "Respect is hard to get, but easy to lose. It takes discipline, energy, and maintenance to get."

Not every horse will respect you. If he learned bad habits through careless handling, you'll have to outsmart him in order to catch, lead, and tie him safely.

Horsemen appreciate animals they can catch easily. The opposite horse — one who sidles away and evades capture — can be one of the most frustrating creatures.

Some horses will move their heads to avoid the halter. Worse is the one who continues walking away from you, not allowing you to touch him.

Don't chase the horse to make him run. You can try bribing him, luring him close to you. Shake a few oats in a bucket, and allow him to eat. Contain him by encircling the lead rope, or a neck rope, around his neck a few inches behind the throat, and secure the halter.

What if your horse refuses to fall into your trap? You can "walk him down," just following him at a walk until he gives up. Then reward him with grain, pet him, and let him go. This retrains him through a pleasant experience.

You can also guide the horse into a "ketch pen," or confined area. Even with a hard-to-catch horse, avoid leaving a halter on him. Grabbing the halter can be dangerous, as the horse could drag you if

Safety Precautions

Memorize these safety precautions, and practice them so that they become automatic behaviors around horses.

Always

★ Move slowly and deliberately around your horse.

★ Wear protective footwear and headgear.

★ Hold the lead rope or longe line with your hand around the coiled rope end.

★ Hold the coiled rope end or bridle reins off the ground when you lead the horse.

★ Talk to the horse when you approach him.

★ Position yourself on the horse's side, near the shoulder, most of the time.

★ Tie your horse to a sturdy object, suitable to hold him if he struggles.

You can discourage a "halter puller" by tying him to an inner tube wrapped around a tie rail. The tube will stretch, then pull the horse back to the rail.

your hand is caught in the straps. Or the horse could snag the halter on a fence, tree, or his own hoof, causing him to panic. (Leave only a break-away halter on a loose horse.)

When you lead him, he might lag behind or charge forward. Tap his hindquarters with a whip in your left hand to urge him forward. Restrain the eager horse with a chain lead shank, fitting the chain over his nose. If he tries to lean into you, slap his shoulder and tell him, "Get over."

If he refuses to walk forward beside you but stares at an object, let him stand and look at whatever has caught his attention. Don't allow him to move away from it, but let him think while he stands in place. Give him time, watch his expression, and then cue him to walk forward again.

If you know your horse fights being tied, don't tie him to a solid object. You can discourage the "halter puller" by tying him to an inner tube wrapped around a tie rail, or a strong stretchy lead rope. The tube or rope will stretch under pressure, then steadily pull the horse back to the rail. The horse learns to keep the rope slack to avoid pressure. A training halter also discourages the horse from pulling against the rope.

If you're new to horses, don't endanger yourself by dealing with one that tries to hurt you. Seek expert training help. A few sessions with a seasoned professional can cure many bad habits.

The best way to learn how to handle horses is to observe an experienced horseman. Watch your instructor, trainer, equine practitioner, or farrier. See how he approaches a horse, and copy his attitude and actions.

4-H horse leaders and many college continuing education classes teach horsemanship and safe procedures. Also, expert horsemen teach their own clinics, open to the public. Authorities such as Monty Roberts, Pat Parelli, John Lyons, Ray Hunt, and Art Gaytan often teach basic horse handling in public settings. In TTEAM sessions, you can learn this approach to working with the horse without force.

Tacking Up

Now it's time to saddle and bridle your horse so you're ready to ride. As a responsible horseman, you can make riding safer and more pleasurable by following a regular procedure. Choose correctly fitted equipment, and place it on your horse with care. You'll also want to select comfortable Western attire for your hours in the saddle.

ENSURING A GOOD FIT

No matter how carefully you saddle your horse, the wrong tack can irritate the animal. As the pad and girth press against skin, muscle, and bone, the constant pressure can cause unnecessary discomfort and even pain. Many animals learn to resent their tack during saddling and riding. They demonstrate their discomfort by nipping, kicking, bucking, or even running away.

First, check your saddle to be sure that its tree conforms to the shape of your animal's withers and back. Look for the tree to clear the withers suffi-

ciently. When you sit in the saddle, you should be able to fit two or three fingers between the gullet (under the pommel) and the withers.

The bars of the saddle's tree spread the weight over the back and lift the weight of the rider away from the spine. The bars should match the angle of the horse's back. Don't use a saddle with a narrow tree on a wide-backed horse, or a wide tree on an animal with a narrower backbone. Too narrow will pinch, and too wide will rest too low on the withers.

Test a new or used saddle before you buy it. Many sellers and tack shops will assist you in checking a saddle on your horse. Evaluate the fit both from the ground and while mounted — just a few minutes will let you know if this is the right tack for your particular horse.

The saddle pad is an important component. With a Western saddle, the pad protects the saddle's wool lining from sweat. It should feel firm, not limp. A pad will measure from one-half to one inch

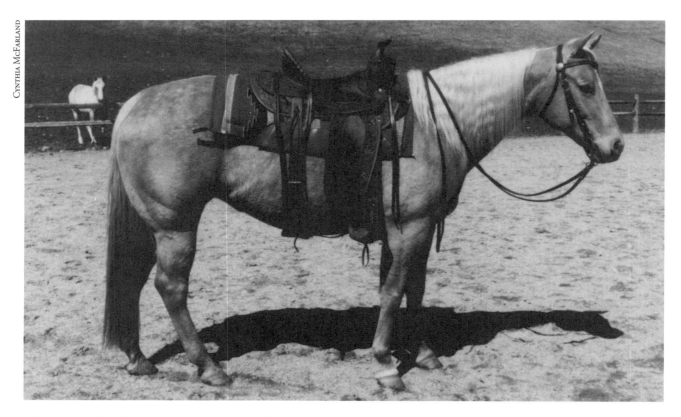

Choose tack that fits your horse correctly. Ill-fitting tack can irritate him, and he may learn to resent it during saddling and riding.

thick. The material should absorb sweat and wick moisture away from the back.

You can choose a pad (a thick square of felt or fleece) or a blanket, or both. Generally, you place a pad next to the horse. On top, follow tradition with a Navajo blanket of woven wool. The blanket covers the pad as a colorful decoration.

Don't expect pads to make a saddle fit your horse. A pile of thick pads can't really cushion the wrong-size saddle, and they can irritate your horse by increasing pressure on the withers. A therapeutic pad can dissipate pressure more evenly, although the permanent solution is matching the saddle tree to the horse's back.

The cinch should fit the horse, too. Usually measuring about 34 inches long, the cinch should not be too long or short, for both comfort and safety. Cinch rings should rest behind and well above the horse's elbows, positioned from 6 to 14 inches below the rigging, depending on the size of

horse and saddle. If the rings sit too close to the rigging, you'll have to wrap the latigo once or twice more. Rings that are too low, on a short cinch, will rub the tender skin behind the elbows.

Your saddle is only as secure as your cinch. Never use a cinch that's frayed or rotten. A mohair cinch will be strong and soft against the horse, or you might choose one of the new neoprene models. Use a cinch with rings of brass, bronze, or stainless steel.

For safety, you can now equip a Western saddle with breakaway stirrups. If you or your horse falls, the stirrup releases under the pressure and your foot slips free.

BRIDLE PARTS AND TYPES

You can choose from a variety of bridles, also called "headstalls." Many Western headstalls are doubled and stitched. The leather straps consist of two layers, stitched together for durability and to prevent stretching.

For pleasure and schooling, you can use any style of bridle, of plain or tooled leather, nylon webbing, or plaited nylon cord. Most of these are ½ to ¾ inches wide.

Western reins are of three types: open, closed, or roping. The open, or split, rein is the most common, consisting of two separate straps, ⅜ to 1 inch wide and 6 to 8 feet long. They're made of flat or braided leather, braided mohair, plaited nylon cord, or nylon webbing.

The closed rein is actually three parts. Two reins connect to each other by a three-foot-long romal, or quirt. This style is also called the "California," since it originated with the vaqueros of that state. It's still most often used by West Coast rid-

ers, and those who show Arabians or Morgans. The rein and romal can be made of flat or rounded leather, or braided leather or rawhide. The braided styles attach to the bit with snaps or with the self-locking bit ends.

Contest riders often use the roping rein, one continuous strap from 6 to 8 feet long. With no loose ends, the rider can't drop the rein while working. It's made of leather or nylon webbing, and the leather style may be braided in the center for better grip.

Because bridles are adjustable, you'll find a limited choice in sizes. You can select from pony, Arab, and horse, or full size. If your horse's head seems to be in between, measure the distance from the corner of one lip, over the poll, and to the other lip corner. Compare this measurement

A traditional hackamore, which uses a bosal (noseband of plaited rawhide) with a mecate (tied horsehair reins), is unique to Western riding. With it, you use a pull and slack motion, exerting leverage against the horse's nose and lower jawbone.

Type	Varieties	Uses
METAL MOUTHPIECE OF IRON OR STEEL		
Snaffle	O-ring D-ring Twisted wire	Basic bit for schooling and everyday riding Direct action
Gag	Snaffle Shanked	Timed events, for training and correction Mouthpiece has sliding action
Curb	Grazing bit Loose-shanked bit	Basic Western bit for a trained horse Used in all types of riding Leverage action A curb with a jointed mouthpiece is a very severe bit.
BITLESS BRIDLE		
Hackamore	Bosal Rawhide noseband	Schooling a colt
Mechanical Hackamore	Flat nosepiece Rounded nosepiece Hackamore gag combination	Roping Timed events Pleasure riding Distance riding
Sidepull	Nylon rope noseband	Schooling a colt

with the bridle you're considering, so you're sure it will fit your horse.

CHOOSING A BIT

Western bits developed from the styles introduced by Spanish horsemen. First forged of iron, bits later became popular in styles manufactured of steel or aluminum. Most contemporary bitmakers produce bits of stainless steel, although horsemen claim that a sweet iron mouthpiece is superior. Quality bits may feature cheeks of stainless steel, for an attractive appearance, and a sweet iron mouthpiece. The iron will rust, but horses seem to prefer the flavor over steel.

Many bits also feature copper, either inlaid in iron or steel or as a coating that forms the entire mouthpiece. Proponents feel that both sweet iron and copper encourage the horse to produce saliva. A moist mouth is more responsive to the movement of the bit.

Riders of the West consider the bit a valuable tool for producing a schooled horse. The finished horse performs on a loose rein, wearing a curb bit in the Spanish tradition. Whether the bit is of the Texas (grazing bit) or California (loose-shanked) style, the trained horse responds to a light touch on the reins.

The curb bit operates on leverage, created by the pressure between the mouthpiece and the curb

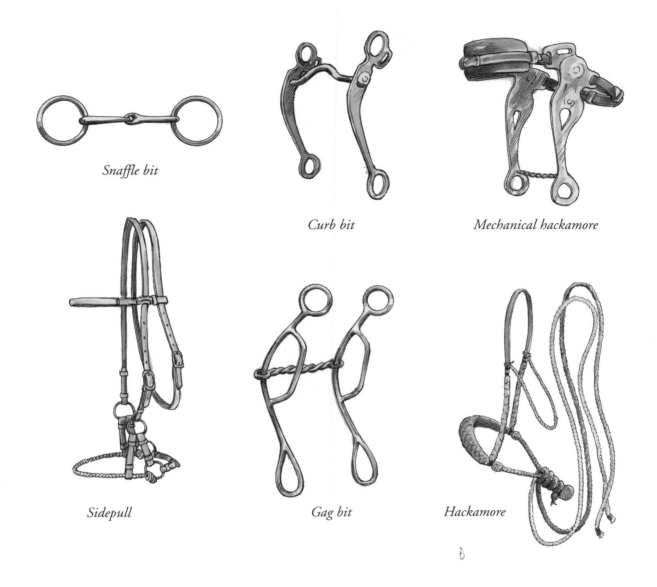

Snaffle bit

Curb bit

Mechanical hackamore

Sidepull

Gag bit

Hackamore

strap or chain. Its severity is influenced by the ratio between the shank above and below the mouthpiece. It must include a curb strap or chain, which also affects the bit's action through its adjustment. The mouthpiece shape helps the bit to position comfortably on the horse's bars (gums) and tongue.

Your hands make a bit soft or painful. A horseman learns to use any bit with tact, exerting just enough pressure to cue the horse.

Unique to Western riding is the traditional hackamore bridle, using a bosal with a mecate. The bosal, a noseband of plaited rawhide, is an effective control device. It exerts leverage against the nose and the lower jawbones. The heel knot at the bottom of the bosal adds balance, so the bosal swings free when you slacken the mecate, or tied horsehair reins.

The vaquero used the hackamore as a training device, to school a colt in the basics. He eventually put the colt "in the bridle," progressing to the curb bit.

The hackamore requires a particular kind of touch. You use a pull and slack motion, pulling only one rein at a time. You must know how much strength to apply, and when you need to lighten up the pressure on the horse's sensitive nose and jaw.

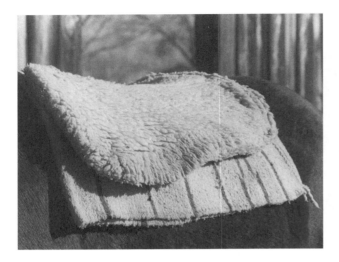

Here, the blanket is placed next to the horse, and the pad is placed on top.

Place the saddle gently on the pad with the stirrup over the horn.

BEFORE YOU SADDLE

Most experts agree that you should tie your horse for saddling. He might spook while you connect the cinch, then run off with the saddle sliding off his back. This situation could terrify the horse and cause a serious accident.

With the horse tied to a rail or in crossties, groom his coat to remove all dirt. Pay close attention to the areas that the saddle will touch — withers, back, girthline, and belly. Stretch up to curry and brush the top of the withers, and squat down to clean the belly.

As you groom, check the withers, back, sides, and belly for swellings or scrapes. If you notice a large swelling or break in the skin, treat the area immediately and skip riding for the day. The weight of you and your tack could cause a gall, which will be even more difficult to treat. Galls often cause the white "saddle marks" you see on many horses' withers and backs.

You might choose to saddle the horse anyway, protecting the swollen or scraped skin. You can cushion the cinch with a fleece cover over the strap. Or, if the spot is located on the withers or back, cut a hole in the saddle pad over that place. Ideally, the hole will keep weight from pressing directly over the problem area.

Inspect saddle and pad for safety and cleanliness. Never use a cracked latigo or stirrup leather, or a frayed cinch. Turn over saddle and pad to check the undersides for cleanliness. Remove any burrs or other sharp objects that could irritate the horse's skin.

PLACING THE SADDLE

Traditionally, you saddle from the horse's left (near) side, but your horse should accept saddling from either side. Some people find it more convenient to saddle Western style from the off side. You only have to lift the latigo with the near-side stirrup, instead of the entire length of the cinch, which you leave buckled to the off-side billet, or strap.

Whichever side you choose, stand slightly behind the horse's shoulder, with your shoulder about 12 inches away. This position makes it difficult for the horse to bite or kick you. It helps to have "eyes in your feet," which will keep your toes safe from a front hoof.

You'll always use a pad or blanket under a Western saddle. Position the pad partly over the withers, then slide it onto the horse's back, leaving the first inch or so over the withers. By sliding with the hairs, the pad lays the coat flat for a comfortable fit. If you use two blankets or a pad with a blanket on top, hold both as one unit as you place them on the back.

Lift the pad slightly above the bone of the withers. This allows air circulation along the horse's back after you add the saddle.

The pad folds along the center of the horse's backbone. Position the fold so each half of the pad covers an equal portion of the back. Walk around to check from the front or rear and the other side.

Pick up the saddle and arrange stirrups and cinch away from the saddle's underside. Most people hang one stirrup over the horn, and the latigo or cinch over the seat.

Next, carefully lift the saddle over the horse's back and set it in place. Never throw it onto the horse. The sudden weight could surprise him, and he could kick or step on you. You also could cause him to cringe and drop his back. If you repeat this thoughtless behavior, he can become "cold-backed." You'll make future saddlings much more difficult, as he retaliates against abuse.

The Western saddle is heavy, and you might not be able to lift it high enough. In this case, lightly swing the saddle onto the horse, using momentum to help you raise and place it.

Position the saddle where it naturally fits behind the shoulder blades. The cinch will hang about 4 inches behind the point of the horse's elbow. If the saddle looks too far forward, slide it slightly back. You may need to move the pad as well, or lift the saddle to move it separately.

If your saddle sits too far back, don't scoot it forward without lifting the pad above the back. If you don't, the movement ruffles the hairs of the coat. This could cause the weight of you and the tack to make sores on the horse's back.

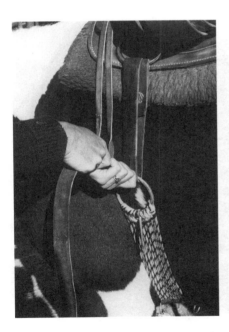

Run the latigo down and up through the cinch ring.

Once the cinch is tightened, it should fall 6 to 14 inches below the rigging, depending on the size of the horse and saddle.

Never use a cinch or latigo that is frayed or rotten. A traditional mohair cinch is both strong and soft. Cinch rings should be made of brass or stainless steel.

Securing the Saddle

Don't spend too long arranging gear before you secure the cinch. The saddle is merely resting in place, and an abrupt movement could dump it onto the ground.

Quickly make sure that the pad is lying smoothly against the horse's back. If you need to, lift the front again to maintain an air channel. Walk around to the off side to verify that all parts of the saddle and pad lie flat. If you've left the cinch over the seat, carefully lower it. Try not to let the buckle swing against the horse. Back on the near side, loop the stirrup over the horn to uncover the latigo.

Securing the cinch can be the most hazardous part of saddling. Some horses will express their resentment by trying to nip or kick. Protect yourself by scanning the horse's expression, and also keep an eye on his feet. Be prepared to chastise him with a sharp word or slap.

Bend over slightly to reach underneath the belly for the end of the cinch. As you place your-

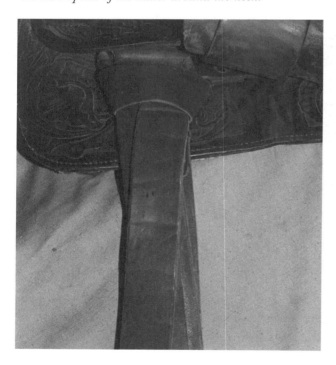

To control your horse while you put the bridle on, buckle the crownpiece of the halter around the neck.

Instead of using a buckle on a cinch ring, you can knot the latigo through the ring on the saddle. Shown are two knots.

self in this dangerous location, keep an eye on the horse. It might help to touch his shoulder with your free hand; you can feel any movement.

Some martingales and breastplates slide over the cinch. If your cinch needs to fit through a connecting strap, attach the tack now, before you buckle the cinch. When you lift the cinch, you'll position the connecting strap mid-belly.

Bring the end of the cinch up toward the latigo. It is best to shorten the strap slowly and smoothly. Your horse will appreciate the gentlest pressure possible, and you'll avoid making him "cinchy."

The large buckle on the cinch fits through holes on the latigo. You will loop the latigo down through the buckle's metal ring, up to the rigging, and down again to fit the buckle's tongue into a hole in the latigo. A short free end of the latigo can hang down from the rigging, or you may run it through a loop strap on the saddle's pommel. Pull the latigo down solidly, so the tongue fits securely into the hole.

You can also secure the latigo by tying a knot instead of using the cinch buckle.

When you snug the cinch, check that the skin and hair under it lie flat, with no pinching. You might lift each foreleg up and forward, to eliminate any wrinkles of the skin under the cinch.

Also compare both sides of the cinch rings. Each should reach to the same height on the horse's sides, for equal pressure.

Preparing the Bridle

With the saddle in place, you're ready to replace the halter with the horse's bridle. Your goal is to handle the tack deftly, while gently guiding the animal's head into the headstall.

Before you start, pick up the bridle by the crownpiece to check all parts for safety and cleanliness. Look for any cracked or torn places, especially where the metal or nylon contacts metal hardware.

Examine where the cheekpieces attach to the bit. Your bridle will probably connect to the bit with either Chicago screws, buckles, or leather ties. These fasteners must hold the bit securely.

If you haven't used this particular bridle before, check its style. Western bridles fit onto the horse's head with an earpiece or browband and throatlatch. The earpiece holds the bridle around an ear. A split-ear bridle is a crownpiece with a long split in the leather through which the horse's right ear fits. Variations are the shaped-ear and sliding ear. The browband is a strap that attaches across the horse's brow, below the ears and above the eyes. Another strap, the throatlatch, secures the bridle under the jaws and against the throat.

Wash the bit if it's encrusted with dried saliva or feed, and check its condition. A bit can break or wear out. Never use a bit that has cracks or sharp edges, because the metal could injure the horse's lips, tongue, or bars.

Holding the bridle by the crownpiece, arrange the reins in your other hand, or drape them over your shoulder. Shake the bridle so the weight of the bit pulls the straps to hang vertically. This should disentangle any twists in the cheekpieces.

In cold weather, warm the bit just before you ride. You can breathe on the chilled metal, or rub it between your hands.

Placing the Bridle

Always bridle from the near side. You'll adjust the throatlatch or curb strap from that side, and your horse has been trained on that side.

Maintain an alert attitude as you bridle. You place yourself in an awkward, possibly hazardous position, close to the horse's forehand. You have to juggle halter, tie rope, bridle, and reins. Some clever horses have learned to wriggle free during this task.

Standing next to your horse, unfasten the halter and slide it off his nose. Keep the halter against his neck while you rebuckle the crownpiece around the neck. This allows you to control the animal in the moments before you slip the bridle over his ears.

Keep a calm, purposeful attitude when bridling your horse. Pick up the bridle's crownpiece in one hand. (You might choose to drape it over your shoulder, so you can quickly grab it when you remove the halter.) With your other hand, place the

Bridling

To fit the bridle, move your right shoulder near the horse's throat.

Hold the crownpiece in your right hand, and the mouthpiece in your left palm. Bring the crownpiece close to the horse's forehead and reach it up toward the ears, while you guide the bit into the mouth.

You can modify the basic bridling method if you are short or your horse is tall. Reach your right hand under the horse's neck. Grasp the bridle together and raise it up toward the forehead. With your left hand, slip the bit into the horse's mouth. Now both hands are free to continue.

After the bit is in place, both hands are free to move the crownpiece over the ears. With the left hand, slide the crownpiece over the forehead, and with your right hand, gently flick the ears forward at the base as you fit the crownpiece in place. Reach over the poll to fit the off side first. With a tall horse, you will have to do this by feel. With an earpiece, slide the right ear into the slot or loop.

reins over the horse's head to rest partway down the crest. If he starts to move, you can restrain him with both the reins and the buckled halter.

Whichever method you use to hold the bridle as you bring the bit into the horse's mouth, be sure to keep the crownpiece raised with your right hand. If you let it slip down, the horse might open his mouth and drop the bit. The upward pressure of the crownpiece helps keep the bit in place while you fit the bridle behind the ears. Be careful not to force the bit against the horse's lips and teeth. As you pull the crownpiece upward, your left hand will merely point the bit in the right direction. Stretch a finger or two to keep the curb strap underneath the bit, out of the horse's mouth.

Reach under the crownpiece or earpiece to smooth back any loose mane hairs. If the bridle has a browband, pull the forelock over the strap.

With a throatlatch, attach it by threading the short top strap down through the buckle on the long strap hanging from the offside. Connect the buckle so the straps lie flat and somewhat loose. You should be able to slide four fingers between the strap and the horse's jaw.

Most horses will cooperate and open their mouths. Yours might choose to evade the bit by clenching his teeth or moving his head. Encourage him to open his mouth by sliding your left thumb or a finger between the lips, into the toothless space on the bars. He should respond by chewing, so slide your finger out as you slip the bit between the parted teeth.

Respect your horse by sliding the bit gently into position. Never shove the bit against the lips or teeth, which can train him to evade bridling.

If he does raise his head high, lips pressed tightly, remain patient yet determined. Urge him to drop his head as you carefully bring the bit into position. Time the insertion of your finger into the mouth so you can quickly move the crownpiece up and the bit in place.

As a last resort, you might wipe a dab of molasses or peanut butter on the bit's mouthpiece. Resorting to this enticement might save some time, while it rewards (and hopefully retrains) the ornery horse.

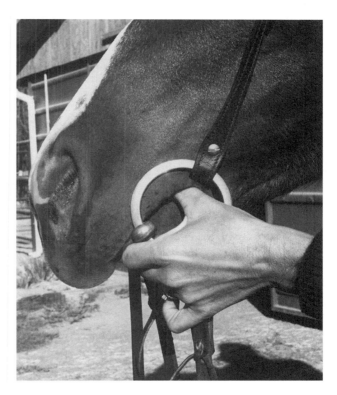

You can encourage your horse to take the bit by inserting your left thumb between his lips, into the toothless space on the bars. Slide your thumb out as you slip the bit between the parted teeth.

A better way to soothe the head-shy horse is to rub the sides of the horse's mouth and ears. Soothe him by gentle massage with your left hand, as you hold the bridle in place with your right. Drop your left hand to the bit, and easily "swoop" the bit into the horse's open mouth.

Carefully place the crown behind the ears. Flick them gently from the base, without bending them. Reach over the poll to fit the offside portion first. If your horse is tall, you'll have to do this by feel. With an earpiece, slide the right ear into the slot or loop.

BRIDLE ADJUSTMENT

Look for all straps to rest flat against the horse's face. The browband should rest close to the ears.

Cheekpieces should position the bit snugly, not too tight or too loose. A *curb bit* fits into the corners of the mouth without forming any wrinkles there. Adjust the buckle on the nearside cheekpiece to raise or lower the bit. If you have to adjust it more than one hole, move to the off side to shorten or tighten that cheekpiece. Ideally the buckles sit the same distance from the bit on both sides, so the bridle fits evenly.

The curb strap should hang so you can fit one or two fingers under it when the reins are slack. Test the strap's action by pulling back on the reins. As the bit's shanks move back toward the saddle, the strap should exert pressure. Release the reins, and the shanks swing freely forward.

A *snaffle bit* should fit right into both corners of the mouth, forming one wrinkle on each side. Don't make the bit fit too tightly, with two wrinkles, or too low. A horse can put his tongue over a loosely fitted snaffle.

With the bridle adjusted, remove the halter from around the horse's neck.

To check the length of your stirrups, hold the base of the stirrup against your armpit. Stretch the leather along the underside of your arm. Your fingertips should touch the top of the leather, where it attaches to the saddle tree.

READY TO RIDE

Just before you mount, check saddle and bridle for security. Tighten the cinch so it's snug but not overly tight.

If you have to shorten it quite a bit, space the tightenings over two or even three times. Many horses have learned to combat the compression by holding their breath, which forces you to readjust the girth several times. You can combat this by prodding the horse to exhale, using your knee against his belly.

With your saddle in position, you're almost ready to mount. You might want to check the length of your stirrup leathers, to gauge that they're adjusted correctly. Hold the base of the stirrup against your armpit so you stretch the leather along the underside of your arm. Your fingertips should touch the top of the leather, where it attaches to the saddle tree.

Use the stirrup buckle to adjust the length of the leathers. Unfasten the top section of the metal buckle by sliding it upward. Lower or raise the lower section, to fit into a different pair of holes in the leather. Lower the top section so it clicks back over the lower part, fastening the buckle securely in place.

Count the number of rows of holes up from the tip of the stirrup leather. On the off side, repeat the process so both stirrups are the same length on both sides.

If you use a rear cinch on a Western saddle, buckle it loosely. Allow about three fingers' width between the cinch and the horse's belly. It's wise to fasten the middle of the rear cinch to the front one with a connector strap.

Pick up the reins close to the saddle horn. Check the cinch a last time before you mount, sliding two or three fingers underneath the cinch or latigo. This permits the horse to breathe easily while still holding the saddle securely.

During a long ride, give your horse an occasional rest from the constant pressure of the tack. Dismount and loosen the cinch a few holes. Remind yourself about the slack cinch by hooking the near stirrup over the saddle horn.

Back at the Barn

Most riders remove the bridle, then the saddle. With the bridle replaced by the halter, you can tie the horse for unsaddling and after-ride grooming.

After you dismount, bring your horse to the tying area. Locate your halter where you left it. It is often convenient to drape it over your shoulder for easy access.

Leave the reins over the horse's neck, and unbuckle the throatlatch, if equipped. With your right hand, bring the crownpiece over the ears, slowly lowering it over the forehead. When you see your horse open his mouth, continue lowering the bridle so the bit easily slips free. Avoid moving too quickly or letting the bit hit the horse's teeth.

Hold the bridle in one hand while you slip the halter in place and fasten it. Before you connect the lead rope or cross ties to the halter rings, bring the reins over the head. After you've secured the horse, hang the bridle on a nearby hook for cleaning.

You'll encounter few problems when you unsaddle your horse. Most animals appear relieved as you remove the tack, but remember to do it gently.

Reverse the saddling process, and always undo the rear cinch first. Avoid banging your horse with a swinging cinch or stirrups by laying them over the seat before you lift the saddle.

Place the saddle on a rack or fence rail. If you have nowhere to store it temporarily, you can prop it against a wall or post, with the pommel on the ground and the cantle resting against the wall.

Care for a sweaty back by rinsing or massaging the wet hairs. You can use a sponge or water from a hose. Wipe off excess water with a sweat scraper.

Tack Care

Before you store your tack, brush off loose hairs. You should saddle soap leather components after each use, and wash fabric pads and girths often. Also, if you notice any loosened stitching on your saddle, have it repaired as soon as possible.

Brush or vacuum loose hairs from your pad. Wash it occasionally, before the fabric becomes stiff with hardened sweat.

Dip the bridle's bit into a bucket of water to wash off the metal. Store your bridle on a rounded hanger, not a nail that can crease the leather so it cracks. Let the reins hang down or loop loosely.

Because it's your primary means of control, keep your bridle in top condition. Clean leather both inside and outside, ideally after each use. Sweat, saliva, and the rubbing of metal parts can damage leather. If you notice cracks, have the bridle repaired or replace that section. Watch for wear on metal parts, too, especially the threads of Chicago screws on Western bridles. It's quite a shock to have a screw give way so the bit falls from your horse's mouth!

Traditional Western attire evolved from a need for protection from the elements, livestock, and long hours in the saddle.

Your Attire

Western riding would seem to imply cowboy gear, though you may wear any comfortable riding apparel. In competition, rules and traditions usually require distinctive Western attire. For pleasure and distance riding, choose any outfit that offers protection and comfort.

Western wear styles continue to evolve, with rodeo contestants influencing the fashions. The basic articles fulfill the function of riding wear, with two items important for safety in the saddle — boots and headgear.

A horseman always wears boots when handling livestock. A boot gives support to the foot for long hours in the saddle, and it pro-

 WESTERN RIDING ATTIRE

Garment	Popular Varieties	Description
BASIC RIDING ATTIRE		
Jeans	Wranglers	Dark blue or black Starched
Boots	Riding boots Ropers Lace-ups	Stiff, high tops, scalloped, stitched for decoration Reinforced arch, high heels
Hat	Felt Straw	Of wool or beaver fur
Shirt	Rodeo style	Plain cut, long sleeves, button front Brilliant colors in solids or patterns Starched
OPTIONS		
Vest	Blue denim	Adds warmth
Chaps	Shotgun Batwing Chinks Woollies	Protect legs from brush, ropes, fences Loose fitting, wrap around legs Knee length for warm weather Fur for warmth
Bandana	Classic red	Use as a handkerchief Tie loosely around neck
Belt	Tooled leather Horsehair	Adorn with a trophy buckle or silver buckle set

This Western safety helmet meets current safety standards and is available in felt or straw styles.

Chaps protect your legs from brush, ropes, and fences.

tects the leg from chafing against the stirrup leather.

On the ground, boots protect your feet if a horse or cow steps on you. Large heels won't slide through the stirrup, so you won't catch your foot if you or the horse falls.

The look of your boots also implies you're a horseman. Your spurs will leave gray marks on your boot heels. This mark of distinction tells the world you're "a ridin' man (or gal)."

The cowboy's traditional hat has generated controversy in today's safety-conscious society. In all equestrian disciplines *except* Western riding, horsemen recognize the value of protective headgear. When jumping, all riders wear helmets that absorb shock in case of a fall. Western riders who gallop and turn at speeds faster than most jumpers stick to their hats of felt or straw.

You can buy a felt hat with a protective shell inside. Several manufacturers offer models that meet current safety standards. The style disguises the shell, which features a chin strap.

Manufacturers report that younger riders and seniors tend to be the primary customers for this protective headwear. Unfortunately, the idea hasn't caught on with the majority of riders. Trail riders, especially distance riders, have been the only group to adopt protective headgear. In Western riding, trail riding may be the riskiest discipline, with more opportunities to fall from a moving horse.

In the Saddle: Learning the Basics

Your body language, and that of your horse, express your equestrian skill. By your seat — the way you sit on your horse — you communicate your competence.

You don't need to look perfect. You just ride efficiently. In most Western riding, you ride for function rather than form.

Watch an expert ride. He sits firm, straight, and solid, yet relaxed and supple. He exudes confidence. His movements are fluid as he moves with the horse — just as a cowboy appears glued to the saddle.

To ride like this, you need to develop balance and timing. Through balance, your body flows with the horse as you feel his motion. Balance relates to your center of gravity, just like the horse's balance. Instructor Sue Cummins has used the term *centering* to describe that balance: "It's where all the energy and the flow comes from."

A balanced rider sits firm, straight, and solid, yet relaxed and supple.

She has described the centered rider as authentic. With a genuine balance, you sit in the saddle with your legs falling down relaxed over the horse. Your arms hang down softly, also relaxed, and your vision is straight ahead.

Riding resembles other sports, in which the athlete moves from a base without rigidity. If you pose, hold your breath, move from your shoulder or chin, or stare, the tension makes you look and feel tight and rigid rather than relaxed and elastic.

Your horse feels your body language. You communicate your tension to him, often without realizing it. Cummins has cautioned against concentrating too much on sitting "correctly." "When you ride stiffly 'in position,' your horse doesn't like it. The horse wants to feel a softness on him. He wants to feel a flow. He wants to feel a partnership."

Learning balance and timing does demand a focus. Before you can experience that fluid feeling on horseback, you need to develop physical skills.

When mounting, aim for a continuous, smooth movement, and ease gently into the saddle.

MOUNTING UP

With your horse ready to ride, check your tack one final time. Lead your horse by the reins to a clear, level area. You'll usually mount on the left (near) side, although the Western horse should be trained for you to mount from either side.

Make sure that the horse stands quietly and balanced on all four legs. While you mount, he must stand still. You're in a precarious position between the ground and the saddle, and a sudden movement could cause you to fall. Maintain control by keeping a hand on the reins at all times.

Stand with your left shoulder beside the horse's neck, and place the reins over the horse's head so they rest on the withers. With separate (split) reins, you can drape the near rein to the off side, and the offside rein to the near side. Shorten them just enough so you have control.

With your left hand, hold onto the reins and a fistful of the mane. You can mount facing the saddle or slightly toward the rear so you're looking over the horse's offside hip. Facing the saddle, you can watch to make sure he doesn't move, and use your right hand to twist the stirrup toward you. Place your left foot in the stirrup and hop up with your right foot.

As you push off the ground, shift your rein hand from the mane to the saddle horn. Swing your right leg over the saddle and gently settle yourself in the seat. Place your right foot in the right stirrup.

Aim for a continuous, smooth movement. Try to alight into the saddle; do not plop down with all your weight.

If you suspect that the horse might move while you mount, maintain a lateral flexion with the reins. Shorten the near side rein so the horse bends his neck toward you, and say, "Whoa."

To dismount, you reverse the steps. Remove your right foot from the stirrup. Stand up and turn toward the horse's offside hip to swing your right leg behind you. As you move toward the ground, keep your left foot in the stirrup. Remove it as your right heel touches the ground, and step down.

During the dismount, keep the reins on the horse's neck so you maintain control. You should face forward, standing beside your horse's neck, to complete the movement.

SITTING CORRECTLY

Your seat is where you gain security and softness, blending the two sensations for a graceful posture. Sit in a comfortable, natural way, in the middle of the horse.

You should look as comfortable as you feel. Sitting from your center, you sit vertically — an imaginary line from your ear down through your shoulder and hip would touch the back of your heel. Hold your back straight and flat, yet not arched so you look stiff.

Imagine that the horse has disappeared, and you are standing on the ground, and maintain that same posture in the saddle.

California trainer Mack Linn has taught: "Riding a horse is just like standing here. Stand up and sit straight down without being stiff. Stand up, drop back, and keep that position. You bend only at the knee and hip." He advises that to loosen up, you can stand up, turn right and sit, then stand up and turn left and sit.

With an ideal stirrup length, your knee is bent slightly so your heel is lower than your toe. Your legs hang down at or slightly behind the cinch. If you feel as if you're reaching for the stirrups, or your knees are bent too much, test the length by standing up so your weight is off the horse's back. You shouldn't have more than an inch or two between your crotch and the seat of the saddle. If more or less than that, dismount and adjust the length on both sides.

Place your foot in the stirrup so your weight rests on the widest part of your foot. Flex your ankles to absorb the shock, but don't press hard on the stirrups. Pushing will tense your body and brace your legs so they move to the sides, away from the horse. You should be able to feel the warmth of contact with him, along your thighs, knees, and upper calf.

In this balanced position, you can move with the horse, yet remain steady. You effectively con-

To sit correctly, imagine a line from your ear down through your shoulder and hip to the back of your heel.

trol him with your body weight, hands, and legs. You feel close to him, and you can meld with his movements.

Hold the reins in one hand, your left. (If you're left-handed, switch to holding reins in your right hand.) Adopted from the working cowboy, this style leaves your dominant hand free to open a gate, swing a rope, or crack a whip.

You can hold the reins in a fist, with the lines coming up through your fist. Or, hold your first finger (or two fingers) between the reins. Whichever style, most trainers advise to keep your thumb up and knuckles facing forward. This gives you effective control and an "elastic" hand.

Hold your rein hand slightly in front of the saddle horn so it's parallel to the ground, in line with the horse's neck. Try to keep your hand in that spot, slightly ahead of your hip. You can rest your free hand on your thigh, let it hang by your side, or hold it at waist level.

You sit in the center of the saddle, and you feel the horse through your seat bones. You also have contact through your legs and hands.

Maintain a guiding contact, not too tense or too passive. Hold the reins so that with only a light movement, you contact the horse's mouth.

Hold your rein hand steady, but not completely rigid. Don't worry about keeping your elbows in, or you'll tense the joint. Let the joint relax and go with the horse, absorbing the shock.

Learn to sit down, so you won't move and pull on the horse's mouth. You maintain the vertical position at all three gaits. You move slightly back and forth with the horse's motion, and you appear fluid and supple.

REINING

You guide the horse in the saddle as you do on the ground. Your body language cues the horse to respond.

"A cue is a signal between you and your horse," trainer John Lyons has said. "You set up the condition often enough so you get the correct response to happen. If you don't get your response, go to a point where you set it up and repeat, repeat, repeat, until the response becomes automatic."

For the signals, you use the aids of hands, legs, body weight, and seat bones. Every horseman aims

The Western horse steers with the neck rein, turning away from the feel of a rein laid on his neck.

for good hands, a give and take. When you apply a cue, the horse answers and you instantly stop the cue. Although you work on a loose rein, at times you'll ride on contact. You maintain a sensitive feel of the horse's mouth and keep the horse "between the reins."

You'll spend many hours in the saddle learning the right amount of feel. On contact, your hand will move with the motion of the horse's neck. You'll gently let your hand go forward and back at the walk, to keep the pressure consistent. Don't hold your hand rigid, so the reins alternate between taut and slack. If you pull on the reins as the horse moves forward, you're clashing your aids.

The Western horse turns with the neck rein, turning away from the feel of a rein laid on his neck. If you want to turn right, first you look to the right. Keep your hand low, but move it to the right to lay the rein on the left side of the neck.

Try to move your hand only as far as the distance over your saddle swells. Any further, and you'll start "cranking" the horse's neck with the opposite rein. The horse might tilt his head to the outside, instead of bending in the direction of travel. You want him to follow his nose as he walks forward in an arc.

Trainers consider the neck rein an indirect rein. A direct rein is a direct pull, toward the direction you want to go. (Western riders often call this the "plow rein.") Texas educator Terry McCutcheon has taught students to understand the concept of the indirect rein.

"So many riders tend to pull across the neck, which gets the horse's nose turned to the outside. We teach how the horse moves in one direction with the direct rein, his head and neck in position. Then you use the indirect rein to follow that, and use the leg to push the horse in the direction set by the rein. You need to understand the combination of a leg and the indirect rein."

Lay the rein, release the pressure, and lay it again on the neck. The horse should move his neck and body to turn the corner. If he doesn't, squeeze your outside leg (the leg on the side away from the direction you're turning) against the horse. This reinforces your rein cue. Squeeze and release.

Halting

The understanding that develops between you and your horse begins with "Whoa." You know that when you give the command, the horse willingly obeys. Your horsemanship depends on this mutual understanding: "Whoa" means stop right now.

Use your voice first, and easily take up the rein. This cue relies on pressure and reward, just as in handling the horse on the ground. You give, or release pressure, to reward him for a correct response.

Ideally, he responds to the halt cue because he wants to please you, not because you have forced him. He's learned the path of least resistance, which is to submit his will to yours. He also anticipates that you will respond by rewarding him with lack of pressure.

Both of you gain mutual confidence through this simple response. The two of you read each other. The way your horse halts tells you how he's feeling — willing or resistant. The way you apply and release pressure tells him what kind of rider you are. You're working with your horse so he performs, regardless of what he wants. You'll expand that feeling at each gait, and then develop the comfort and relaxation of a secure partnership.

Walking

Nudge the horse to walk. Either touch him with your heels, or squeeze with your calves. As he moves, you absorb his motion and remain one with him. Keep your shoulders square and your head up.

To gain that authentic seat, don't force your body into a posed position. Texas trainer Nancy Cahill has advised learning by sitting on the horse and feeling your own balance. "Just go ride, without someone saying 'Do this, do that,'" she says. "Ride in a safe place. Ride smart and don't abuse the horse, and it's okay if you bounce. You'll find how to sit in the middle some day, to sit in the middle and find your balance."

Sit down in the saddle on your seat bones, and think of the seat as your spine. With an ideal seat, your spine fuses with the horse's spine. You feel the support of the horse's hind legs with your seat.

There's a feeling of togetherness, with no gap between you.

When you relax, you feel what the horse is doing. His back ripples as he moves in the four-beat walk, and he swings his neck up, down, and sideways. With a loose rein, he swings the neck in rhythm with the legs.

Learn to feel the horse, so you can respond to his movements. Trainer Terry Berg has advised: "You're going to feel it before you see it, or feel it in your hands when he starts to slow down, or he starts to speed up."

While holding your body vertical, start absorbing in your foundation, your feet. Pull your legs back under you, breaking at the ankle and lifting the toe so you drop your heel.

Instructor John Richard Young has coached riders to keep their seat steady, using their legs while releasing the rein: "Control your legs in order to control the horse."

With your heels dropped, you'll find it natural to hold your calves against the horse's barrel. This position will help keep you steady and secure and your legs quiet. Feel the insides of your calves

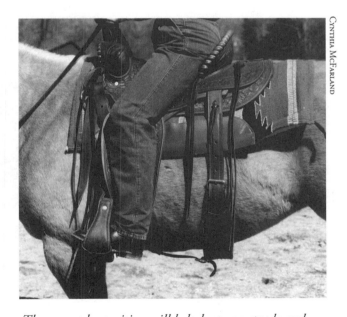

The correct leg position will help keep you steady and secure. With your heels dropped, hold your calves against the horse's barrel. Your feet should point forward or slightly out.

against the horse, with the upper part of your boots touching his sides. Your feet point forward or slightly out.

Your knees point forward, without grabbing. Grabbing establishes a pivot point. Your lower leg will tend to swing back and forth instead of remaining quiet. You can maintain contact with your entire leg, keeping it "open."

If you push too much weight against the stirrups, you push your crotch out of the saddle. Let your weight settle in your seat. Sitting still helps your horse move smoothly.

You might find that you slouch, propping your buttocks against the cantle. You lose that vertical line, so aim to remain forward rather than back. Your torso remains in line with your leg and hip.

California trainer Dave Rhodes has said: "Remember to keep your feet still and quiet, and keep the top half of the body still and quiet. Let the hips move with the horse's motion. Don't get to rocking with the motion like you're riding down the trail on a Saturday afternoon."

Look where you're going, with your eyes up so you look between the horse's ears. Looking down can cause you to lean forward, out of balance.

JOGGING

Moving from the walk to the halt involves a transition. To move out of the walk, you practice upward transitions into faster gaits like the jog or lope. Downward transitions occur from the jog to the walk, or the lope to the jog.

Achieve transitions through your voice, hands, legs, and seat bones. Keep your back strong when you change gait, to absorb the shift in movement.

Coordinating aids takes practice. You want to use your "gas" to push the horse forward with energy, yet you channel that energy with aids that "brake" and guide the horse.

To absorb the jogging motion, relax and let your hips go with the horse.

Coordinate your balance with your timing. "Timing is to get the horse to respond and to make the corrections at the right time," Arabian horse trainer Jim Porcher has said. "Balance is the confidence to know that you're there and will take charge of the horse. You have that kind of balance so you don't act after the fact."

Allow the horse to go forward. Integrate your cues so you don't confuse him. Keep your arm and fingers elastic on the reins, so you don't pull back while urging him forward.

For this simple acceleration of gait, check your balance. Drop your legs back and under you. Depending on how your horse is trained, nudge with the inside leg or both legs and cluck (click your tongue) to ask for the jog. Make your cue subtle, yet definite.

The horse jogs in a two-beat gait, which varies in roughness from horse to horse. Some are smooth, so you can easily sit with minimal motion, your seat glued to the saddle. You'll move with the horse. Other horses move roughly, jostling you back and forth at each step.

To absorb the motion, relax and let your hips go with the horse. Your upper body remains relaxed and quiet. Dave Rhodes has suggested that you concentrate on the bouncing up and down. "Not to post, but to go up and down with the motion. When I judge riders and see them coming down the rail, I see a lot less motion on the up and down rider than when I watch one who goes back and forth."

This is a conscious movement that counteracts the movement that's already happening. Rhodes suggests that you tap your feet on the stirrups, because that foot movement will work against the horse's motion. Tapping helps your feet become still, and you absorb the motion.

Jim Porcher has offered a different suggestion. "Take the shock in your hips, sideways — left hip, right hip. Your upper body shouldn't bounce more than your horse's topline. If you tighten up, you start to bounce."

Learn the rhythm of the jog, and concentrate on maintaining it. Your horse may try to escape you, by speeding up to a trot or slowing down to a walk or halt. If he trots fast, don't lean forward or pinch with your knees. Stand up in the stirrups if you feel yourself wobbling, with your body vertical or slightly behind the vertical.

To move down to the walk, sit tall, say "Whoa," and apply rein pressure. Release the reins as soon as he slows.

Don't let your horse "die" into a downward transition before you have given the cue. If you feel him start dragging, squeeze him lightly with your heels and release. You might also make a clucking noise.

With practice, you'll keep your legs steady as the horse jogs. You'll learn to ride the gait's diagonal motion with your body, absorbing in a fluid manner that's somewhere between rigid and rubbery. Your joints — ankles, knees, hips — should feel strong yet elastic.

LOPING

When you want to lope to the left, bend the horse's nose slightly to the inside. This moves the hindquarter to the left, which affects the lead he'll take.

You'll use your outside leg, in this case your right leg, to tell the horse to lope. Keep him slightly bent in the direction of the lead you want him to lope on. Trainers call these "diagonal aids," when you combine aids on two sides of the horse.

Your horse may only respond to more basic lateral aids, where you apply both rein and leg aids on the same side. Here you'd bend the head to the outside when you press with the outside leg.

You'll feel your horse thrust forward as he strikes the lope. Keep your body back. Pull your shoulders away from your hands to sit tall. Your back should feel strong in this upward transition, and your seat should remain square, with weight in your heels. Avoid rocking forward into the lope.

Sit the lope. If your horse lopes smoothly, without rolling or rocking his back, you can easily keep your seat so only your pelvis, seat, and thighs stretch forward with each stride. On a rougher horse, you may feel that your buttocks pound against the saddle at every stride.

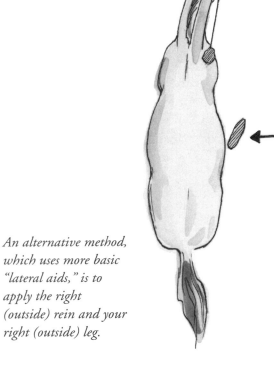

To lope to the left, apply the left (inside) rein and your right (outside) leg. The use of aids on both sides of the horse is called "diagonal aids."

An alternative method, which uses more basic "lateral aids," is to apply the right (outside) rein and your right (outside) leg.

At the lope, you should be sitting tall with your seat square and weight in your heels.

You want the motion to flow down into your heels. Dave Rhodes has suggested that you try standing in the stirrups and pushing your hips forward, while holding onto the saddle horn. "Push with the lower part of your back. Push from the back of the saddle to the front. You do it in time with the horse's movements."

Once you learn this pushing movement, you can slide lightly back into the saddle and absorb the circular, longeing motion. You let your hips go along with the horse's back, and the horse accepts the weight of your seat.

"The top half of your body will stay still and quiet, and your feet will stay still and quiet. You'll have that good base of support, and you'll be right up with the motion of your horse," explains Rhodes.

Learn to follow the up and down motion, as the horse seems to rise and fall. Florida trainer Andy Moorman has used the image of a Ferris wheel to explain the movement. "Understand what

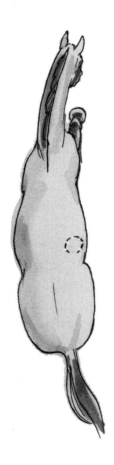

On the right lead, the right front and hind feet "lead" the left and hit the ground before the left feet.

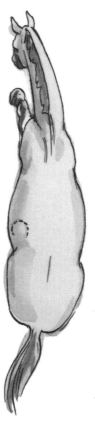

At the lope on the left lead, the left front and hind feet hit the ground (or "lead") a moment before and ahead of the right feet.

the gait does, what legs are doing what, and that the horse will come up and come back down. You don't fall forward or back. You just stay right in the middle. As the horse comes down, keep your legs in place so the horse comes back up again."

Nancy Cahill has explained that you need to feel the full stride of the lope. "I count a full stride, one, two, three. Don't count *one*-two-three, *one*-two-three, or it's a 'Lawrence Welk' waltzing feel. Get into the cadence and rhythm with your body."

Your horse should not gain speed in the lope. If he does move out more quickly than you want, open the angle of your upper body to a position slightly behind the vertical. This tells him, "Wait for me," while you "bump" him with the reins.

From the lope, you perform a downward transition to the jog, and then to the walk. Use your voice to say "Whoa" (or whatever word your horse responds to) and sink into the saddle for the change in gait. Make your lower leg grow longer with

weight in your heels. Raise your toes up to absorb the changed movement. Don't press down with your toes, because you'll push yourself up out of the saddle.

LEARNING YOUR LEADS

Four-footed animals lope (canter or gallop) in the same way, in a three-beat gait with a period of suspension. They lope with front and rear legs on the same side moving in unison.

When a horse lopes on the left lead, he moves his left hind and left front legs forward in a sweeping motion. The left front and left hind feet hit the ground a moment before and further forward than the right feet.

On the right lead, the right feet strike the ground ahead of the left ones. The horse chooses which lead to take, depending on the direction of travel.

You direct your horse to take the correct lead. You maintain the animal's balance by selecting the side that you will turn. If you are circling a pen in a clockwise direction, you should cue for the right lead.

If a horse is on the wrong lead for the direction he's bending, he'll have to work harder to maintain his balance. He might shift into what's called "cross-firing," or a disunited lope, such as leading with the left front and right hind. If he does this, you'd feel a rough, bumping motion, not the smooth rocking of the correct lope. Stop your horse immediately and cue him to lope again.

Whenever you signal your horse to lope, check to make sure he started in the correct lead. At first, you'll have to look at his shoulders to be able to tell which lead he took. If you're loping to the right,

his right shoulder should extend slightly farther forward than the left. On a horse that takes long strides, you can see his hoof reaching forward.

Don't lean far forward to check, which compromises your balance and might bother the horse. Learn to glance down to determine the lead, and continue riding. Eventually you'll learn to sense by feel, and you can tell the moment your horse strides correctly into either lead.

GALLOPING

The gallop is a faster lope, usually not an all-out run. (You should only run a horse on a racetrack.) Ride only as fast as you feel comfortable. Don't gallop to see how fast he can run; the all-out speed can turn your horse into an uncontrollable runaway.

With a balanced seat at all gaits, you refine your position. You can adapt to a specialty sport that requires a more forward posture, such as reining.

Humane Riding

Pay attention to how your horse feels when you ride. When you first start on a ride, let him relax at a slow walk on a loose rein. Don't make him go to work right away, but allow his body and mind to warm up.

Listen to his body language while you're in the saddle. An alert animal should feel businesslike and purposeful. He moves forward confidently, yet he listens to your aids.

Blend compassion with authority. Know what your horse can do, and don't ask him to perform the impossible.

If you feel his gait become uneven, stop and dismount to check his feet. He may have stepped on a rock, or injured a part of his leg.

Recognize boredom and fatigue. Don't always ride the same way in the same place, and avoid wearing out your horse. If he seems too slow, shortens his stride, or stumbles, he may be tired. Slow down, or stop and rest for a moment. A tired horse can hurt himself, or even stumble and fall.

At the gallop, maintain control of your speed, and ride only as fast as you feel comfortable.

KEEPING YOUR BALANCE

Whatever discipline you follow, you move with the horse, with a straight posture. You stabilize your seat so there is no excess motion or wobbling, yet you feel strong and elastic, not rigid.

Overcome any natural tendencies, mainly leaning in the wrong direction. This affects the horse's performance, as well as puts you in a precarious position.

Trainers agree that the novice rider focuses on a fear of falling. In fact, if you distill the essence of equitation, it's to keep your balance so you don't fall off.

"Riding a horse can be a very frightening experience," Terry McCutcheon has said. "Beginners will literally throw away the reins when they grab the horn. That scares them, because no matter how hard they pull or push, sometimes they can't gain control."

Counteract the leaning by keeping your shoulders square, pulling them back. If you start to lean forward, reach back and pat the horse on the rear. This also steadies your seat.

Never use your hands to control your balance. Your arms and hands must operate independently of your seat. A hand that flaps or bounces — or a tense, gripping hand that fights the horse's movement — demonstrates poor horsemanship and lack of control.

As you ride, continually check your position and adjust yourself. By maintaining your seat, you'll improve your equitation. Adjust your seat or hands when you discover they've moved.

If you feel your saddle veering right or left, you can use your weight to shift it back to the middle of the horse's back. On the "low" side, grip slightly with your knee and hitch the weight of your hip and leg to move the saddle over.

Also check your rein length, your position in the saddle, and your feet in the stirrups. Review your body angle and foot position before and after a transition to another gait, and at set locations around your riding area. By adjusting your position, you establish the habits of an effective rider. Both you and the horse stay comfortable.

Keep a light touch on the reins. Never use a tense or gripping fist — this will only fight your horse's movements. Your free hand can rest lightly on your thigh.

FEELING THE RHYTHM

As the horse moves through his three gaits, your body moves softly in rhythm to the footfalls. You instinctively develop a sense of timing.

"You as a rider are an integral part of that balance and rhythm of the horse," Andy Moorman has explained. "If you cause the balance to go away, or the rhythm, then you lose the feel. If the horse starts to lose his rhythm, you have to be able to enhance it."

Moorman advises counting with the horse's strides. This helps you to relax down on the horse's back and to feel his rhythm. She says: "That's when you know that a person is starting to be a rider, when she begins to exhibit the feel of knowing where she is, and where the horse is. It's a language. You have to speak to the horse in a language he understands."

Safety in the Saddle

Riding is a risky sport, and riders do fall off. You can prevent this common accident by developing a secure, balanced seat.

Ride in a ring, under supervision, until you feel your horse responds obediently to you. Learn how to fall safely by practicing vaulting off at a walk. You should be able to swing your right leg over the back and slide to the ground, away from the horse.

An accident can occur at any time, so don't let your attention wander. As you adjust tack or your riding gear, maintain control over the horse. Never drop the reins to adjust your spur; loop your arm through the reins to retain control.

Riding past a frightening distraction tests your safe riding skills. If your horse is afraid, you'll feel his heart pounding under your legs. Here you must project a feeling of confidence, to override the horse's fear. Demand that he focus on you, not the fearful stimulus.

Keep your heels down in the stirrups. This position strengthens your foundation and also allows you to slide your feet out of the stirrups if you do lose your balance and start to fall.

Any horse might slip, even when walking. Allow him to have his head if you feel him stumble or lose his footing. If he does fall, slide off on the side toward which he's falling. You'll land away from his legs, avoiding a kick as he thrashes.

Practice safety in the arena, around other riders. Wait to enter the ring until no one's near the gate. Quickly move into the arena's center, so you don't obstruct riders on the rail. Walk your horse on the inside track, allowing faster riders the rail, and halt in the center. If you pass riders going in the same direction, call "Passing" as you pass them on the inside. Stay to your right if you pass in the opposite direction.

Always maintain one horse's length — 8 feet minimum — between your horse and others. Never let your horse bite or kick another animal, and watch out for neighboring horses yourself.

You also protect the horse's rhythm. If you feel him "stutter" at the lope or jog, or begin to lose his forward energy, squeeze with your legs for a moment.

Your mind can affect the horse's rhythm. Many trainers use visualization. Trainer Pat Parelli has described this as "having a clear picture in your mind, then getting that picture to go through your body to your horse." Whether you count the rhythm of a gait or simply imagine slowing down or speeding up, your horse can sense your thoughts.

"Horses are smart by how they feel, not smart in the sense of scientific intelligence tests," Terry Berg has said. "They are extremely sensitive. Even the dullest horses are much more sensitive than people realize."

MAINTAINING CONTROL

Most horses want to please their riders. They respond to seek comfort.

For the horse, comfort may mean he's in charge. As the horseman, you need to radiate the sense of authority. You're riding the horse — the horse isn't riding you!

In your handling, seek a balance between firm and gentle. You want to keep the horse soft and responsive, submissive and obedient. In return, he learns to trust you.

You exert authority, just as you do on the ground. Yet, you must keep your seat to maintain your control.

Terry Berg described how a rider can easily let her horse have "the upper hoof." "If the horse starts to do something, you lean forward. That's probably the worst place to be at that particular time, because then you've let the horse have his own decision, as opposed to thinking about your decision."

Because of the horse's attention span, you must resolve each action immediately. Don't realize a moment later that your horse ignored you.

Even a trained horse can evade your command and need a reprimand. You answer by correcting the horse, then rewarding him with a loose rein. You leave him alone when he's correct. He learns that a free rein rewards him, and when you pick up the reins, you'll maintain your aids until he performs to your standards.

This give and take relates to the principle of pressure and reward. When you have to take up the rein or use your leg, you follow up by giving, or removing the pressure.

You must recognize when your horse responds. "If you question yourself whether the horse responded or he didn't, then he probably didn't," Berg has said. "It's a yes or no situation, and you ride with that definite feeling. You have to follow through, to answer."

The horse may duck his head, or "root," to gain a looser rein. Don't "jerk his face," but react with a fixed hand. When you feel a stiffness, close your fingers on the reins and brace your back, or make your back less flexible. You don't let him dictate to you to soften — you wait for him to accept your hand and stop pulling.

You may need to "bump" your horse. Tighten contact for a moment, then release to reward. Don't take hold and irritate the horse.

Gary Ferguson, a California Arabian trainer, has noted that riders have trouble with balancing control and softness. "You need to understand that

This horse is working toward collection, based on the rider's insisting leg aid.

when you use pressure, you get pressure back. The first thing riders do is grab and not relax."

Control means command of the hindquarters. The horse moves his feet through impulsion from his hindquarters.

Your horse must go forward at your command. John Richard Young has said: "When you squeeze with your legs, he should instantly take off. A horse needs impulsion, and a horse that has impulsion is a free goer. He doesn't pull, but he goes freely. You can't work a horse if he won't go forward. Your horse will be behind the bit and only go backwards. You can't do anything."

Get the horse to focus on his job — to move you forward. He goes in the direction you want with minimal cues from you. You shouldn't have to move your upper body or exert yourself, because the horse should respond to your leg aids.

How an Instructor Can Help

An instructor can coach you and help you form good habits through precise explanations and timely suggestions. A good teacher allows you to gain confidence. He challenges you to polish your abilities and to learn new skills, but he keeps you in a safety zone so you don't get physically scared.

Can anyone learn to be a competent rider? Most instructors say yes. Nancy Cahill has compared riding to playing the piano. "There are natural talents, and there are those who have to work harder than the average person. All you have to do is want to, because desire can overcome."

The person who helped you find your horse might be an instructor. Or, you might take riding lessons from a person who specializes in your type of riding. You can also attend riding clinics, hosted by local or visiting professionals.

A sympathetic teacher has to adjust to your learning style. He should inspire you through basic methods of explanation, demonstration, and instruction. He should articulate what he expects.

Instructors find different ways of explaining physical sensations. Many use visual imagery and analogies to illustrate what you should feel. Andy

Moorman has found that a novice can watch and imitate a good demonstration rider. "I point out to students exactly what's happening all the while, and they really see it. A lot of times it's just seeing what the person doesn't do. 'See how still she is?'"

Cahill has said: "You learn a timing and feel that don't come into words. When you get close, I say, 'Did you feel that? That's what you want to feel. Whatever you felt then, that's what looked the best.' I can hardly get those words out of my mouth fast enough, and it's gone."

Make the most of lessons by respecting your teacher's advice. Listen closely and trust him or her, and try to respond honestly.

Moorman has challenged pessimistic riders who fear trying a new exercise. "They find out they really can do something. When they quit worrying about not being able to do it, they start figuring out *how* to do it. The only reason you can't do it is you don't think you can. Think in the positive, not the negative."

When you're a beginner, your teacher should walk you through the basics and move you through phases. He should patiently support you through positive feedback.

A teacher breaks down riding skills into fundamental steps. Your instructor might put you on a longe line to help you relax your stiffness and acquire a secure seat. This is an accepted method, often used by instructors throughout the world. You learn to refine your balance, without having to worry about controlling the horse's speed, straightness, or rhythm at the same time.

Appaloosa trainer Alpha Russell starts all students on the longe line. "You learn to balance at all gaits with no reins. You see if your body's twisted, or your leg is weak. Your body is trained so you won't support yourself with the reins. You can focus completely on your leg or shoulder, so you're a safe rider."

When you get to a certain level of skill, you reach a plateau where you begin to act instinctively. You can feel the horse's responses and distinguish correct from incorrect. You don't need a person telling you every step. A teacher can step back and suggest what to do, and then let you experiment.

Riding Bareback

Some instructors feel that riding bareback, without a saddle, helps you develop a stable seat. Without the pommel, cantle, or stirrups to hold you, you gain an exceptional sense of balance through your entire body. Balance is what keeps you on the horse.

"We start our students bareback," explains McCutcheon. "So they don't have to worry about control, a partner leads the horse. We ask the rider to feel where those feet are, and what part of her leg is most depending or working the most at any particular time, going one direction or another. Knowing where those feet are supposed to be, you start to understand the horse better and become more confident.

"We're trying to develop a muscle memory. Instead of relying on the saddle horn, you kick in a particular part of the body to help you adjust to whatever comes up."

You'll also learn to feel every step the horse takes. To become a true partner, you must understand the sequence of footfalls in the three gaits. You'll move closer to him, and you'll be able to influence him more subtly as his body language communicates with you.

Bareback, your seat feels the forward strides that begin in the hindquarters. All horses move their four legs, but the action begins in the powerful muscles that propel the hind legs forward.

When a horse walks, trots, or lopes, he first moves a hind foot forward. You may not be able to see this from the ground, but riding bareback, you can feel the shifting of weight begin behind your seat.

To mount, either use a mounting block or position your horse beside a fence. You can also mount by springing across his back, if he'll stand. Try to jump so your upper body rests over the horse, and then straighten up.

Sit with your center of balance over the horse's center of balance. You should maintain a vertical posture, and avoid letting your body angle ahead or behind the vertical.

As the horse moves, you move with him. You're not right over his withers, but slightly back so you feel the motion of the hindquarters close behind you. Don't move your body and expect the horse to catch up with you.

The first time you ride bareback, you'll feel tense and insecure. Resist the urge to grab with your knees or heels. Gripping won't keep you in place, and the movement can excite the horse and start a chain reaction. He speeds up, you grab tighter, and you lose your sense of balance while pulling back on the reins.

Absorb the horse's motion through your thighs. Drape your legs so you contact the horse lightly with your calves, and keep your heels out of his sides until you need to cue him to move or turn.

Riding bareback can give you a poise and confidence you may never experience otherwise. You can truly share the sensation of two beings moving in unison.

Riding bareback can help you develop a stable seat.

FRAN D. SMITH

Your instructor can put you on a longe line to help you relax and acquire a secure seat.

You find solutions within yourself. Thinking on your own, you feel the horse and figure out your next move.

You can also learn through group lessons. Here you ride with one or more riders at your same level of expertise. Observe the others, and listen to what your instructor tells them.

YOUR HORSE, YOUR TEACHER

Master horsemen agree that the horse is the ultimate teacher. Even the equestrian with decades of experience continues to learn from each animal's unique responses.

Like people, horses share similarities and individual differences. The more horses you ride, the more you'll learn about equine behaviors.

An instructor should have you work with horses that will teach you. Terry McCutcheon has explained how he builds a rider's confidence by matching him or her with a horse: "We put the most experienced horses with the least experienced people. The horse's level of performance will gravitate toward the rider's ability. Especially old school horses will do as little as possible, but as much as they're asked. The intermediate or advanced rider has the horse with the least experience, so she has to look for a particular result."

Becoming a Horseman

With practice, any rider can become a horseman. As you develop physical balance and coordination, you can also learn how to influence the horse to achieve a superior performance.

You are the dominant partner, but you don't control the horse by brute force. You lead him, just as you do on the ground, by maintaining mutual respect. When he's amenable to your commands and willingly performs as you expect, you leave him alone to concentrate on his job.

When you are working with your horse, you seek finesse. In the saddle, your timing will be crucial, because you must sense when and how much to apply your aids.

When you're patient and take your time, you'll gain a closer partnership. The two of you agree on a subtle yet powerful communication. You feel him being light and loose, not scared or resistant. You let him show his athleticism and style, moving with energy and brilliance.

TEACHING THE HORSE

Although you don't claim the title of horse trainer, you teach your horse every time you ride him. You set up specific conditions, and he responds. Your reactions to his responses train him.

Whenever you handle or ride your horse, you're always teaching him a good or a bad habit. You want to instill and reinforce good habits, for steady and consistent movements. You can achieve this through reprimands. When he makes a mistake, you correct him. You consistently repeat the correction, and these reactions direct him to improve what he's doing. Training the horse relies on the animal's motivation. He responds to you primarily to avoid pain.

Trainer Terry Berg has used the word *finished* to describe the broke horse. "Can you easily rein him? Will he stop and turn around easily? Will he lope off when you kiss to him and squeeze?"

Use as light a pressure on the reins as the horse will recognize. As he learns to respond to a light signal, he will avoid the heavier ones.

She added that most horses aren't finished, or trained, to this level of partnership. Whatever the level of your horse, you need to determine what responses you want from him in every situation. He learns to work for you, to surrender to your request. He knows that if he doesn't submit, you'll repeat your cue and even get after him.

Berg has stressed that when you pick up a rein, you don't release the rein cue until your horse responds. You know what you want to communicate, you move your hand or fingers, and you concentrate on that reply to your request. She explained: "If you pick your horse up and put some pressure on the reins, at that point in time you need to make an automatic decision. The horse tells you something. If he's real soft and gives to you, that's probably the end of it. Whatever you asked for has occurred. But if he leans on you, and you haven't responded to him, he's told you something. You've lost authority right at that point in time."

Establish credibility with your horse. For every action, you expect a reaction. You don't ignore his action, because he'll learn a bad habit. When you act with authority, the horse knows that you mean what you say.

"Learning to ride is learning to be quietly assertive," trainer Gill Swarbrick has said. "The inner confidence has to come from you. If you're a person who has respect for yourself and your capabilities in other areas, you won't lack confidence."

Because the horse is sensitive, don't confuse him with constant signals. "Picking" at him, or fiddling with the reins or repeated jabs with your heels, can make him "dead" to the aids. Assert yourself with a decisive, definite command, and repeat the signal more strongly if necessary.

The definite command doesn't need to be harsh. Use as light a pressure as your horse recognizes, as most horses respect their riders and want to avoid a reprimand. He's learned that if he responds to the light signal, he avoids the heavier one that you'd apply. He stays comfortable, you leave him alone, and he's less likely to rebel.

Vary the intensity to teach and test responses. Trainer Casey Hinton has advised: "Start out with five pounds of pressure. When the horse limbers up, go down to two pounds." Or if you have to intensify the amount, the reprimand teaches the horse to react with the maneuver you've requested. He learns not to make the mistake again.

Hinton has noted that you can make your horse better by allowing him to make a mistake, and fine-tuning the response. He calls this, "Daring your horse to fail to respond. If you ask with less, you can reprimand, and your horse gets lighter as he starts to read your mind. You want him to wonder what you're going to do next, and to wait for you."

The amount of pressure should fit the situation. Trainer Pat Parelli has called this a "just" attitude. "You cause responses, and you don't force or plead. If you have to get firm, you do it without getting mean or mad. You trust your horse to respond, and you're ready to correct. It's not more of one than the other."

A good teacher is firm, consistent, and understanding. A good horse trainer learns the horse's limitations. He doesn't force or abuse the animal to make it perform movements beyond its ability. A horseman lets the horse know when it's done well. The horse acquires the trainer's disposition, so a steady trainer produces a steady horse.

For you to communicate with your horse, practice the communication system he knows. Find out how much of a cue you need, and how sensitive he is. Aim for subtle signals, starting by visualizing what you want him to do. Follow up your expectation with a physical cue. If he resists or doesn't respond, assert your request by repeating the cue, and then increase the strength of your signal.

You teach him to be lighter and more perceptive, so he feels soft and relaxed. Terry Berg has explained: "When you're on a good horse, it's like you think the movement and it occurs. To me, that is the ultimate. And it's fun!"

LISTEN TO YOUR HORSE

In the saddle, you can anticipate your horse's behavior by tuning into his body language. Watch his ears, because he points his ears where he looks. Does he signal what he's thinking before he acts?

Your aids tell him to gather himself for a change in direction or gait, or to move on with more impulsion or speed. Test your horse's responses to you. Lean forward and back to see if he'll speed up or slow down. Reach down to touch your toe, or back to tap the croup. Move into a jog on a loose rein, and think about the halt. Does the horse tune into your thought and slow down on his own? Ask for the halt, and see if he responds quickly or seems to ignore or evade your aids.

You can also feel what a horse is thinking, and you can learn to feel how he expresses anxiety. Anticipate any behavior, and ride assertively. Horses tend to repeat their reactions, so you can correct incidents of shying, rearing, or bucking before the misbehavior occurs.

He may test you by evading or resisting. Know how much to press, and when to back off. Here you

The amount of pressure you apply to the horse should fit the situation. A good trainer is firm and consistent and gets to know the horse's limitations.

maintain your self-control, because you don't want to start a fight. While you don't want to submit to his behavior, you do want to preserve his respect.

You can break the cycle of misbehavior through channeling the horse's energies into work. Your basic goal in riding is forward motion, cueing the horse to move forward.

When in doubt, go forward. In motion, you've gotten the horse's attention and he's submitted to your will. For example, instead of making a nervous beast stand still, put him into a long trot (an extended jog) to take the edge off. This gets his muscles moving freely.

Trotting is the easiest gait for the horse and an excellent warm up exercise.

Pat Parelli has emphasized the trot as an excellent exercise: "Let him trot on a loose rein until you get rid of that impulsiveness. Turn the impulsiveness into impulsion. The trot is the easiest gait for the horse, the middle of the road — not as slow and boring as the walk, and not as fatiguing as the canter."

Terry Berg adds advice about using the trot, noting that some riders make the mistake of trying to jog first. "Warm up at a posting trot. When your horse is ready to think about jogging, put his head and neck and body in frame [rounded] and long trot for a while. You're not pulling him or picking on him to jog slow."

ANALYZE THE RESPONSE

Your horse teaches you. By observing his reactions, you can apply equine psychology to figure out the cause of resistance. Once you identify the reason and modify a situation, you'll change the response.

Trainers say that a horse's primary motivations are fear, social order, laziness, and food. A frightened animal reverts to its primary defense to run from a threat. You can habituate him to a stimulus so he accepts a sight or sound that would normally frighten him.

Because your horse naturally seeks a leader, you've placed yourself high on the pecking order. Even though most equines are basically lazy and will evade work, you exert authority. When you tell him to do something, he accepts your dominance and submits.

When he doesn't behave as you expect, you take command and think through a problem. Why did he do what he did?

Pat Parelli has explained four scenarios of a horse's response: "He does the right thing for the right reason, and you reward him. He does the wrong thing for the right reason, and you correct him. He does the right thing for the wrong reason, and you correct him. He does the wrong thing for the wrong reason — I might get strong with that."

You're responsible for your horse's actions. Instead of blaming him, first consider what you did or didn't do.

Instructor Andy Moorman has said: "No matter what happens, it's up to you to have to change it. You take the blame on yourself, and you keep working on your own ideals and goals. If you want to be good at riding, you have to criticize yourself. When something goes wrong, you ask, 'What happened? Where did I lose it? Where did I fail to do the right thing?' And you don't let that happen again."

By changing your habits, you can teach your horse to perform as you want. You've identified the cause, and you seek the solution.

Arabian trainer Jim Porcher has explained what he tells riders about getting responses to their cues: "You ask the horse the first time, and it could be you or the horse. You ask him the second time, and it's your fault because you weren't strong enough. The third time you ask him, that's the time you get serious."

VISUALIZE THE RESPONSE

Scrutinize riders to observe their horses' body language. What does the horse tell you about the rider's cues? Does he move freely forward and appear soft and relaxed? Do you ever see the rider "block" the horse's forward motion, so the horse gaps his mouth and wrings his tail?

Any horse should move "on the bit" or on the aids, so he travels smoothly in balance. Andy Moorman notes the challenge of understanding this concept. "Most of the riders I teach aren't far enough along to be able to put a horse on the bit. You need to take enough feel to collect a horse, but not be stiff and rigid so you lose the feel, or break what I call the circle of energy."

Although Western riders don't always ride on contact, with a straight line from the hand to the bit, the horse should move forward willingly. Like a dressage horse, the Western horse engages his hindquarters to propel himself forward. When he's active behind, he becomes round and drives up underneath himself. He moves with his body weight distributed equally on both ends.

Horses don't naturally carry themselves this way under saddle. When you watch them move,

The equestrian aims to get the horse to work from the hindquarters forward. A horse moving this way performs in balance, reducing the pounding on the front legs.

you'll see many go "on the forehand," or "strung out." They tend to carry more weight on the shoulder rather than on the hip — they travel with more weight on the forehand.

The hindquarters have two kinds of power: the ability to carry weight, and propulsion. Blending these two forces produces the horse that moves in balance.

In all forms of riding, the equestrian aims to get the horse to work from the hindquarters forward. The rider encourages the animal, "Engage the hindquarters to carry your weight and propel yourself forward."

A horse moving this way performs in balance. He lessens the burden on the shoulders, and this reduces the pounding on the front legs. Because he naturally weighs more in his front end, shifting weight backwards equalizes the concussion. He moves lightly and softly, pleasing the eye through an athletic appearance.

You achieve this by transferring the weight back, driving the horse into the bridle with your leg. You guide him with light rein aids so he's "soft in the face." You can cue him to collect (gather himself) or extend, so he willingly adjusts his stride, speed, and direction. He can gallop, stop, and turn. If you're chasing a cow or running barrels, he should be able to shift his weight safely, at any speed.

"The horse always moves from behind forward," trainer John Higginson has explained. He continues: "You don't concentrate on bridling your horse so much that you forget about the hind end. You keep your horse between your seat and your hands, and you'll always have his hind end driving forward."

While guiding the horse, the horseman does not move aggressively. She cues firmly, without force or anger. Pat Parelli has described this as being "passively persistent. You cause your idea to become the horse's idea, but you understand his idea first."

To succeed as a horseman, you refine your aids. "You have to ride the whole horse," Jim Porcher has noted. "It takes a lot of leg and back, and subtlety with the hands."

EDUCATE YOUR HANDS

Expect to take time learning how to use your aids. Although skilled riders don't rely on their hands, as a novice you'll focus on overcoming a natural tendency to grab with the reins for security.

"It's important not to take hold and choke a horse down," trainer Gary Ferguson has said. "But it's natural. A person's first instinct is to grab and pull back."

Respect your horse by not over-riding him. Aim to balance contact with lightness. When you need to apply pressure, make a smooth adjustment and ask quietly.

You're seeking softness and artistry in the way you handle the horse. If he responds to one pound of pressure, you apply no more than that.

You want to keep him soft at the poll, or willingly yielding to pressure. "The horse must be able to break over the poll and be soft," Arizona trainer Tony Boit has pointed out. "I feel the front legs, the lower jaw, everything is connected to the poll. If the horse is stiff in the poll, he's going to be stiff all over."

Casey Hinton has noted: "You want the horse to always give his chin. If he doesn't surrender his chin to you, he's not surrendering his body, his back, or anything else. When I pick up the reins, I always want the horse to yield."

Know when to give, to loosen the rein, and when to take, to shorten or "bump." You also need to understand how much pressure to apply, a pull or a bump. (A bump doesn't mean a jerk, or a sudden "chop" that you apply with force.) For example, a pull with a snaffle could mean taking a feel of the mouth and squeezing with your legs. When you feel him round underneath himself and lighten, reward him by sitting still.

You don't want your horse to hollow out, or sink his back and fall onto the forehand. In a transition, you might feel this if you overflex him, using too much hand so he comes behind the bit. Increase leg pressure to drive him forward, and lift your inside hand slightly.

Instructor Larry Gimple has explained: "Sensitivity comes with savvy. The rider finally gets a feel of the horse, but she has to establish it herself. It can't be taught. You have to know the proper length of rein, when to bump or not to bump."

"You've got to adapt to the horse's ability," is the way Texas trainer Nancy Cahill has explained it. "A good hand is what you're working toward all the time. How to use the hands, and when to quit, are probably most difficult. You learn timing and feel that don't come into words."

When practicing, most Western riders ride two-handed, with a rein in each hand. Hold the reins so a half-inch will shorten enough to take a feel. Check the position of your upper arms, which shouldn't be behind the vertical.

Learn the difference between two types of hands, the fixed and the following hand. When you ride on light contact, you'll usually adopt the "following" hand.

Find contact without pulling or hanging on the horse's mouth. You want a feel between your hand and the mouth, to help the horse. If your hands bounce, practice holding them steady by putting your little fingers on the saddle's pommel. Hold them there, no matter what your body does.

With the reins too loose, the unfinished horse has a tendency to drop his shoulders. The finished horse should move into a gait, and when you drop your hand to give him a loose rein, he maintains his impulsion and frame.

You want your horse to stay in position between the two reins, so he follows his nose. You rein him into a turn by guiding, not steering. Aim for light, subtle use of the reins when two-handing or neck reining.

EDUCATE YOUR LEGS

A horseman rides more off the legs and seat than off the hand. Learning this principle requires you to take command and resist grabbing first and legging second. You can't balance a 1,000-pound horse through pulling his head.

Andy Moorman has noted a tendency among novice riders. "If the horse fails to respond, the rider typically responds with her hand instead of her leg first. It's a habit. She clutches instead of

drives, and then she's in trouble. You have to train yourself to react with your leg first.

"Whatever you feel you need to do with your hand, you need to do instead with your leg. If you start to use your leg in place of your hand, pretty soon your hand can be still and soft. Most people with bad hands don't have an educated leg."

You learn to use your leg independently of your hand, but this doesn't imply that you throw the horse away with the hand. Your hand is ready to support while you push him with your legs. Your leg controls his legs. It cues him to move from the hindquarters, and it keeps him "in front of" your leg.

Even when you back up, you ask with the leg. The horse has to shift his weight back to move in reverse. California Arabian trainer Tom Sapp has explained: "Make sure you drive to the bridle, then

To apply the leg aid, slide the lower leg behind the cinch, and use a soft squeeze.

bring him off the bit. Don't gag him back without asking him to collect, or he'll start backing off the forehand instead of the rear."

Use your leg so the horse engages his hind foot first, at every gait. Harold Farren has noted: "To lope, the horse has to engage his inside hind foot to the ground and get it under him. That puts him on the front axis of the hip, so he can move off the inside hind and start loping on 'the short stride'

[not strung out]. By always engaging that hind foot first, he will respond to the lope cue without trotting in the transition."

With engagement, the horse won't drag his hip or fall into an incorrect, four-beat lope. His driving hip supports his forehand and your weight.

To use your leg, drop it back behind the cinch so your horse can feel it. In some cases, you'll squeeze with both legs, and other times you'll use

The Horseman's Tools: Bit and Spur

Your tools will teach, control, reinforce, and refine your horse's responses. The value of any tool depends on your attitude.

Because you want the horse to respond to less pressure, use a mild bit. Master trainers rely on the snaffle, and return to it to reinforce skills.

Pat Parelli has advised using the snaffle. The milder, direct action of this bit avoids causing fear. "The snaffle is for lateral flexion. The plain snaffle is ancient and proven. You don't need anything more."

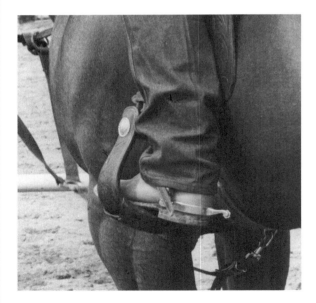

Pick a spur that matches you and your horse.

Trainer Harold Farren has recommended only the plain snaffle. He says: "Because the horse tends to move toward pressure, he'll just push more against the action of a strong bit, like the twisted wire. I've found only one spot on a horse's body that isn't affected this way – the recess under the chin. This spot isn't utilized during schooling with the snaffle bit."

"Use the snaffle to get your end results," Casey Hinton has advised. He prefers the snaffle because the horse can feel the cue and the reward. "It's harder to train to get the result with the snaffle, but you have a better final product."

You will probably show your horse in a curb bit, which can make him respond stiffly. Some horses learn to fear the curb and will push against it if the rider allows no release. "It's a tool of refinement, but you must be more delicate to produce a more delicate response," Parelli has advised.

The spur is an extension, an aid that refines your leg cue. You touch the horse with the spur only if he ignores a squeeze from your legs, and then a bump with your calf. Don't jab or prod, but nudge or roll the rowel lightly. The horse learns to listen to your suggestion.

Pick a spur with a shank to match you and your horse. If you have long legs, you might need a longer shank to reach the horse's side. Choose a shorter shank if you're short, so you won't "grab" the horse too high.

only one, or one more strongly than the other. Hold your legs still while you ride, unless you're applying a definite aid. If you continually tap against the sides every step, you can make him "dead" to your leg.

Your leg needs to feel strong, yet not rigid or clinging to the horse. A strong leg is a controlled leg, where you can apply the appropriate pressure. You can strengthen your leg position by riding without stirrups. This improves your balance, as you rely on your seat as a base.

Use your leg with proper timing. Your leg indicates the cue before your hand. When you want to round your horse, squeeze lightly with both legs so he moves up to your hand. Aim to increase the pressure slightly on your inside leg, to move him up to the outside rein. Your fingers feel him seek the rein, and you release the leg pressure.

If you need to reinforce your leg aid, bump with the calf. Your pressure in leg and hand match in intensity — follow a firm leg with an increased rein cue. Lighten leg and rein to teach the horse to respond with greater sensitivity.

Tony Boit has described leg pressure as a cue and release. "Don't hold the leg. Leg, get it off, leg, get it off. It's like a punching bag. The degree of the punch is the degree of how much the horse listens to you."

To turn, press with the leg, either inside or outside depending on your horse's training. Instead of using the hand, you indicate the direction with your leg. Press the leg in rhythm with the horse.

The amount of leg pressure also influences the horse. A soft, massaging squeeze can gather him without making him increase his speed. When he willingly steps forward from behind, you feel a wave of energy, not necessarily an acceleration.

Andy Moorman has commented: "If you use your legs without involving your body, then you only change the horse's legs. You won't change the horse's rhythm. The horse will lengthen his stride, but he won't increase his rhythm if you use the leg properly. The horse collects, but he doesn't speed up. If you use your leg incorrectly, the horse will speed up."

TRAINING EXERCISES

Warm up at the walk. Andy Moorman has said: "I like to lengthen the walk on a loose rein to begin with, until the horse comes through and swings his back. He says, 'Okay, I'm ready.' If you always start that way, then he'll accept what you do."

Practice adjusting your horse's stride, beginning with the walk. Instructor Terry McCutcheon has said: "Using your legs, you impulse the horse into a longer, extended stride. Then keep the horse balanced, so he's in a position where he travels equally in his stride. One step leads to another, and the basics from a walk apply to the trot and lope."

From the lengthened walk, use your legs to ask your horse to gather himself for a more collected walk. Move into the trot, lengthen the trot, and move back to the jog.

When you're moving at a faster gait, try using your seat to slow into a downward transition. Exaggerate your weight cues, to allow your horse to have time to respond to them before you use any rein pressure.

How he moves from the lope to the halt points out the quality of your horse's connection between forehand and hindquarters. Jim Porcher has commented: "Stabilize the lope with your outside leg. To halt, use your calf to push the horse to your hands. Don't let him brace into it, but pick him up with your hand."

Casey Hinton has explained a simple exercise to use in the downward transition, from the lope to the halt. Use this in conjunction with his suppling exercises, described later in this chapter.

The halt reinforces the basic message of "Surrender." You look for the horse to give to you with his poll.

Say "whoa" once, then as you repeat it, put your rein hand straight down as you reprimand. Take out the slack, and pull back to your hip. Leave your hand down, and don't raise it at all during the transition.

"Concentrate on a more perfect head position, not how quick the horse responds," cautioned Hinton. "Don't pull on the reins too soon. It takes a horse longer to digest a thought and respond than

Wrong

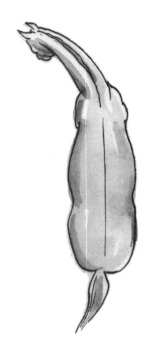

Right

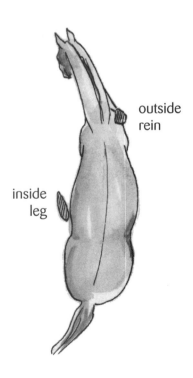

outside
rein

inside
leg

*Practicing arcs will help you coordinate your aids.
Press with your inside leg, and use your outside rein,
as diagonal aids. The body follows the forehand.
Don't let the horse "rubberneck."*

it does a person. Your horse needs two seconds to react to the whoa.

"When you take his head, [you want your horse] to say, 'How much?' not, 'Make me!'" Hinton has explained. "Don't quit until the horse gives in to you."

Backing up can help the horse stop, when used carefully. Hinton doesn't rely on this movement as punishment. "He can start thinking about being punished for backing up." If your horse "trickles" to a stop, use an equal amount of backing steps as a reprimand. For example, you ask for the stop, and he lopes four steps after your cue. Back him up four steps, then lope again.

PRECISION IN YOUR AIDS

Knowing how to use aids to influence the horse distinguishes the horseman from the passenger. The horseman performs a change of gait with his horse's hindquarters engaged and both shoulders lifted. His horse moves gracefully in any direction and bends equally to right and left.

Your horse might carry himself well on a straight line but fall apart on turns or circles and lose the equal weight distribution between inside and outside, front and rear. Practicing arcs will help you coordinate your aids to shift your horse's body right or left, to move the shoulder out and then in. When arcing, press with your inside leg to keep the ribcage lifted. Your leg aid assists your inside hand and pushes the shoulder out and around. Remember that the body follows the forehand, and don't let the horse "rubberneck."

Using diagonal aids — inside leg and outside rein together — can help. Andy Moorman has used the image of doors on the horse's shoulders and hips. "You can't let the doors come open. You keep the horse balanced between your two reins and two legs. You always have something going on with both hands and both legs. One may be passive, another active, and that changes."

In the lope, Moorman teaches riders to focus on the sequence of footfalls and think of the aids as a "U" that follows the horse's body. "Start with your inside leg, inside rein, outside rein, outside

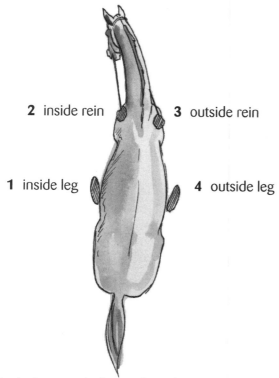

2 inside rein   **3** outside rein

1 inside leg   **4** outside leg

In the lope, get the horse soft on the inside leg and inside rein. Then close the outside rein so the shoulder doesn't leak out. Finally, push in the hip with your outside leg.

Used in combination, the brace rein and flexion rein cue the horse to bend correctly, with a relaxed neck.

leg. With the diagonal aids, you have to get the horse's outside leg under him, because that's the leg that he's going to rock back on to step up. Get him soft on the inside leg and inside rein. Then close the outside rein so the shoulder doesn't leak out, so he will listen to your outside leg. The final thing you do is push the hip in with the outside leg. And the minute he starts to pick up the inside hind leg, then you have to increase with your inside leg to make that hind leg come deep under the horse. It's just a set of doing this, over and over."

Practice isolating the horse's front or hind end. Here you cue the horse to move his fore- or hindquarters only. He moves his front end around his rear, or his rear end around the front. This exercise helps you coordinate your aids, and helps your horse to balance and connect from the hindquarters to your hand.

You use two reins here, called the "brace" rein and "flexion" rein. The brace rein is a combina-

tion of outside leg and hand, to steady the horse; the flexion rein is a combination of inside leg and hand to flex the horse to the inside. Used in combination, your aids cue the horse to bend correctly, with a relaxed neck. He moves his shoulders, keeping them lifted so his forehand remains light. A dropped shoulder means he shifted more weight onto his forehand and won't move in balance.

Practice isolations at the standstill, which results in a turn on the forehand or hindquarters. For the turn on the haunches, use your outside leg and hand as the brace rein. Apply inside leg and hand as the flexion rein. Your outside leg cues the horse to move. He bends around your inside leg, which maintains him in balance and keeps the shoulder up. Coordinate the pressure so you don't overbend.

In a correct arc, you should be able to see the horse's inside eye and ear. You should feel his balance shifted to the rear, and see that the shoulders are up. If you feel the inside shoulder get heavy,

By practicing circles, you can improve your bending aids and your horse's balance.

raise your inside hand to pick up the rein and bump the mouth.

With your outside leg, you can tell the horse to move his shoulder over. Your inside leg positions the hindquarters, encouraging him to bunch up and move underneath himself.

For the horse with a weak loin that resists engagement, Jim Porcher suggests combining the turn on the haunches with the downward transition. He coaches: "When you halt, use your outside leg to make the horse move away from the rail. Your leg transfers his weight back to ask him to turn. Hold him to pick him up and make him strengthen himself as he transfers."

The horse might evade your cue by swinging his hindquarters and trying to walk out of the movement. Apply a firmer leg aid to arc him up, so he engages the hindquarters.

"The horse will naturally want to move his rear end, because his weight's on his forehand," says Porcher. "You pick up the front end and move it around the rear end. You have to be light and still have some contact with the horse's face."

Practicing circles will help you improve your bending aids and your control. Circles combine a figure with an animal's body, and a perfect circle is very difficult. The horse must arc his body without resistance.

The circle also can help correct a problem. If your horse is strung out, moving heavily on the forehand, put him in a small circle to collect him. With a more acute bend, you can feel his movement, and he's less able to "cheat" on you. When you feel him moving more from the hindquarters, let him move onto a larger circle.

You use both reins and both legs in a small circle. The outside rein turns the body. The outside rein is dominant and it regulates the horse's frame.

Pat Parelli has explained: "When you use the outside rein, you're getting a hold of the hindquarters. Pull that rein, and you talk to the hindquarters. Then look where the forequarters go. It's like turning the wheel of a boat, where you turn the wheel and the rudder follows."

You should feel that connection as the outside rein holds the horse going forward yet bent. The inside rein dictates the bend to the inside, or flexion.

Nancy Cahill has told riders to make a perfectly round circle like a figure skater. "See if you can stay in your tracks. It teaches you — you used too much left hand, or too much right, or he dropped a shoulder. The hardest thing for anybody to learn is where every piece of that horse's body is."

Some horses cut in on a circle, or bulge to the outside. Bend the horse to the inside to prevent cutting in, using your inside leg to move the ribcage out. This can produce a bulge, so here your outside rein can receive the bulge, block it, and keep the horse curved in a smooth arc. You should feel him slightly bent, working against the outside rein. He angles his body weight to the outside in order to keep balanced.

Most trainers feel the horse bends in three places — neck, shoulder, and ribcage. The neck and shoulders should be square and lifted. Gary Ferguson has said: "You always move from the hip forward. The shoulders and ribcage definitely have to give to bend away from your leg around the corner. The horse arcs correctly and follows his nose where he's going."

You want to think in terms of your horse as an extension of yourself. He responds to your aids when he's attuned and synchronized to you. He yields to your aids because he wants to, not because you force him.

SUPPLING THE HORSE

When you ride your horse, you'll continually remind him to submit to you. Trainers rely on exercises to train the horse to obey with the mind while performing as an athlete.

For that soft feel, you can flex the horse's body and mind. In past centuries, European masters of classical riding used doubling, a training exercise that brings the horse's head back to the saddle or the rider's leg in a willing fashion. This helped the young horse learn submission.

Today the exercise is used mainly in Western riding to help teach a horse to turn quickly. Many trainers use it along a fence line, doubling the horse into the fence so he pivots on his inside hind leg.

At a slower speed, you can follow a three-step program as taught by Casey Hinton. He has used this technique to supple any horse and to control the animal 100 percent.

Step 1

First you ask the horse to surrender his head and lighten the forehand. "The reason for training the head is that it's the horse's steering wheel," explains Hinton. "Everything you teach the head to do, the body has to follow, whether it's stopping, spinning, or changing leads. I want to move the front end by telling the head to do it.

"Take the slack out of your left rein, and pull toward your hip. Pull out and back to make the horse's feet step across. Just hold the rein and let him decide."

Lighten your rein hand and keep your fingers soft, without clenching or jiggling the reins. Hinton describes this as "pulling relaxed."

When the horse obeys by moving his nose and near forefoot to the left, flexing to you, immediately

Most trainers feel the horse bend in three places — neck, shoulder, and rib cage.

Here the horse is resisting the arc and moving heavily on the forehand.

In the suppling exercise, take the slack out of your inside rein and pull toward your hip to make the horse's feet step across. Hold the rein and let him decide to move. Don't force it.

the rein, and let your horse rock his head and bump the bit until he responds, then take away the command. He'll give in, put his head down, and surrender."

For a 100-percent response, you want to see the poll lower and feel the feet stepping across as the horse swings his shoulder. However, your horse might cheat by moving the head and not the forehand, or swinging his hip instead of his shoulder. Any such response shows you that you control only a small portion of the horse.

What about the horse that steps without dipping his poll? "Take his head all the way to the side, and get more forward impulsion on a larger circle. A horse that just turns will drop his shoulders at the lope."

Forward movement also improves the response in Step 1. Here you can add a squeeze with the calf. Hinton says: "I want to move the front end by telling the head to do it, so I use the leg more as a reprimand than a cue. If you don't need the leg, don't use it.

"Make the horse's feet go better with his head. Use your outside leg and speed up the front end. Drive the horse forward on a bigger circle. While you continue walking, get the chin a little bit at a time. Make that head move, to come to you and to flex to your side."

Your horse discovers how to avoid the pull of the rein. "The only spot where I leave the horse alone is when his head is correct. Every time he straightens, I take his head back. He finds the spot where it's easiest to surrender, and when I leave him alone, he stays in the position I want."

Step 2

Teach the horse to "push away," or shove his shoulder to the outside. With his moving forward, you flex the body and teach him to flex his poll.

You teach him to move out, still stepping across with the front feet. Hinton: "At this point you're going to use your other rein more. The inside rein's going to push, and the outside rein pulls a little bit. Pick up your inside rein, and push both hands across the neck to the outside. You want the horse to move between the bit, between the reins."

pitch the reins to him. Hinton says: "Give the horse slack when he makes the decision because of the pressure. Hold it there until he decides to give in. When your horse starts stepping with his feet, tip your hand down and release. Walk straight forward, make him follow the rein and step across, and walk straight again, so you end up doing a circle."

You must wait, holding the rein, until the horse gives to you and steps. Tell him that he moved away from pressure, so the pressure went away. Hinton cautions: "Don't force it! Don't bump it! Just hold

Teach the horse to shove his shoulder to the outside —
you teach him to move out, still stepping across with the
front feet.

Apply agitation with both reins for direct flexion. You
want the horse to move between the bit, between the
reins. His ears should tell you he's waiting for you to tell
him what to do.

The horse steps his feet to the outside. When you circle right, you should feel him stepping his left foot over the right.

To keep forward momentum, experiment with the amount and timing of leg pressure. Look for your horse to appear relaxed. His ears should tell you he's waiting for you to tell him what to do. "Every time you get a result, give a reward," Hinton stresses. "Teach your horse to push away, then leave him alone. If you constantly pull, or bury your hands on your horse, pretty soon he'll push right back. You want him to soften, because you're going to release that pressure."

Use this shoulder-out exercise as a progression, and work in both directions for a light, supple attitude. Even if the shoulders move only one step, quit asking, relax, and allow your horse to walk forward on a slack rein. Next time, try to get his chin to flex a little more, and increase the exercise to two steps. If you get three steps at the walk, begin working at a jog.

Look for the horse to flatten his neck when you take hold. When he resists with his poll, you lose control. Hinton advises: "When your horse gets away in his face, he won't react with his feet. Take your time, but make it definite. Look where he hangs his head."

If you're tracking right, your horse's hip might drift left. Apply your left leg and take the head further with your pull and release.

Try to increase the intensity of the response. "Make your message more extreme with forward motion, which will get the response for you," Hinton says. "Dramatize your cue and reward, and see how much more flexibility you get."

Step 3

Here you change the direction of the shoulder on the circle, to push it to the inside. Tracking left, use your right leg and right rein to shove

Change the direction of the shoulder on the circle, to push it to the inside. When tracking left, use your right leg and right rein to push the shoulder to the inside.

the shoulder. Your horse should respond by moving on two tracks, limbering his backbone.

Hinton notes: "Only get a couple steps, and drop the reins when the horse moves his shoulders. After you do it in a circle, let him relax and go on a straight line."

Adjust your timing to the reaction. Decide if you need to slow it down to calm a nervous horse.

Keep forward motion because with too much rein pressure the horse might back up. Hinton explains: "The horse has the willingness to surrender because you release the pressure and allow him to walk forward."

In Steps 2 and 3, you might encounter what Hinton calls a "sticky spot," or a slight resistance going one direction. Concentrate on this weaker side so you achieve equal control on both right and left sides.

LIFELONG LEARNING

Becoming a horseman means work. Trainer Sue Cummins has compared riding to life. "It's a challenge. What is life but one obstacle course after another? It causes you to move to the next level of who you are. It's fun, the fun of learning, self-esteem, building confidence, and overcoming the obstacles."

Western riding poses a challenge unique to horsemanship. Gill Swarbrick has compared Western riding to dressage. "People don't realize that Western is harder. The horse has to be trained to work on a minimum amount of contact. You don't just get packed around!"

Trainer Art Gaytan agrees, comparing the bits and seats. "Both disciplines use a snaffle bit, and later as the horse becomes proficient, both go to almost exactly the same curb bit of a 5 to 2 ratio. The seat is the same, straight up and down in Western and dressage. But the Western rider asks his horse to perform and then maintain that gait until he asks it to change. You shouldn't have to move the horse up, or slow him down."

With the horse moving on minimum contact, the classical equestrian principles apply: *rhythm, relaxation, connection, engagement, straightness,* and *collection.* Horsemen the world over pursue this natural progression.

7

Trail Riding Pleasures

The beckoning trail inspires you to saddle up, humming the old Roy Rogers tune, "Happy trails to you . . ." What delights lie ahead, as you and your horse tour the world beyond the barn. As you develop your horsemanship skills, riding outside brings you new pleasures to share with your equine partner. Together you'll wander along quiet paths and canter across grassy slopes or deserted beaches. After a long uphill climb, you'll arrive at the summit and survey the landscape on the other side. Trail riding offers a range of benefits besides being fun. The world looks different on horseback. You can explore familiar and unfamiliar sights. You and your horse share the adventure, as he travels with a purpose. Most animals enjoy the relaxation of wandering along paths.

You can experience trail riding just about anywhere — around the neighborhood, on dedicated trails, along a waterway, through a pasture, or across public lands. Your trails can be solitary excursions or social occasions. With fellow riders, everyone savors a closeness with nature while riding at a leisurely pace.

Trail riding can help condition your horse's muscles and bone density, so he's ready to tackle more strenuous work. A workout intended to muscle him up — to "work his tail off" — can change his behavior by releasing tension or boredom. Choose varied footing and terrain for your travels, such as riding in deep footing like the sand of a dry riverbed. Riding up hills helps settle a nervous horse.

Unpredictable footing can teach the horse to watch where he's going. If you ride in the desert and have to cross a patch of rocky ground, you encourage him to drop his head to pick his way through. Mountainous terrain lets him find his own way of going, as he puts

Ride Type	Location	Description	Organizer
INFORMAL DAY RIDE	Town, suburbs, country, wilderness	Ride for fun Ride to a destination Ride in a loop, from start to finish, or meet at an arranged pickup point	Riders
ORGANIZED DAY RIDE	Country, wilderness	Planned itinerary Sponsoring group charges entry fees or horse rental	Riding club Breed organization Wrangler at guest ranch or resort
OVERNIGHT RIDE	Country, wilderness	Horse camping Pack gear on horses Gear trucked to sites	Riding club Breed organization Trail guide Wilderness outfitter Riders

his feet down correctly and maintains his natural balance.

Work up to such challenges, because not all horses are coordinated on the trail. In steep, uneven terrain, a few animals will stumble and have trouble maintaining their footing.

CURTIS MARTIN

A trail-wise horse is sure-footed, nimble, and balanced.

THE TRAIL-WISE HORSE

A capable trail horse usually moves with a long stride and carries a naturally low headset. He should be rugged with strong bones, but he does not have to be heavily muscled. An overly muscular type may not move as freely over rough terrain. A horse should have prominent withers to hold the saddle in place. Mules tend to have low withers, so a crupper helps keep the saddle from sliding forward. For hill climbing, many horsemen look for an animal with powerful hindquarters.

You want your trail horse to be sure-footed and to negotiate any incline or uneven footing. Look for feet that are large enough to support the horse's weight and to "grab on" in a crisis. Mules, famed for their agility, often excel when you're going "down trail."

The trail-wise animal is nimble and sensible. He knows where to place his feet and how to pick his way deftly over loose gravel, jagged shale, or slick granite. When traveling along a tough section of trail, he carefully maintains his balance.

You could be climbing along a pile of rocks or traversing a narrow ledge. On a tortuous path, this equine athlete twists and turns to keep his feet in place. Because he's broke for the trail, he surmounts obstacles with a casual attitude.

The trail-wise mount trusts you and goes where you guide him, regardless of the behavior of his equine companions. He isn't herd bound and will work alone or in company, traveling at the front, rear, or middle of a group.

A safe trail horse remains calm and responds instantly to your aids, no matter what. He stops and stands where you want. When you ask, he slows to a quiet walk or moves at a brisk six-mile-per-hour stride. He doesn't rear, bolt, kick, or spook, and he'll tolerate the sound of gunshot and the smell of game you ask him to carry or drag. When you have to tie him up at a lunch stop or overnight, he'll cock a hind foot and relax. You could even praise this horse as politically correct, because he respects the environment. When you tie him to a tree limb, he doesn't paw the ground to damage a tree's root system. A perfect trail horse will ground tie and wait till you return. (A pretty good one will stand tied to a bush.) A trail horse may not express his love for you, but he won't abandon you, either. If he finds himself loose, he waits for you to find him. (He wouldn't consider hightailing it for home!)

The Misbehaving Horse

You may find yourself on a mount that lacks the above trail-wise attributes. Your horse might be broke — until you join friends for a trail ride. If you're an authoritative rider with a less-than-ideal mount, you can still enjoy excursions. Most wrecks on the trail involve equine misbehaviors, such as kicking, spooking, or being barn sour. You can figure out the reasons for each action, and prevent misbehavior or retrain the horse.

Your partner might never kick, except when you're riding in a group. Then he decides to dominate his neighbors, especially if they incite him by "tailgating."

Fellow riders won't welcome your kicker, as a flying hoof aimed at another horse endangers the other rider as well. The targeted animal dodges, and the hoof impacts upon your friend's knee, shin, or foot. Ouch!

If you ride alertly, you can discourage a horse from kicking his buddies. Remain cautious at all times, on the trail and at rest stops. If anyone approaches the kicking zone, warn the person with a verbal, "Watch out; he kicks." Or, tie the traditional red ribbon around the top of your horse's tail.

Watch out for other horses kicking or biting yours, too. Keep a distance — at least a horse's length — from the horse ahead of you, and stay away from tailgaters.

Pay attention to your horse's attitude. If his ears go back and you see he's on the defensive, correct an impending kick with your voice and legs, or even a crack of the whip. If you feel him shift his weight forward or to one side, reprimand him firmly before he lifts one or both hind feet.

The spooker is the most common terror of the trail. Realize that an unpredictable sight or sound can "booger" any horse. The intensity of his reaction depends on the fearsomeness of the object and the horse's athletic ability.

You can't predict spookiness until you begin riding outside. Many horses will never shy in a familiar environment, but they transform into "fraidy cats" 50 feet down the road. As you explore different roads and paths, you'll learn by experience which sights, sounds, or even smells strike fear into your horse's heart.

Expect him to question such common sights as dogs, pigs, cows, sheep, trash, trash cans, flapping clothes on clotheslines, railroad tracks, and helicopters. When you travel to more remote environments, you could encounter backpackers, mountain bikers, burros, llamas, or large rocks that resemble bears.

Because you're the leader, you determine how to guide your horse through a scary situation. At his clinics, trainer John Lyons teaches horses to stand and face a threat, without turning away or running from it. In many cases, you can comfort your horse with a calm pat and by saying, "Easy."

Equestrian authority Linda Tellington-Jones has taught ways to help the horse overcome his fear of a common terror like water. Through using her Tellington-Jones Equine Awareness Methods (TTEAM) groundwork exercises, you can teach your horse to deal with fear of the unknown. He learns to think rather than react while you calmly let him cope.

Watch your horse's ears along the trail. This is how he will alert you to wildlife, other domestic animals, and people as you travel. When you see him intently focus his ears toward something, remain confident and cue him to continue moving forward.

If you haven't done your homework and trained him to overcome a specific fear, you can take two approaches when he becomes spooked. Some experts suggest riding your horse up to the supposed threat; others contend you should ignore it and continue normally. Whatever you do, breathe normally and continue to ride assertively. Don't convey anxiety to your horse. Never allow him to use the object as an opportunity to back up or to turn around and return to the barn. Con-

tinue moving forward, even if you have to go out of your way, or, as the absolute last resort, dismount and lead him past it. (Tip: Try distracting him by cueing for a shoulder in. Or, make him rein back, still progressing in the direction you have set.)

Shying endangers both of you. If your seat isn't secure, a whirling horse can dump you before you realize what spooked him. Also, he could slip and lose his footing, or slam into a hazardous object such as a fence or car. In the back country, this character could even fall off a narrow ledge, far from the search and rescue team. (Now you see why trail riding is so risky and why protective headgear is so important.)

You can outride spooks by developing a strong seat and predicting your horse's responses. Remind him that you remain in control and that he must obey your commands despite his fear.

You can desensitize him about a persistent phobia by surrounding him with the very objects he fears. You could stable him temporarily beside a pen of potbellied pigs, hang plastic bags beside his corral, or ride a noisy motorbike back and forth past the stall.

Hopefully you'll never ride a barn-sour horse — one that doesn't like to leave the barn. Any horse will want to hurry home, seeking rest and food, but a brisk walk should be the fastest gait you permit.

TRAIL EQUITATION

Ride in a balanced seat, so you can move with your horse. Usually you'll ride on a somewhat loose rein or with light contact, so your horse carries his head and neck at his natural balance point.

Trail riding involves climbing and descending slopes, hills, or even mountains. Your mount has to carry your combined weights uphill. Check your cinch again before scaling a steep hill. As you start up a grade, help your horse by maintaining your balance. Get your weight forward off his loins, without leaning forward from the waist so you crouch over the withers. This can overload his neck and forehand, inhibiting his impulsion to pull up the hill. And if you sit back too far, you'll put too much weight on the hindquarters.

To ride at the ideal angle, sit over the horse's center of balance. As a guide, look at any trees alongside you, and match your backbone to the vertical trunks. Push down in the stirrups so you shove your feet forward in line with the girth. You'll avoid hitting your feet against the horse's stifle or gaskin, and you'll find this position helps him negotiate the incline.

Avoid hanging on to the saddle horn, because you increase the pressure on the girth if you pull on the horn. Grab the mane if you need to balance yourself.

Don't let your horse race uphill — teach him to conserve his energy by stopping partway up the grade to rest. When you stop, pick a place where you can turn him right or left, so he stands level. On a long, steep grade, you may make several short stops so your horse can catch his breath.

Riding uphill rewards you with a sense of achievement. Yet what goes up must come down. When you start downhill, keep contact so the horse doesn't increase his speed or lose his balance on the grade. He should keep his feet and hocks under him.

Again maintain your weight over the horse's center of gravity, and stand slightly in the stirrups so you're light in the saddle. Your seat should just brush the saddle, so you're in what hunt-seat riders call the "two-point" position.

Place your free hand on the saddle's pommel, or the horn, and hold your weight steady by keeping your ankles bent so your heels are down. You absorb the concussion in your legs.

With most of your weight in the stirrups, keep your legs close to the horse without gripping. If you tense up, your body will start to sway. This could put your horse off balance down a steep hill.

As your horse tilts down the incline, he drops his head and neck. Those ears just seem to disappear!

You'll naturally want to lean way back to keep from going over his head. Resist this tendency, because you'll make it harder for your horse to keep his balance. If you plant your seat firmly in the

To ride downhill at an ideal angle, sit over the horse's center of balance. Push down in the stirrups so you move your feet forward in line with the girth.

saddle, his hind feet will dig further into the ground. He may start to scoot down the grade, sliding on his hocks, because he can't get his hind legs out from under himself. Watch for difficult inclines on slippery ground, such as slick rocks or deep sand. If you do feel your horse slide or tilt dangerously, be ready to bail out. You don't want to roll down the hill with him, because you could end up underneath him at the bottom.

Watch that your feet don't swing too far forward or back. You can use an alternating leg to counterbalance the motion — put slightly more weight in the opposite stirrup at each step. When your horse steps forward with his left front leg, put weight on your right stirrup.

Few riders sit too far forward downhill, but this can overbalance the horse's forehand. He can stumble or even fall.

TRAIL SMARTS

With your determined attitude and balanced seat, you'll bond with your horse as you ride the trails together. He learns to trust you outside. In a demanding situation, you decide whether to continue, go around, or turn back. When you feel him hesitate, you only push forward if you know it's safe to do so. When you ride bravely, you communicate your attitude to your horse. You're "driving," and he goes where you guide him. Brave doesn't mean careless, however. Combine common sense with forward motion. You can learn trail smarts from experienced riders and trail-wise horses. Ride with a group, and follow the lead of the best rider or the trail guide. If you ride at a guest ranch or on a rented horse, pay attention to how the horse handles himself.

On any trail, the first rule is to watch where you're going. Scan the landscape ahead so you're prepared for any changes in the earth below your horse's feet, on each side, and above your head. When you ride under a tree, be sure you can duck under branches without scraping your back. Lean forward and hold onto your hat.

On a narrow trail, you'll navigate through the tight space. Rein your horse around brush, scanning ahead for gaps. You might have to take your feet out of one or both stirrups when you move next to a bank or large rock. You don't want to get your foot stuck between your horse and a rock, or brush your knee against a snake sunning itself.

Besides watching for snakes, be ready for pheasants or rabbits that can surprise both you and your horse. Other natural irritants can include ticks (which land on you or your horse when you touch bushes) and the temptations of plants at your horse's level. Don't let him grab at trees or brush. This is an irritating habit, and he could possibly eat a poisonous plant.

Horses must get used to crossing unfamiliar terrain, but it's your job to check for the footing. Don't push fast through deep sand, and inspect wet or loose footing. In a marshy area, watch for quicksand and sinkholes. If the ground ahead seems boggy, consider going around on firmer terrain. The two of you weigh 1,100 to 1,300 pounds, and that weight can sink much faster than you alone. Could you rescue your horse if he became trapped? Never cross a cattle guard. A horse can easily catch his foot and find himself in a deathtrap.

A horse raised on flat ground may fear crossing a ditch or arroyo. When you encounter a steep ditch, keep him moving but not plunging forward to try to jump the gap. Keep him facing the ob-

CURTIS MARTIN

If your horse fears crossing water, start him across a shallow creek so he learns to trust you and the water.

stacle and cue him to walk forward. By your attitude, you let him know there's nothing to be afraid of.

Consider your momentum in such situations. Increased speed could carry you down steep terrain, but will you be able to get back up?

Many horses fear crossing water. Because they can't sense the depth of a puddle, stream, or pond, they tend to distrust any water.

Before you cross running water, you have to know its depth and current. If possible, start your horse across a shallow creek with a solid bottom. He learns to trust you and navigate obstacles, and you can move on to more demanding water crossings.

Allow your horse to drink water during these encounters, which also familiarizes him with it. If he's hot, let him drink a reasonable amount, and keep him moving for at least half an hour before you stop, to avoid possible colic from the cold water.

Some horses want to roll in water. If your horse drops his head down and paws, move him forward immediately. An abrupt dunking is no fun, and you could lose control of the animal. Don't take chances if you're unsure. In rough terrain, stay away from the edge of ledges. Stay back from the horse ahead — he could balk, spook, or fall, and you'd be part of the wreck. Judge every obstacle. If it could hurt the horse, then he has reason to question you next time, and you've lost trust. Trust his judgment too, such as crossing a rickety bridge. A sensible mount recognizes whether or not he can go down a cliff. The trail-wise horse will hesitate, whereas a dull-witted one may not.

Changing weather conditions can also endanger you and your horse. If you're caught in a lightning storm, dismount and lead him away from water, trees, or fences. Try to wait out the storm in a dip, gully, or below a hill.

Finally, know when to stop by listening to your horse. If you plan to tackle a strenuous route or a long ride, estimate his fitness level. Never ride a soft, out-of-shape horse hard, or you could cause permanent damage. An exhausted horse is more likely to stumble or slip.

Your horse might seem fine, but then quit on you. Figure out the reason why he refuses to go up a hill, or spins and tries to head downhill. He could be in pain, in his back or legs.

In some situations, you might need to dismount and lead your horse to safety. Or, up a steep grade, take the burden off his back by "tailing," following him while you grasp his tail so he pulls you up the hill.

When you dismount or mount on the trail, always use the uphill side. The broke horse should not mind your using the off side, and sometimes off side is the only side.

Riding through Suburbs

Whenever you ride through a residential or commercial zone, realize that you and your horse are "on stage." Ride with respect toward the inhabitants, and keep a low profile. Crossing through a horseless neighborhood is a privilege, not a right. Polite riding will keep horses welcomed. Ride in single file at a slow gait. (Never ride faster than at a slow jog on pavement.) Stay on the road, not the sidewalk, so you don't interfere with pedestrians.

In a populated area, you risk the embarrassing event of your horse dropping manure. This is probably the reason suburban homeowners and in-town businessmen object to equestrian traffic. In the saddle, you can only apologize if someone complains about your horse's functions.

You'll have more fun riding in less populous neighborhoods, where you can follow a path or trail along the road. Keep your horse along the road, avoiding private property. Never cross a lawn or garden, and don't let your horse nibble hedges, bushes, or trees. Besides leaving shrubbery untouched, this safeguards his health. Many ornamental plants, such as the popular oleander, are poisonous to horses.

Day packs can carry small items for a short ride, or you can use a saddle pad with built-in pockets, stationed behind your thighs.

Gear for the Short Ride

When you plan an expedition, specialized equipment can add to your comfort and the comfort of your horse. On a short, casual trail ride, you'll carry only what you need. Plan your equipment according to the climate and length of the ride. A brief tour with no stops can mean simply the same tack you use in the arena — saddle, bareback pad, or even bareback.

"Day packs" can stash small items you'd need on a short ride. You can use a saddle pad or bareback pad with built-in pockets on the back, stationed behind your thighs for a wallet, sunglasses, or camera. Or, wear a close-fitting fanny pack.

You can increase the comfort of any type of saddle with the addition of a seat saver. This fleece pad is shaped to fit over the seat and cantle, providing extra cushion between your seat bones and cold, hard leather. A strap underneath the seat holds it securely in place.

Some trail riders like the extra security of tapaderos, or hooded stirrups. On a long ride, these help you maintain your foot position without concentration.

In mountainous terrain, outfit your horse in a comfortable breast collar, strap, or breastplate to prevent the saddle from sliding back. Avoid adding a tiedown, which can hinder the horse's balance. In deep water, a tiedown can even cause a swimming horse to drown.

On a trip lasting several hours with stops along the way, you should bring a halter and lead rope. The easiest way to carry it is to bridle the horse over the halter, tying the lead rope loosely around the neck. Or, use a combination halter-bridle.

Tie the horse to a tree short and high, with a quick-release knot. You might loosen the cinch during the break, but remind yourself by hanging the near stirrup over the horn.

When you dismount, it's safer to control the horse with a lead rope than the bridle reins. Even

Riding on the Road

When you venture out, you won't always ride in remote areas. You may even find that most of your trail riding requires you to use roads designed for motor vehicles. Reaching the peace of "unimproved" roadways might mean a half-hour's ride beside a busy thoroughfare.

As you ride on or alongside roads, you will realize that the public sees your horse as an unusual, nostalgic form of transportation. You must ride defensively, ready to cope with unexpected events.

First, observe all state and local traffic laws that apply to equestrians. Like other travelers, you have certain rights on public roads. Some states give equestrians the right of way, or they require you to ride on the right, with traffic. All expect you to obey regulatory signs and signals. Ignoring laws endangers you and your horse, and you're not exempt from receiving a traffic citation. This includes riding a horse while intoxicated.

Probably most drivers are unaware of the laws regarding equestrian traffic. On roadways, keep your horse as far from the pavement as possible. Just seeing a horse makes some drivers act silly. Hopefully you will never encounter one who purposely honks to see your horse jump, but these clowns do exist. Anticipate traffic hazards that might impede your progress. Even if you know your horse wouldn't be bothered by a narrow traffic lane, you would obstruct motorized traffic. Try to avoid roads under construction, major bridges, and commuters' favorite shortcuts.

Besides staying alert for motorized traffic, watch out for other forms of transport. Keep a safe distance from bicyclists and skateboarders. Respect pedestrians you encounter along the roadway.

When riding on the road, stay to the far right.

CURTIS MARTIN

if you don't plan to tie him along the way, a halter makes it possible for you to remove the bridle and allow him to munch grass while you relax, holding the rope.

Behind your cantle, you can tie a rolled-up slicker with the saddle strings. A cantle bag or pommel bag can hold a water bottle, day's lunch, hoof pick, first aid kit, camera, and jacket. Tie it behind the cantle by threading the saddle strings through the metal D rings attached to each end of the bag. Be sure to stow any litter in your bag, and pack it back to the barn.

To carry more items, saddle bags are the traditional choice. You can use the traditional style of two large bags connected by a wide yoke, which lies across the rear skirts of the saddle. The bags rest behind your thighs and fasten onto the saddle and rear cinch.

One design, called the "packing" saddle bag, combines the cantle pouch and the gusseted bags.

Here a zippered pouch is added onto the yoke. Whatever bag you choose, don't overload it so the weight irritates your horse. Balance on both sides the weight of items you pack.

Specialized containers are shaped to fasten single items to the saddle. You can find cases designed to carry pliers, wire cutters, a hoof pick, or a camera. A hoof pick case might strap around the flank

Saddle bags are a good choice for carrying a variety of items you may need on the trail.

To be prepared for bad weather, you can tie a rolled-up rain slicker behind the cantle using the saddle strings.

MINIMAL TRAIL EQUIPMENT

You Need This	List of Items	Check for
HORSE		In good condition Shoes secure
TACK	Saddle Bridle	In good repair Adjusted correctly
	Halter and lead rope Extra leather strap or shoelace	
PERSONAL ITEMS	Bag to carry gear First aid kit Hoof pick Camera Whistle Watch Compass and topographic map Sharp pocket knife	
CLOTHING	Hat Boots Outerwear	

cinch, and a padded camera bag can rest against the saddle's swells.

Carry food and drink in functional cases. Choose the old reliable canteen, or a plastic water bottle, which can strap onto another bag.

If you tote a rifle while hunting on horseback, you'll probably carry it in a scabbard. This leather case straps to the rear cinch ring and latigo of the front cinch, to hold the gun at a diagonal angle. Whenever you cross a stream, turn the scabbard to face straight up to protect the gun from water.

When you travel in the high country, even for just a day, dress for changes in weather. Backpackers know to avoid cotton, because wet cotton won't wick water away from your skin. Your body tem-

The Wide Open Spaces

Ride only where horses are allowed. On some public lands, you may need to buy a permit to ride the trails.

If you plan to cross private property, observe property owners' posted signs. Don't assume that a "No Trespassing" sign applies only to vehicles. Always close any gates you open, and be sure you have latched the gate securely.

Farmlands offer unpaved roads for trotting and galloping. Be courteous by skirting the grower's fields. Do not allow your horse to damage any crops, terrain, or equipment. Don't cross irrigation ditches or pipes, as one misstep can block the water flow.

Riding away from traffic gives you a sense of freedom. It also brings you into competition with other users of open space. You and your horse must share paths with hikers, mountain bikes, all-terrain vehicles, off-road motorcycles, 4-wheel drivers, or even skiers.

Rarely will you confront all these hobbyists on the same trail. And, yes, you can co-exist with fellow pleasure-seekers. Many drivers of off-road vehicles will courteously slow down, pull aside, or even stop to allow you to pass.

Again, ride defensively by expecting to deal with varied responses to your presence. Thank the polite drivers, and stay away from the rude ones.

Maybe you're fortunate to have access to bridle trails, dedicated only to equestrian use. Here you'll confront only other riders. Follow the same guidelines you would in a riding ring, keeping a safe distance between horses and alerting riders as you pass at a faster gait. If you pass an oncoming horse, stay to the right as you would when driving a car.

Always close any gates you open, and be sure you have latched the gate securely.

perature can drop rapidly. Choose synthetic fabrics for inner and outer layers. Gaiters can protect your legs, because jeans can get soaked in a sudden rainstorm. Carry a lightweight, waterproof slicker, to direct water off you and your saddle.

OUTFITTING LONGER TRIPS

For overnights you can carry camping gear on your saddle horse. By toting your complete outfit on one animal, you reduce the impact on the wilderness environment. Instead of destroying a campsite, you preserve it through limiting yourself to one animal per camper. You also avoid the hassle of securing gear on a packhorse and the constant distraction of worrying about leading him over rough trails.

For this type of packing, choose specialized equipment that applies backpacking technology. Certain manufacturers design large, sturdy bags

OVERNIGHT EQUIPMENT

HORSE	Horseshoe repair items or Easyboot Hobbles, overhead picket line equipped with tree saver straps, or picket stake and rope (only if horse is accustomed) Nosebag Horse brush and sponge Antiseptic powder Insect repellent
BACK-PACKER'S CAMPING GEAR	Dehydrated food, utensils, stove, water Matches, flashlight

that attach to saddle and crupper and do not bounce. Such bags can carry your clothing, camping gear, cooking utensils, and dehydrated food, yet still distribute weight evenly. Compression straps keep the load in place.

Whenever you plan to add extra weight onto a horse, practice riding or leading him with all equipment loaded before the trip. This will allow the animal to become used to any unusual shifting, and you can be sure you've fastened all items securely.

By adopting the backpacker's ethic, you'll tread lightly and treat the wilderness with care. Proponents of low-impact horse camping find that they can enjoy the peaceful isolation of the back country and leave minimal trace of their travels.

If you do choose to load extra gear onto a pack animal, use a horse, mule, burro, or llama. The pack animal hauls its load in large bags or canvas-

LARRY SANDERS

Certain manufacturers design large, sturdy bags that attach to the saddle and have a crupper to prevent bouncing. Such bags can carry your gear yet still distribute weight evenly. Compression straps keep the load in place. For a longer trip, you can outfit your pack animal with a pack saddle — a combination of harness and saddle tree that allows the most secure arrangement of the greatest load of gear. The mule at the far left is outfitted with pack bags. The mule to his right is outfitted with a pack saddle.

wrapped packs (known as "manties"), usually one on each side of its back.

You could substitute canvas saddle panniers. These look like oversized saddle bags, with a wide strap that fits over a Western saddle. A front and a rear cinch fasten over the saddle's regular cinches, and a web breeching strap keeps the panniers from shifting. Avoid overloading your animal. Some horses will only be able to handle a total burden of 100 pounds — 30 pounds in each pannier hung on a 40-pound saddle.

To pack in for a longer time, you'll outfit your beast of burden with a pack saddle. This combination of harness and saddle tree allows the most secure arrangement of the greatest load of gear.

The most common types of pack saddle are the Decker and sawbuck. The Decker is easier to pack. You wrap each portion of the load in a manty and strap a manty on each side of the saddle. The load ties to the Decker's D rings.

On the traditional sawbuck, you tie the load to two pairs of wooden cross pieces. Both types of pack saddles cinch down with a front cinch (the sawbuck adds a rear cinch) over a regular saddle pad or oversized blanket. The saddle stays in place with a breast collar and breeching, pronounced "britchen."

Outfitters rely on the pack saddle and harness to be in top condition. They depend upon pack animals to transport gear during the expedition.

Horse packing is an art, best learned from an expert. Sloppy packs can cause problems ranging from a minor gall to a major disaster on the trail.

ORGANIZED GROUP RIDES

Riding with a group, you'll travel 10 to 25 miles a day. The ride can go from one point to another, or form a circular loop back to the starting point. If you start from a ranch or base camp, you can take different excursions each day. Rides can be casual or fancy. You might set up a rustic camp in the wilderness, or you can enjoy catered meals at an elaborate tent city with all the comforts of home.

Be sure your horse is well shod and in shape for the ride. You don't want to hold others up or cause your horse to suffer an injury or loss of a shoe. The ride description should include the type of terrain and the distance, and some rides require health certificates for the horse.

Whether you'll ride for a day or a week, follow the rules of ride officials. The trail boss is the captain of the ride, and his word is law. He knows the route and has permission of landowners, or he's made reservations when you travel across public lands. All riders must remain behind the boss when on the trail, and ahead of the drag riders who bring up the rear of the column of horses.

On a typical ride, the boss leads you out in the morning. Have your horse ready to go before the announced start time. Some rides meet a water truck at designated stops along the trail, so you can offer your horse water (and enjoy a soft drink or beer). You may carry your own lunch or meet the lunch truck at the noon stop.

JEFF VANUGA

Trail riding allows you to enjoy the scenery of the back country.

On a group ride, you'll enjoy scenery of the back country. You'll enjoy wildlife in pine forests, marvel at the desert in bloom, follow historic trails, or see the fall colors. Remember that riders share public lands with other pleasure-seekers, so minimize your horse's impact on the wilderness. Hooves do cause erosion, so always stay on the marked trail and never cut across switchbacks.

FRAN D. SMITH

A guest rider assists the cowboys during the excitement of a cattle drive.

Resort or Guest Ranch

A resort or guest ranch usually hosts short, all-day, and possibly overnight rides. During your stay, you'll ride a horse assigned to you by the wrangler or outfitter. The horse will be fully equipped, so your dress is your only concern. Overnight rides provide all camping gear, along with a cook and packer.

These rides attract all levels of "city slickers." The wrangler or trail guide might consider his job baby-sitting, but he wants to make sure you ride safely and enjoy the trip.

On a guest ranch, you may start with riding lessons in the corral. The wrangler might ask you about your riding background, or just assign you a horse and watch you meet the animal. He'll know how much you know about horses by the way you approach the horse, so don't overestimate your horse-manship or you might end up looking like a real tenderfoot.

You may choose a ride with a specific focus, such as one led by a naturalist. Or you might experience the excitement of a cattle drive, where you ride alongside working cowboys. After a long day pushing steers to new pasture, you'll relish supper served from the chuckwagon.

Trail Safety

When you saddle up for the trail, examine your tack on both sides of the horse. Secure your cinch before you start, and check it again about 30 minutes into the ride.

Riding on the trail is an adventure. Keep it fun by riding on safe ground. Avoid glass, cans, holes, or loose wire. Keep a distance between your horse and any possible hazards, such as other animals, a cliff or drop-off, wire fence, or narrow path.

On a group ride, courtesy makes the ride more pleasant and safe. Before you start, wait till everyone is mounted and then walk as a group. If anyone has to stop on the trail, everyone should halt. Horses don't like to be left behind.

Ride only as fast as the least experienced rider can handle. If you see glass on the trail, warn riders behind you with, "Beware glass." Never gallop past another rider — pass no faster than at a trot and call out "Passing." When someone passes, control your horse by angling its head toward the other animal.

Consider your fellow riders and be a good citizen. Stay up with the column of riders. Don't "barge or charge" in the group, and keep the pace set by the trail boss. If you need to stop, move to the side of the trail.

When going through a gate or crossing an obstacle such as a stream, the first riders should walk slowly to maintain an even pace. After crossing, the trail boss should halt the group until everyone arrives on the opposite side (and the last drag rider closes the gate). The horses at the end won't have to trot to catch up with those near the front.

On an overnight ride, the trail boss leads you into camp in late afternoon. You'll unsaddle and care for your horse, letting him rest before offering water and feed. Organized rides will haul feed to the camp, along with your camping gear. Tie your horse to the picket line or to a tree. Station him a safe distance from others, and tie him securely so he won't get loose in the middle of the night.

8

Trail Riding Competitions

Organized distance rides combine the fun of group riding with the challenge of competition. You ride with a goal in mind, and you measure your performance against fellow riders.

Distance riding demands discipline. Through weeks and even months of practice, you condition your horse or mule to a high state of fitness. You don't need a fancy mount to excel in this sport. He has to meet one basic requirement — to cover ground efficiently.

If you like camping and the out-of-doors, distance riding adds the thrill of a contest. If you want to compete but don't like the pressure of the show ring, trail riding provides an ideal equestrian sport. While you prove your ability against other riders, you'll also gain the satisfaction of going "down trail."

Whatever distance they travel, distance riders show "grit," or the heart to continue. You're on the move continuously with the clock ticking, and you cover a range of territory. You aim to ride every

mile, and you and your equine companion become partners who respect and understand each other.

You can participate in various types of rides, with challenges from a few miles to a hundred. In each event, you ride a measured course, marked with signs such as flags or ribbons, from start to finish. Men and women compete equally.

Distance riding differs from other horse sports because the horse's welfare comes first. You prepare your horse by conditioning it for the course. Veterinarians monitor the sport at checkpoints. The ride veterinarian advises you on your horse's physical well-being, and this official can pull you from the contest if your horse displays signs of stress.

The vet analyzes him in four categories: *systemic, locomotor, attitude,* and *lesions.* She evaluates his system by his recovery rate, or how quickly his pulse and respiration (P & R) return to normal. If she judges your horse as exhausted or deyhdrated, you're out.

Type	Goal	Duration	Association
COMPETITIVE TRAIL	To ride a marked trail within a set time period. Judges score horse on time, distance, and stress, and rider on trail equitation and horse care.	1–3 days 15–90 miles total	North American Trail Riding Conference
ENDURANCE	To complete a marathon in a fast time, while maintaining the horse's well-being	1–3 days 50–100 miles a day 25–35 miles for Limited Distance rides	American Endurance Ride Conference 600 rides a year
RIDE AND TIE	To complete a marathon in a fast time, with two people sharing the same horse. One runs while the other rides.	1 day 6–40 miles	Ride and Tie Association

In distance riding, you and your equine companion become partners who respect and understand each other.

She watches him move, to see if he's "ouchy" or lame. She checks for sole bruises and signs of muscle fatigue. She considers his willingness to keep going, and she checks for any sores caused by your tack or trail injuries.

THE DISTANCE-RIDING HORSEMAN

All events challenge you in four ways: your animal's physical fitness, his mental attitude, your physical condition, and your strategy in completing the course. Strategy means you plan ahead to meet the event's requirements. You control certain elements, such as conditioning your horse, analyzing the trail, and determining the pace you'll maintain over every mile of the course.

You train your horse to accept the obstacles he's likely to meet on this particular trail. For a level trail on dirt roads, practice in familiar territory. If the course starts on a ski hill, find a mountain trail or steep hill as your training track.

The challenge arises from those factors you can't control — the terrain, the weather conditions, and your competitors. You condition your animal

What's His P & R?

During your training and competition, your horse's pulse and respiration, or P & R, indicate his well-being. A normal horse at rest has a pulse of 32 to 44, and a respiration of 40 breaths per minute. As he exercises at walk and trot, uphill and downhill, his heart beats faster and he breathes faster. When you slow down and eventually stop, his P & R slow down. At rest, they recover to normal.

The rate of recovery is an important systemic factor, but you don't need a degree in veterinary medicine to calculate it. To measure your horse's P & R, you count the heartbeats and breaths. You can feel the pulse in several places:

* ★ Inside the jawbone
* ★ Behind the nearside elbow
* ★ At the underside of the tail, about four inches down
* ★ Underneath the fetlock, at the back of the pastern

Veteran riders use a stethoscope and wristwatch. You'll stand by his near side, wearing the scope, and gently place the concave bell side on the skin

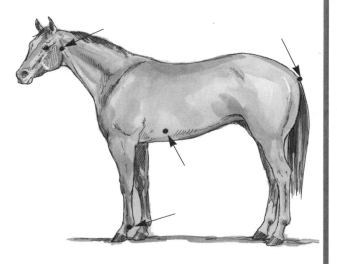

To measure your horse's P & R, you can feel the pulse in several places — inside the jawbone, behind the nearside elbow, the underside of the tail, and under the fetlock, at the back of the pastern.

behind his elbow. Count the beats for 15 seconds, and multiply by four.

For the respiration, count the number of breaths for 15 seconds. Count the number of times the horse exhales, watching the ribs or flank. Or, use your stethoscope on the underside of the neck, about eight inches below the throatlatch.

Learn your horse's normal P & R, at rest and during various stages of exercise. This preparation will help you keep your horse in good shape as you complete a distance ride.

Ride veterinarians also check capillary refill time to evaluate the horse's hydration. You can easily check this by pressing firmly for a moment on the gum above the front incisors. Release the pressure and count the seconds till the white portion resumes its normal pink color. A refill time of 2 seconds is ideal; longer than 3½ seconds may indicate low blood pressure.

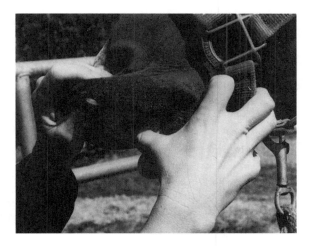

Capillary refill time is checked by pressing the thumb on the gums, then timing the return of a normal pink color.

to withstand the stresses he'll undergo, and get yourself in shape to stay alert before, during, and after the ride.

You'll also learn the most important aspect of distance riding — how to pace yourself so you complete the ride in good shape. On the trail, a horseman thinks for the animal — she knows her animal's abilities and knows when to ride conservatively. She doesn't push too much on first rides, because the horse could resent the pressure. When she senses the horse is in pain, she retires from the ride rather than stress the animal unduly.

Your form influences the horse's comfort and your enjoyment. You sit straight in the saddle, adjusting your upper body angle to help him over the terrain. You never sit crooked or sloppily, as your weight influences his efficiency. Dead weight

Your form influences the horse's comfort. Sit straight in the saddle, adjusting your upper body angle to help him over the terrain.

or uneven pressure inhibits his movement and can result in back injuries.

Ride on light contact, and at even paces. Most riders use trot and walk, with infrequent breaks of loping. The trot requires less energy and covers ground most efficiently. Over good ground, a horse will trot 10 to 12 miles per hour. You might choose to lope to make up time and vary the gait.

In the trot, keep your weight off the horse's back. Either stand in the two-point position, or post as a break from standing in the stirrups.

During the ride, you care for your horse. You keep him hydrated by offering water available at checkpoints. You also carry water with you, so you can offer it to him, drink it yourself, or cool him off by dousing him.

When you join these events, you'll realize that the dedicated riders aim to bring their horses to the finish in better shape than when they left the starting line. Your goal should be to work your horse hard on the trail, and the next day see him bounce back from stress without displaying any adverse effects. Just like the horses of the early West, he's ready for another round.

Other horsemen often label distance riders as "mavericks." The sport can become an obsession, because you must focus on so many aspects of horsemanship — health, biomechanics, tack, and psychology. To succeed, you must know your horse so well that you immediately recognize any unusual behavior and discover the reason.

Distance riders share a unique support system. You may not always ride in a group, but most competitors willingly offer help to one another on the trail.

Tack for Distance Riding

If you plan to concentrate on distance riding, consider switching to a lightweight endurance saddle. Weighing 20 pounds or less, the endurance saddle can resemble a barrel racing model, without a horn.

Back soreness plagues endurance horses, and a well-fitted saddle is crucial to keeping the horse going through the season. A few American saddlemakers build models designed to eliminate undue pressure on the horse's back and withers. Bars should avoid any edge pressure. The tree and rigging are constructed to distribute weight evenly and to avoid interference with the action of the shoulder blades. One unique brand has hinged bars that adjust to the shape of the horse's back as the horse's muscles develop.

For rider comfort, the seat is narrow and the stirrups are hung directly under your center of gravity. Look for a seat that keeps your back straight so you sit in a balanced position on long rides. If you suffer from back pain, the right seat can alleviate much agony.

The saddle should have metal rings so you can attach a breastplate and an optional crupper. You'll also strap on a cantle bag and two water bottle carriers. Some riders tie a sponge or scoop onto the saddle, for cooling the horse with water.

The McClellan saddle, made famous as the official saddle of the U.S. Cavalry, is a favorite with many trail riders. It was designed for extended travel, so the saddle favors the horse's comfort. Although some people suffer from the saddle's seat, fans of the McClellan saddle claim it is the ideal choice.

Many distance riders use some style of seat saver, such as a sheepskin, on top of the saddle. The padding adds comfort on those long miles. Under the saddle, use a saddle pad that avoids any pressure points. Several manufacturers offer specialty pads that transmit pressure uniformly over a broad area of the horse's back. These absorb shock, and some materials mold to the ever-changing shape of the horse in motion. A pad also must wick moisture from the horse's coat. Natural fabrics like wool or wool felt let the skin breathe and remain cool.

Choose specially designed distance riding tack for your own and your horse's comfort.

Help keep your saddle in place on inclines with a breast collar. A Y-shaped collar keeps the saddle from shifting sideways or backward, and it avoids rubbing the shoulder muscles. You might need a crupper on a mule or a horse with low withers. This tack will keep the saddle from sliding forward when you walk down a steep hill.

Look for lightweight stirrups that will support your feet on the long miles. Stirrups should absorb shock and have wide treads for comfort.

Many distance riders prefer a bitless bridle, such as a hackamore or even a halter (usually with a bit attached). The horse can eat or drink more comfortably on the trail, especially during longer rides when it's crucial to keep his system operating at full capacity.

Be sure to train in the same gear you'll use during the ride. Try out new equipment at home to confirm it fits the horse and stays in place. A new saddle blanket can be so slick it slides off, even with the saddle cinched.

Wear lightweight, comfortable clothing appropriate for the weather conditions. Many distance riders wear spandex riding tights. Faux suede insets keep your leg secure against the saddle. Padded tights add cushioning at crotch and knee. Choose outerwear of synthetic fabrics like microfiber or polar fleece, depending on the climate. Fabric should wick moisture away from your body so you don't overheat or become chilled.

You might choose to wear riding shoes rather than boots, so you can ride and run in your footwear. Riding shoes support and protect the ankle from rubbing against the stirrup leather. Ribbed soles help you keep your foot in position.

Be sure to wear protective headgear. Equestrian helmets are accepted in this sport, with visors to shade your head from the sun.

Veterinary assistants take pulse and respiration counts at planned and unplanned stops throughout the ride.

	Open Division	Novice	Competitive Pleasure
RIDE TYPES	B (1 day) A (2 days) AA (3 days)	B (1 day) A (2 days)	B (1 day) A (2 days)
RIDER CLASSES	Heavyweight (190 lbs & over) Lightweight (130–189 lbs) Junior (no weight limit)	Heavyweight (190 lbs & over) Lightweight (130–189 lbs) Junior (no weight limit)	Only 1 rider class

COMPETITIVE TRAIL RIDING

In North American Trail Riding Conference (NATRC) competition, all horses complete an identical trail in the same length of time. Officials judge the horse's soundness, condition, and manners, along with your horsemanship. In NATRC, the combined weight of rider and tack determines your weight class.

To organize and manage the ride involves a ride chairman and a trailmaster. The trailmaster determines the trail, within the guidelines set by NATRC. She uses a topographic map to track the mileage and timing of the trail. Open and Novice divisions may use the same trail, with different times, lengths of hill climbs, and additional mileage for the Open riders.

The goal is to determine the best trail horses, the animals that can cover the course with the least stress. During a ride, competitors must observe rules about caring for their horses. Rules prohibit treatments with medications or ice, or using any leg wraps or boots. A rider is allowed to use fly spray or apply water.

NATRC also limits the type of horseshoes by width and thickness. You may use only rim pads. In an emergency, you may use an Easyboot as temporary hoof protection.

A ride has at least two judges, who score horse and rider. The veterinary judge rates the horse for condition (40%), soundness (40%), way of going (5%), and manners (15%). The horsemanship judge evaluates the rider for grooming (20%), trail equitation (50%), and trail care (30%).

Under current rules, horse and rider start with 100 points each. Judges deduct penalties for deviations from the ideal. In each division, the winning horse completes the ride with the most points for the best condition. The winning rider is the superior horseman, earning the most points.

Judges examine each animal before the ride and each ride morning, noting his condition on a judging card. To arrive at a baseline, they evaluate health, soundness, and way of going, and they note marks and blemishes.

Officials observe horses throughout the ride, at planned and unplanned stops. Veterinary assistants take pulse and respiration counts at the stops. NATRC requires two P & R checks per day, although some rides or divisions of rides have three or four. After the ride, the horse is checked by a vet that evening and again the next morning.

On an NATRC ride, your goal is to conquer the trail environment and to bring your mount to the finish line safe and sound. You prove yourself a responsible horseman when you keep the horse relaxed and comfortable. To the dedicated rider, awards rank secondary to this goal.

The Competitive Ride

At the ride, you'll receive a map of the trail showing turns, elevations, mileage, and water stops. You leave the starting point individually, usually at a 30-second interval after the previous rider.

You'll set your watch at a zero point, such as 12:00, when you start. Using the map, you see the time you should arrive at the first designated P & R check. If this is an hour and 20 minutes and measures 4.6 miles, you figure out how fast to travel. The map lists the elevations on the route, so you know when to walk and when to trot.

"We time the trail by walking rocks and trotting the good terrain," NATRC National Champion Audrey Taylor has explained. "Open riders trot down some easy hills, and up some slants. Novice riders walk most everything, except they trot good terrain."

Plan your strategy according to the distance, terrain, and weather conditions. You'll use your discretion to ride at your own pace, watching the time so you know what speed to adopt during various stages of the trail. You must remain in the saddle during the ride, not walk or run beside your horse or tail it.

NATRC rules specify that you arrive at designated checkpoints within a 30-minute time frame. You can come in 15 minutes before or after the specific time. Arriving any earlier or later costs you penalty points, one for each minute.

"You have to work as a team," says Taylor. "That's my favorite thing about this sport. If you don't, then you'll be too early, or too late. After a while, the horse gets to know when you would ask for a trot, and when you'd want to walk."

Your horse figures out the pace and learns how to conserve his energy. He tells you how he feels by his energy level, and he tells you when he's ready to move out. If he says, "Let's trot," he's telling you he feels good. "Let's lope" could mean he's tired of trotting and his muscles could use a change. Or if you communicate, "Do you feel like trotting?" you gauge his energy level by his response. He may grudgingly change gait, which tells you he's getting tired.

At a vet check, officials examine the horse to see if he meets the P & R parameters. When you arrive at the check, a timer checks you in, with your check time recorded at 10 minutes ahead. Your horse has that time period to recover.

When the 10 minutes are up, the vet will take the P & R for 15 seconds. Your horse should show a pulse of 12, and a respiration of 6. You earn one point penalty for each count over the parameter.

Depending on the heat, the vet may raise the P & R to a higher measurement. If the parameter is a pulse of 16 and your horse's is higher, the vet will "hold" him for another 10 minutes and then recheck. You have to wait those 10 minutes, with the time added to your end ride time.

With temperature, terrain, and condition affecting P & R, you also concern yourself with how your horse moves during the ride. For example, if he bangs his leg on a rock, you should notice the unusual movement.

You'd dismount, soak your sponge or bandana from your water bottle, and soak the leg to cool it. (If you're out of water, briskly rub the leg.) The temporary pain will cause his pulse to rise, but it should slow as you treat the area.

Competitive trail riding is the only distance riding that includes horsemanship judging. The horsemanship judge observes how you handle your horse, both on the ground and in the saddle. You'll also receive scores for how you groom the horse, how you control him in hand, and your tack. For the veterinary examinations, hold the reins or lead rope while standing on the same side as the vet. Keep your horse under control, because his manners count toward his score and yours.

Judges test your trail skills with obstacles. You might have to walk or sidepass over a log, back your horse (always look first to see if it's safe), or maneuver around rocks. Depending on the terrain, other tests could involve crossing water, stepping down a steep, winding path, or dismounting and mounting on the off side. Judges look for a safe, calm trail horse and a smart rider who thinks through the obstacle.

As you approach the end of the ride, you must maintain forward motion for the last two miles.

Stay on the Trail

A major hazard in distance riding is getting lost. In almost every ride, somebody ignores the map or misses the markers. This rider has to backtrack, losing time or points.

Ride officials post ribbons of surveyor's tape to mark the trail. Usually they'll "ribbon" the course with the ribbons on the right, tied high on tree limbs. Three ribbons means a turn is coming up, and next will be three more ribbons marking the actual turn. For a left turn, you'd see two ribbons on the right, and one on the left.

To follow the route, study your map and watch for the ribbons, or hoofprints of earlier riders. If you get lost, go back to the last ribbon you saw.

If you get lost, blame yourself for failing to pay attention. Don't blindly follow a rider or group ahead of you, because someone else could easily make the mistake first and you could succumb to their error.

If you're tired, you might miss a marker and go down the wrong trail. If you do find yourself lost and your horse hasn't learned where "home" is, wait for the drag riders to find you. Carry a whistle for such a circumstance, and blow it at intervals to broadcast your location.

Judges will score you on how you feed, water, and tie your horse in camp. If the camp doesn't have separate corrals, every rider has to tie her horse to a stationary object (usually the horse trailer).

AMERICAN ENDURANCE RIDE CONFERENCE (AERC) RIDES

RIDE TYPES

Ride Mileage	Time	Checks
50 miles	12 hours	4
100 miles	24 hours	8
150 miles	36 hours	–

CLASSES

Senior Division	Junior Division
Lightweight (160 lbs. and below)	All riders under the age of 16
Middleweight (161–210 lbs.)	
Heavyweight (211 lbs. and over)	

Rules prohibit you from stopping or dismounting along this final segment of the trail.

Base Camp

On distance rides, riders and their horses live at base camp. Usually in a meadow or valley, the campsite resembles a recreational vehicle parking lot. But you don't need a fancy motor home, because you can bunk down in the back of a pickup or on the ground.

In camp, you care for your horse after the day's ride. On some rides, camp also serves as the lunch stop.

Your horse stays tied to the trailer, to an overhead picket line, or in a portable corral. He needs to relax in camp. The freedom of a corral encourages him to stretch out, and as soon as you unsaddle and leave him alone, he's likely to urinate.

Because you concentrate on caring for your horse and planning for (or recovering from) the ride, you probably won't spend much time "camping." These are family sports, and your family or friends come along to enjoy the outdoor life (and take care of the housekeeping while you do the horsekeeping).

In camp, you'll make friends with your fellow competitors. Distance riders share a camaraderie in their love for horses and their obsession with the sport. Most old hands enjoy sharing experiences and opinions, so you can ask lots of questions. Some rides will distribute name tags designating novice and open riders, so you know whom to ask. The experts will also freely offer advice, so maintain an open mind and thank them for their help.

Your horse care in camp becomes part of your horsemanship score in competitive trail riding. Judges can score you on how you feed, water, and tie your horse. NATRC rules govern stabling and limit the hours of horse care. To keep the competition fair, all riders must secure their horses in the same way. If the camp doesn't have separate corrals, every rider has to tie her horse to a stationary object (usually the horse trailer).

ENDURANCE RIDING

Among all equestrian sports, this discipline places the most demanding test upon horse and rider. The horse's physical and mental capacities affect how well he can cover ground cross-country, within a specified time period. Endurance riding is the only international sport open to riders who choose Western style. The U.S. Equestrian Team added endurance riding in 1993.

Because the event originated in North America, riders from the United States have dominated the World Championships. Becky Hart and her Arabian "Rio" have won this title three times.

Inspired by frontier treks, endurance riding reflects the Western heritage. Rides often follow pioneers' trails, yet today's riders apply scientific data to maximize the horse's travel and minimize the stress.

This marathon involves skill and stamina. The American Endurance Ride Conference (AERC) has a motto: "To finish is to win." Riders follow another guideline: "The trail is your competition." To succeed, riders focus on the goal of completing the ride within the specified maximum time. Competition does drive some riders, who concentrate on the race aspect to finish with the forerunners.

As a novice, your goal is to complete the ride. Plan your strategy accordingly, and begin your endurance career with a training ride. Riding competitive trail can teach you horse care that you'd apply to endurance riding.

AERC sanctions rides of varying distances. For beginners, AERC sanctions the Limited Distance ride of 25 to 35 miles. This is held in conjunction with a regular AERC ride.

The ride strategy resembles that of competitive trail riding. The map marks every designated rest stop, or check, set at regular intervals. Study the map to calculate your speed to each check, so you can plan your rate of travel. On your first rides, you'll aim for an average speed of four to six miles per hour.

Your pit crew will meet you at each check. At least one, preferably two or more, helpers will assist you in caring for your horse. Experienced riders may choose to ride solo, without a crew to assist.

During this break, you'll help your horse to recover his pulse to 68 or below. You'll check his shoes, offer feed and water, and dose him with electrolytes to restore his hydration. After removing the tack, you'll sponge him on his neck and legs to reduce the pulse rate. You might drape a soaked towel on his neck, or apply iced leg wraps to reduce any swelling. Many endurance riders use TTEAM techniques to relieve temporary muscular aches.

Each check includes a veterinary examination. The veterinarian determines if your horse can continue the ride safely.

The Endurance Ride

Before you tackle the ride, learn as much as you can about the course. You might ride the entire trail to learn it. Pre-ride the last leg, so your horse learns where home is. This can stimulate his homing instinct on the last miles.

Attend the pre-ride briefing to find out how the trail is marked. Officials will describe specific hazards and explain the veterinary criteria. You can also ask fellow riders about the trail.

AERC has developed rules and guidelines for a standardized format. Strict veterinary controls begin with a pre-ride exam. The veterinarian will determine the horse's starting condition. She checks the cardiovascular system, hydration, gut sounds, and overall soundness.

All riders usually leave at the same time in a "shotgun" start. Before the start, walk and trot your horse slowly. Take your time when you do travel along the trail, letting the faster horses hurry to the front so you can maintain control over yours.

Riders soon spread out, so you can pace your horse so he doesn't wear himself out. You may decide to ride in a group moving at a comfortable pace, but maintain control if others pass you. Don't let the excitement lure you into trying to keep up with faster riders, whose pace might tire your horse before you realize it. And don't let him decide he has to stay with the group; he should be able to work alone and not waste energy fretting about horses ahead of, or behind, him.

You'll usually ride at the trot. As you near a vet check, walk your horse so his P & R will drop.

You'll come into two types of holds, or time spent in vet checks, that don't count in the total ride time. Timers record your arrival and departure times at each check. Some vet checks are mandatory holds, where you stay a set amount of time. You don't have to come into this hold with a low P & R.

Most vet checks have a "gate" into the hold. Before you present your horse for the examination, his pulse must recover to an announced requirement (usually between 72 and 64). The lower his pulse when you near the vet check, the sooner you can pass through the gate into the hold, and the sooner you can resume the ride.

At every check, the veterinarian evaluates metabolic and mechanical indicators. She pulls horses that aren't fit to continue. If you've overridden your horse or pushed him beyond his ability, he won't recover quickly. The vet will check gut sounds and anal tone as indicators of fatigue, along with other signs like inversion (pulse faster than respiration) and panting.

Heidi Caldwell, a rider with 20 years in the sport, was on the pit crew for Teresa Cross at the 1990 World Championships. She explains the use of water at the vet checks. "You must maintain your hydration, so the more water we get in and around these horses when it starts getting warm the more we can keep the jets cooled down. Horses generate a lot of body heat from their working muscles. Their temperature can rise by a number of degrees. So you need to have that extra cooling, and the evaporation of the water helps cool these horses.

"There are certain areas of the body you don't want to put it on when they're working like that. You tend to stay away from the hindquarters and the large muscle masses over the back and the loins. They can cramp up with a heavy dousing of cold water. We usually douse the neck, the shoulders, the legs, and the chest in between the front legs. The rider can use a squeeze water bottle to keep the horse cool while they're moving."

The horse with strength and courage excels in this sport. In a fit horse, the heart rate can increase with exercise to 120 to 200 beats per minute. Within 10 to 15 minutes, that rate should drop dramatically. A horse with a high recovery rate has a pulse that comes down fast.

On the ride, you need to take care of yourself. You can lose 10 pounds on a ride, so keep yourself hydrated. Dunk a bandana in water, and tie it around your neck. Drink a lot of water, before you feel thirsty, and also eat snacks like oranges so you don't get heat exhaustion. If you become woozy and lose your form, it affects the horse.

On a mandatory hold, like an hour lunch break, you and your horse can relax. You may or may not decide to unsaddle. Leaving the saddle on keeps the back muscles warm; removing it cools the muscles. On a longer ride, you might switch to a fresh saddle pad and girth cover, or even a different saddle.

At the completion of the ride, an official will weigh you and your tack. This determines your class in the ride. Your horse undergoes a final vet check, and if he's met all criteria, you've successfully completed the ride.

Famous endurance rides include the World Championships (where riders represent the U.S. Equestrian Team), the Western States Trail Ride (the Tevis Cup), and the Race of Champions. You must qualify to enter the Race of Champions, considered the toughest in the United States. This three-day ride covers 160 miles in the high country.

RIDE AND TIE

Ride and tie originated in the Old West, where two people occasionally had to share one horse. As a sport, this distance race spreads the challenge across three team members — a horse and two riders. While one person rides, the other walks or runs, so runners and riders alternate on the trail in this unique version of the biathlon.

Most ride and tie events run for 10 to 20 miles. The shortest distance is about 6 miles, with the World Championship race at 40.

In ride and tie, you and your human partner decide who rides the horse what distance. If you start riding, you travel the trail as you would in endurance riding. You pace the trail and read your horse, while considering the ability of your teammate. When you've ridden as far as you think your teammate can run, you halt, dismount, and tie the horse to a tree along the trail. You then continue the course at a walk or jog. The horse waits for your partner to catch up, untie him and mount, and then the two of them follow you. The three of you meet, and you agree who gets the horse for the next segment. (Rules prohibit riding double or one tailing the horse.)

Is ride and tie a horse sport, or a people sport? It places unusual demands on the three athletes who make up the team. You have to be in shape for a cross-country marathon, in addition to handling the horse down trail. You'll spend a major percentage of the race time on foot rather than in the saddle. (Riders and runners must switch a minimum number of times.) The horse has to show both mental willingness and physical fitness. Besides being fit for the distance, he must cope with the stop-and-go conditions of the ride.

Ride and tie contestant Lisa Skyhorse explains: "The horse has to be mentally reasonable. You tie him up and run away from him. Meanwhile, other horses pass him on the trail. It takes a lot of athleticism, too. He either sprints, or he stands still."

The standing still part poses difficulties for many equine athletes. The veteran ride and tie horse knows to take advantage of the rest period during his breaks. A seasoned endurance horse, conditioned to maintain constant motion, might fret and fight the tie rope. If he gets untied, he'll run down the trail with the pack, or travel home to base camp. (He'll probably pass either you or your teammate on the way!) All three of you must cross the finish line together to complete the race, so an equine dropout can disqualify you.

The ride includes vet checks, usually about every 10 miles. A pit crew can assist you at the checks. You and your teammate must exchange the horse at least twice between vet checks. Officials examine horses and mules for P & R, capillary refill, soundness, and abrasions, and they pull animals who don't meet the criteria. After completion, the horse must also pass a post-race examination.

The Ride and Tie Ride

You'll probably compete wearing riding tights or shorts in warm weather. (Protect your legs by sprinkling talcum powder over the saddle during the ride.) Racers wear running shoes.

At the starting line, everyone sets off at once in a shotgun start. In a major race of 120 entries, you'll run with 120 horses and 120 runners. (If you start on foot, you'll be wise to position yourself behind the equine racers at the start.)

Some teams plan ride strategy, aiming for the superior runner to handle the tougher parts of the trail. However, you can't always plan your exact trade-off points. Other riders may have used all the available trees for tying their horses, and you'll have to continue till you find a proper spot. You must tie in a safe location beside the trail, where your partner can spot the horse.

Ride and tiers recommend a special rope, measuring about 3½ feet long with strong clips on each end. You don't actually tie the rope, you wrap it around the tree and snap the clip to the wrap. This quick wrap should hold the horse securely.

If you're in the saddle when you arrive at the first vet check, you must present your horse to officials. Your crew helps you by offering water and snacks, filling your water bottles, and helping the horse recover. The horse can't continue until he passes the veterinary criteria and the runner arrives at the check. You can start running as soon as you're ready. Most vet checks use the "hand tie," where a crew member holds the horse's rope instead of your tying the horse to an object.

When the runner arrives, the horse should have passed the check and should be ready to continue. The runner mounts and follows the course.

As you walk or jog along the trail, you don't know exactly how much time and distance separate you from the horse and rider. You may expect them to overtake you within 15 minutes, but a delay could occur if the officials hold the horse. Your crew could ask other riders to tell you what's happening, but you might keep running farther than you had planned.

A top, two-man team averages six miles per hour in ride and tie. They could complete a 28-mile course in 2½ hours. Teams of both genders or two-woman teams usually take longer to complete the ride. You can compete as husband and wife, parent and child, or go for the "Century" category, in which the ages of all three team members add up to at least 100.

A good distance horse must be mentally and physically conditioned. The best ones are lean, streamlined athletes that are fit but not overly muscled.

The Horse for the Distance

Distance riders look for a certain type of equine athlete. This horse is lean and sinewy, with light muscles of the slow-twitch type. The muscles expand and contract more slowly than those of the fast-twitch type. The horse can dissipate heat faster and endure repeated efforts over a longer duration.

Becky Hart describes her World Champion Arabian, R.O. Grand Sultan+\: "The thing that makes him a good endurance horse is that mechanically he's put together very well. He's got short cannons, deep heart girth — all the things you look for in a good endurance horse. Along with the conformation, he's got the heart and the desire. He does it because he loves it."

A successful distance horse flows over the trail with no wasted motion. At the walk and trot, he seems to spring forward. He has substantial feet and correct angles on all joints.

NATRC rules require a Novice horse to be at least 48 months of age; an Open horse, 60 months. AERC requires the horse in a Limited Distance ride to be at least 48 months.

The distance riding horse must have a good walk and trot. One that moves slowly, without expending much energy, can frustrate the rider. This animal may maintain low pulse and respiration rates, but other animals will pass it on the trail.

Champions are "lean machines," streamlined athletes that are fit but not overly muscled. The sport tests these horses against a standard of performance, and some breeders have succeeded in producing animals that have the ability for the sport.

Although individuals of any breed can compete and win, Arabian and half-Arabian horses (and mules) dominate distance riding. Originally bred to endure desert treks, these animals consistently outride the more contemporary breeds.

Besides looking like a distance horse, the animal must have the metabolism to handle the test. He can carry weight, yet he converts energy into forward movement. He has a hearty appetite and readily drinks available water. He also shows a "can-do" attitude, with the spirit to keep moving toward the finish line.

A distance prospect benefits from an early life running free in a pasture. A youngster builds bone density through ranging over a large area of uneven terrain. He learns to cope with the elements and handle himself if exposed early to an environment that contains hills, rocks, and running water.

Benefits of Conditioning

To bring your horse to a state of fitness, you apply both science and equestrian art. You focus on your riding goals and prepare your animal to meet the test.

Distance riders develop a variety of approaches to conditioning, but all require consistent work.

Through increased physical demands, your animal becomes fit. Heart, lungs, muscles, and mind all must function at full capacity in the equine athlete. Fitness implies well-being, a combination of inherited soundness, proper nutrition, and regular workouts.

Conditioning builds your horse up to his genetic potential. The fit athlete is strong, confident, and injury-free. Through a planned workload, he's ready for competition. His muscles are flexible; they stretch and flex rather than pull and tear.

A conditioning program of higher-energy activity improves the horse's strength, endurance, balance, flexibility, and agility. Through planned exercise, you exert muscles, strengthen the cardiovascular system, and build up the animal's basic structure.

Briefly, increased activity overloads the body's cells. Responding to stress, the cells enlarge. You may not see your horse's muscles grow bigger, but the cells can process and maintain energy for longer periods.

Exercise stimulates the cardiovascular (heart and blood circulation) and respiratory (breathing) systems. Stress requires the heart to pump blood faster through the body, and the lungs to inhale faster, sending energy to all cells. As these systems increase in their efficiency, the horse's pulse and respiration maintain acceptable levels during exercise. Increased stress of time and intensity helps the horse build strong bone, thick cartilage, and strong tendons and ligaments.

Your equine athlete will benefit from increasingly stressful aerobic and anaerobic exercise. Aerobics, also popular in human workouts, develop the cardiovascular system. Fast-paced, steady movement stimulates faster, deeper breathing, which stresses the heart and lungs to supply cells with more oxygen. You elevate the heart rate and hold it up in "cruise control" for several minutes.

Anaerobic exercise stresses the muscles by demanding quick energy. A short sprint or a rapid hill climb are anaerobic workouts, which strengthen muscles already toned by moderate exercise. In competition, you reserve anaerobic work for a sprint to the finish line.

Pony your horse by leading him while you ride another.

You can condition a horse without riding it, through ponying. Pony your horse by leading him while you ride another. Be sure you can ride with the reins in one hand, and outfit the ponied horse in a stout halter and a long enough lead rope. School the ponied horse to travel close to your right, its head beside your knee. Practice in an enclosed area before you pony a horse on the trail.

A CONDITIONING PROGRAM

Your program begins with a goal, usually the length of the season's first ride. Develop your program gradually, so your horse can adjust to increased stress. Usually, you want him to peak about 10 days before the ride. Then you maintain his condition throughout the riding season.

Always help your horse stretch before a training session, and warm up at the walk. And vary the terrain you cover in your workouts. As NATRC champion Audrey Taylor has said, "You have to build the whole horse." She recommends hill climbs one day, then resting the mountain climbing muscles and trotting hard-packed ground to build bone density.

You might get by with a three-month program for a short competitive trail ride, but training an endurance horse takes longer. Besides building muscles, you strengthen tendons and condition bone.

If you begin with a horse that is out of shape, you might ride him daily for 30 minutes at a walk, then add the trot, for two to four weeks of legging up. Gradually increase the distance and speed during the next few weeks, with more trot and canter work.

Scrutinize your horse constantly during the training period. Be sure the farrier shoes him for distance riding, with pads if you'll be traveling over rocky trails. Watch for signs of excess stress.

Developing a moderately fit horse takes from three to six months of regular exercise of heart, lungs, and muscles. For example, you could start with four to six miles for two weeks, then move up to an eight-mile ride one day. Encourage your horse to develop a ground-covering trot, and use "long trotting" (about 10 miles per hour) as an ef-

You might save your horse for the sections where he has to pick his way over tree roots or rocky ground, while still maintaining a good pace.

ficient aerobic exercise. This gait will build up his wind and encourage him to move at a steady rhythm. (If you post, change your diagonals frequently.) Gradually increase the time you trot, and move up to trying 10 to 12 miles one day a week. You'll probably ride the horse five or six days a week to get him in condition. For more than moderate fitness, you must work daily, or six days on, one day off. Check the P & R after a long trot, aiming for him to recover after a 10-minute rest.

Measure training trails so you can calculate your speed. Post mile markers, and move them to different terrain to learn how your speed changes as you move up or down, or across difficult footing.

Conditioning bone takes longer than conditioning muscles and requires low intensity, long duration work. Include this type of exercise in your regular conditioning program. The time required varies according to the horse's condition, age, and your adherence to a daily schedule. Avoid rushing or shortcuts to prevent stressing body or mind.

For a more strenuous ride, increase the mileage and add more stressful anaerobic work, also called "interval training." Usually this would be short sprints at a gallop, either on the flat or up a grade. Mountain trails shorten the time to get a horse fit. For hill climbs, you might start with 200 yards, then work up to a half-mile climb.

By stepping up the duration and speed of workouts, you'd need about 8 weeks to ready a moderately fit horse for a 2-day, 75-mile trail ride. Try a 30-mile test as a conditioning ride.

When the horse is fit, some trainers feel you should work him hard one day, then give him some time off for muscles to rebuild. The fit horse could go on a 20-mile ride every other week. You can probably keep him in shape with about 25 miles a week. This might be through one, two, or three rides a week. You could go 10 to 15 miles on a weekend, with two 5-mile rides during the week. Becky Hart says she keeps her horses in shape by riding 4 to 6 miles three times a week, for 45 to 60 minutes.

Work on your fitness, too. You need to maintain your alertness on the trail so you can guide your horse. Endurance riders spend time on the

CHECKLIST FOR A DISTANCE RIDE

Site	Item	Use
ON THE HORSE	Hoof pick	Pick out the horse's feet
	Easyboot	Apply if horse loses a shoe
	Vet card in plastic bag	Present at vet checks
	1 or 2 water bottles	Drinking and cooling (pour water over the horse's poll as needed)
	Stethoscope	Taking P & R
	Sponge	Cooling horse at water crossing
THE RIDER CARRIES	Wristwatch	Keeps track of riding time
	Fanny pack	Contains rainwear, knife, whistle, flashlight or glow bar, high-energy snacks

ground, leading or tailing. In tailing, you help your horse surmount a hill by dismounting and holding on to the horse's tail. Don't pull the tail as he walks up the hill, but let him tow you.

Downhill, you may choose to walk beside your horse. This groundwork demands that you be in shape. You may find yourself jogging alongside during your training sessions, and you can also swim or work out to toughen your legs for those hours of trotting down trail.

Test your conditioning program with a novice competitive ride or a limited distance endurance ride. Besides evaluating your horse's fitness, you'll discover how he adapts to the campsite, the ride officials, the other horses, and unfamiliar terrain.

COMPETITIVE STRATEGIES

Distance riding presents a challenge because you must pace your horse to conserve energy as you ride against the trail. Winning strategy begins with training your horse, both on the ground and in the saddle. He has to accept handling from strangers, as he'll undergo veterinary examinations during the event. You may have conditioned your animal to a high level of fitness, but he also must cooperate to allow the ride officials to check his pulse and respiration.

Distance riding tests your horse, so plan how to maximize his strength and fitness. By balancing the effects of distance, terrain, altitude, and weather, you'll know when to "motor out," or push ahead, and when to slack off and ride conservatively.

You need to know how much horse you have left, especially if the hardest part of the trail is in its second half. Here you might save your horse for the tough sections, so he's mentally and physically alert enough to pick his way over tree roots or rocky ground, while still maintaining a good pace.

Your horse will tell you how he feels. If he stumbles once or twice, he may be tiring. If he's breathing hard during a trot, slow down so his respiration rate drops closer to normal.

During training, you should learn what type of trail he prefers. He could thrive on hills but lack speed on the flat. Or if he hates trudging through sand, plan to make up lost time on an earlier or later section of the trail.

In distance riding, you develop a close rapport with your horse. You learn every aspect of his physical state and normal behaviors, and you're attuned to any variation. You can tell when he moves easily, and a slightly different feel could indicate he's sore or fatigued. When your horse moves differently in the mountains, you have to decide if he's suffering from altitude sickness, bored with his job, or simply tired from struggling up hills.

Through pitting yourself against the trail, you learn the limits of your horse's abilities, and you'll discover when he "hits the wall" and has nothing left. You don't want to push him too hard, or he may sulk and not want to leave the base camp.

If he falls on the trail, try to determine what caused the fall. He might have slipped and lost his momentum, or fatigue might have caused him to stumble. Some horses don't seem to care about losing their footing, which endangers both you and them.

Critics challenge distance riding, especially endurance, citing the stress that riders inflict on their animals. However, most contestants do put the horse's welfare first, often above their own. You'll see weary riders who struggle to stay awake, while their horses appear fresh and ready to continue. AERC rules prohibit the use of any drugs during a ride, even forbidding the use of liniment until after the final vet check.

A conditioned endurance horse thrives on his task. He receives better care than most equine athletes, and probably more veterinary attention. With veterinarians monitoring the events, a 100-miler has as many as 10 examinations before, during, and after the ride.

The distance horse proves himself through competition. It may take 1,000 miles for an endurance horse to begin to thrive on competition. The champion develops a will to win. He wants to stay ahead of the pack, and he knows when other horses travel in front of him.

Distance riding also concentrates on trail preservation. Enthusiasts cooperate with government agencies to ensure open space and dedicated trails. Horsemen prove they're responsible users of public lands and aim to conserve natural resources.

Horse Show Basics

Throughout history, horsemen have competed among themselves to see who had the fastest or most polished horse. Today's Western events follow equestrian tradition. Competitions have evolved into two basic types, horse shows and arena contests. Generally a show involves subjective judging, and in a contest, the clock determines who wins. Some shows do include timed rodeo events like roping and barrel racing, but a rodeo would rarely include horse show classes.

Why would you compete in front of spectators? In a show, you can:

* Prove your ability
* Test your skills
* Dress up
* Win prizes (and even money)
* Beat the competition
* Have fun

Yes, horse shows can be fun. You'll savor memorable moments when you and your horse perform for a crowd of spectators. That first ribbon is one you'll never forget, no matter what its color. At shows, you'll also mingle with horsemen and learn more about horses and riding.

Showing presents a challenge — you act out a role in an artificial situation. In a 10-minute class, you demonstrate the work you've accomplished over months of practice. You and your horse also demonstrate the bond you've developed. You assume responsibility for your horse's smooth, willing performance in the show ring, which Western riders call "the pen."

This chapter introduces you to the pleasures of showing, concentrating on the pre-show preparations and three popular events. Subsequent chapters explore how you can polish your showmanship and progress to the more sophisticated show classes.

	Western Pleasure	Western Horsemanship (also called "Stock Seat Equitation")	Halter
JUDGE SCORES	Horse	Rider	Horse
IDEAL PERFORMANCE	Horse moves smoothly and obediently; holds head and neck at height of withers; pretty; shiny coat; rider appears comfortable.	Rider remains calm and quiet; cues horse without visible aids; immediately responds to horse; appears in control at all times; has good hands and seat; is fairly athletic.	Horse presents an ideal picture of the breed standard; poses well; responds immediately to cues. If a color breed, judge looks for perfect shade, coat pattern, or dun factor (Buckskins only).
USUAL CLASS ROUTINE	Horse walks, jogs, lopes both directions of the pen. Riders line up and back up for the judge.	Judge directs group of riders to perform on the rail. Individual riders perform a set pattern of maneuvers.	Entries pose, trot for the judge, and line up for final judging.

BEGINNING SHOW CLASSES

Competitions challenge Western riders at all levels, from a local "shaggy show" up to World Championships for each breed. When you launch your show career, you'll probably start at a moderate level to test your horse's abilities. You don't need a fancy, expensive horse, and you can see if showing satisfies your competitive urge.

These entry-level events listed above are the starting point for most beginners in the show pen; they test how you and your horse meet the standards of performance.

MATCHING YOUR HORSE TO THE EVENT

The entry-level events appear elementary. Yet these sedate classes can deceive by their simplicity. The more you examine the intricacies, the more complex even basic performance seems.

Before you enter a class in a horse show, consider if your horse will be competitive. Yes, just about any horse can follow the class routine, but how suitably does your animal meet this particular standard?

To decide how you'd fit in, attend a show of the type you envision entering. Observe class routines carefully, and picture yourself in the pen alongside the horses competing. Do you feel you could match the winners? Or would your horse even place above the worst? Your honest comparison will tell you if you're ready to show in that level.

In any show, you'll feel more secure if your horse resembles the others. If you don't conform, you'll look out of place. You want the judge to see you and score your horse, but not in a negative way. If you exhibit an unusual animal, like a pony or mule at an all-breed show or a Paint in a class of bays and sorrels, people will notice.

Can your horse do everything the class requires? How reliably can he perform the basic

Entry-level events can help you launch your show career by testing how you and your horse meet performance standards.

requirements? List any weaknesses, and plan how you'll improve them.

Is your horse bomb-proof? He has to tolerate the "hurry up and wait" atmosphere of the show-grounds. Most of the time he stands tied to a trailer, or in a temporary stall. Then you suddenly appear, anxious about getting ready for the class. Meanwhile, he has to ignore strange horses, cars and trucks, loudspeakers, baby strollers, and flapping flags. (Some shows add hot air balloons, elephants, and cows!)

Ask for advice from your instructor or mentor. If you're taking lessons from or have bought your horse from a trainer, request this professional's opinion about your show direction. Chapter 10 discusses how a coach can assist you.

Qualifications

The show premium (also called the "prize list") is a guide to the show. First check the show's title. If you see "Schooling" or "Training" in its name, this

is a casual event geared toward practice for horses and riders. The informal show usually offers ribbons as the only prizes.

The more prestige a show offers, the more intense the competition becomes as exhibitors compete for association points. Look for the name of the show sponsor, and note if the show is recognized by a local, state, or national organization. Bigger prizes attract seasoned amateurs as well as professional trainers. A show can be part of a circuit, or a series of shows at the same location or in a time sequence. The circuit may offer its own awards for exhibitors gaining the most points during the series.

On the prize list, study the type of classes offered. Unless a class says, "Open," the show management has restricted entrants by age, sex, experience (of horse or exhibitor), or the horse's breed. Most of the distinctions should be clear, but notice some specific terms.

Here's a partial prize list, showing typical classes for an open show:

1. Halter, Stallions, all ages. Open to any horse of that sex.
2. Halter, Mares, all ages. Open to any horse of that sex.
3. Halter, Geldings, all ages. Open to any horse of that sex.
4. Showmanship at Halter, 19 and over. Handler is at least 19 years old.
5. Showmanship at Halter, 18 and under. Handler is 18 or younger.
6. Walk-Trot, 9 and under. Rider is 9 or younger and doesn't have to lope.
7. Walk-Trot, Beginning Rider. Rider's first year of showing and doesn't have to lope.
8. Western Pleasure, Green. Horse's first year of showing in this event.
9. Western Pleasure, Maiden Horse. Horse has never won a blue ribbon in WP.
10. Western Pleasure, Novice Horse. Horse hasn't won more than 3 blues in WP.
11. Western Pleasure, Junior Horse. Horse is 4 years or under.

12. Western Pleasure, Senior Horse. Horse is 5 years or older.
13. Western Pleasure, 19 and over. Rider is at least 19 years old.
14. Western Pleasure, 14–18. Rider is between these ages.
15. Western Pleasure, 13 and under. Rider is 13 or younger.

If you're inexperienced, you should look for classes like the Maiden, or ones for beginning or novice riders. Avoid open classes, where you'd be up against skilled riders (and even professional trainers) who don't qualify for the classes restricted to less experienced horsemen. Even amateur classes can be highly competitive.

Horse show age starts on January 1 of the current year. If you turned 19 on January 2, you're considered 18 for the entire year. A horse's age changes on January 1, regardless of his actual birthday. If your horse turns 5 on December 30, he's considered a 6-year-old on January 1.

LEARNING THE RULES

Every show observes a set of written rules. In Western events, a local show would probably follow AQHA rules, unless another breed sponsors the competition.

Whether large or small, a show follows a set structure. You choose classes, complete an entry form, pay fees, and prepare your horse to compete in a certain class on the schedule. Arriving at the show, you tie your horse to the trailer or release him in a temporary stall. You groom him, dress in your show duds, and warm up.

A well-groomed horse has a shiny coat and long, flowing tail.

An announcer broadcasts the call for the class, often giving a "10-minute" call, and exhibitors gather near the pen's in-gate. At the final announcement, the gate opens and you enter the pen. Every show pen is rectangular or oval in shape.

You perform in a group on the rail, or individually in the center of the pen. If you perform alone, you may draw for a working order or informally agree who goes first. The announcer calls the action like this: "Number 54 is next. 33 is on deck [to go after 54], and 17 is in the hole [to go after 33]."

In the show pen, you ignore the spectators and concentrate on your horse. You focus on staying on the rail, or performing the pattern according to the judge's directions.

After everyone has performed individually, or after the group has completed the judge's instructions, you line up in the center of the ring. (This is usually your horse's favorite part, because he learns the class is over.) The announcer calls the numbers of award winners, and you accept your ribbon. If your number's not called, you leave the pen.

PREPARING TO SHOW

Whatever class you enter, you present a picture to the judge. The judge expects to see your horse well groomed and you neatly dressed. He can tell if you just pulled your horse out of a dusty corral and knocked off the dirt.

First comes a shiny coat. The ideal show coat gleams as one surface rather than individual hairs. A healthy coat begins with sound nutrition, and you augment the shine of the hairs by daily rubbing. Curry the coat from 10 to 30 minutes each day, and add a final polish with a brush or towel. Stroke with the hairs to flatten them against the skin.

Most show horses wear blankets or sheets throughout the year. Blankets add warmth in winter, and in summer protect the coat from the bleaching effects of sunlight. The lining also rubs lightly against the coat, enhancing the shine.

You might bathe your horse for the show, in addition to daily grooming and blanketing. A bath would include a rinse, shampoo, and a final, thorough rinse.

If you show year-round, you might body clip your horse. (This can change the horse's color.) Use full-size electric clippers with new or newly sharpened blades. Before clipping, bathe the horse so you clip a clean coat.

Most breeds require a short mane and forelock. For the desirable flat mane, shorten and thin by pulling long hairs from underneath. (Don't trim a mane with scissors, or it will look chopped off.) This encourages the shorter hairs on top to lie close to the neck, so you end up with a mane three to five inches long. Tame flyaway hairs by dampening the mane with hairsetting gel, or apply a mane tamer.

The forelock hairs should lie neatly against the forehead, and the mane should press against the neck. You may decide to band the horse's mane, separating the strands into many narrow hanks and wrapping a colored band around each section.

Treat mane and tail hairs with care. Instead of combing to separate hairs, use a soft brush or even your fingers. Shampoo and condition the mane and tail more often, and treat the hairs with moisturizing products.

Every showman aims for a long, flowing tail. Protect your horse's tail by wrapping it to guard against hairs being broken off or pulled free. Wrapping also encourages growth. The usual method is to braid the hairs below the tailbone into one long braid. Fold the tail and place it inside a tube sock or tail pouch. When you unwrap and unbraid, the tail will look wavy.

Beauty treatments accentuate the horse's face and legs. You'll trim your horse with electric clippers, starting with the bridle path, or the section of the mane just behind the ears. The bridle path positions the mane away from the throatlatch. Trim a section about three to six inches long and run the blades both directions, close against the crest.

Also trim protruding hairs along the jawline and whiskers on the muzzle. A smooth clip job results in a naturally smooth appearance, and "shaving" all hairs to the same length defines the bones of the face.

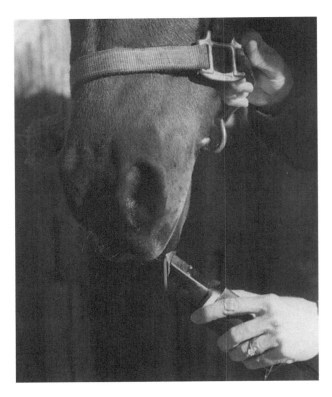

Trimming the hairs along the jawline and on the muzzle helps define the shape of the face and gives a smooth appearance.

Clipping is a craft and an art. Develop an eye for the desired results, and run the clippers with the grain of the hair. Try to blend the clipped areas into the parts of the coat you leave unclipped, and blend abrupt changes of color.

You can "defuzz" the ears to different degrees. You might choose to shorten the hairs simply by folding the ear and trimming only the fuzzy hairs that protrude. On furrier ears, carefully run the clippers along the edges to define them.

You can also clip the ears closely, shaving inside and out. "Peel out" the ear by turning it inside out and clipping down to the surface. (Hold your thumb over the inner ear opening to protect it from loose hairs.)

You'll also clip the longer hairs from the horse's feet and lower legs. If you're new to clipping, use these areas to practice. It's simpler to clip these contours than those of the face, and any mistakes will be less obvious.

Like the ears, you can opt for a touch-up or a full-blown barbering. Perform a quick job by running your clippers down the fetlocks and pasterns, or add more refinement by trimming upward on the coronet. If you feel confident of your clipper control, try the elaborate booting-up, in which you trim from hoof to knee or hock.

Whenever you clip, consider your horse's comfort. Clipping too close on sensitive skin can cause irritation. If you clip a white muzzle or bridle path, keep the horse out of the sunlight to protect against painful burns.

On show day, perform any final preparations of the mane and forelock. You might want to tuck the forelock under the bridle's browband or ear loop. Dampen the hairs with hairsetting gel and pull the forelock to the side.

Control any flyaway tail hairs by dampening them and applying a tail wrap. If your horse has a long tail, knot the hairs to avoid the horse's stepping on them during your warmup.

If you want, add hoof polish just before the class. Stand the horse on a hard surface, and paint his hooves with either clear or black polish. Allow the product to dry thoroughly. And don't forget to protect your horse with fly spray just before you leave for the ring.

In those last few moments, scan your horse one more time. With a towel, wipe out the nostrils, and remove any traces of saliva or sweat before you approach the in-gate.

Show Tack

Use the best tack you own. You'll notice that Western riders use flashy show tack, often decorated with engraved silver trim. You don't have to show in silver equipment, but most riders do.

You can show in the same pleasure saddle you ride every day, after cleaning it thoroughly. Your saddle should place you forward, over the center of balance. Stirrup leathers allow you to sit with your feet directly underneath your shoulders, so you won't bounce in Western Pleasure.

You might have a saddle with an "Equitation" seat. The deep seat with a slight rise helps you

ONE MONTH BEFORE	Practice show maneuvers, concentrating on what's difficult for you or your horse.
	Practice show grooming techniques.
	Gather your show tack and buy or borrow items you lack.
	Check condition of all tack and make any necessary repairs.
	Gather your show outfit and plan exactly what you'll wear.
	Arrange your horse's transportation to the show.
ONE WEEK BEFORE	Practice riding in your show clothes and tack.
	Arrange for farrier to trim or shoe your horse.
	Trim your horse with electric clippers.
ONE DAY BEFORE	Bathe or thoroughly groom your horse.
	Clean tack.
	Pack car or horse trailer.
SHOW DAY	Arrive in sufficient time to enter classes, groom, tack up, and warm up.
	Add final touches to show grooming.

Western riders often use show tack that is decorated with engraved silver.

SADDLE	Light oil color Silver trim Visalia stirrups Neoprene girth Woven wool saddle blanket
BRIDLE	½ to ⅜ inches wide, rounded or flat leather One- or two-ear, or browband Silver trim (conchas, bars, buckle tips, buckles) or decorated with plaited rawhide Flat harness leather reins If closed reins, braided leather, decorated with silver or plaited leather or rawhide Curb bit of stainless steel, meeting association rules in the type of mouthpiece, shank length, and curb strap
BREASTPLATE	Flat leather to match saddle, silver-trimmed

adopt the desirable position for Western Horsemanship, without rolling you back too far.

In a show bridle, appearance is as important as a comfortable fit. For instance, if you equip your horse with closed reins, American Horse Shows Association (AHSA) rules require that you attach hobbles to your saddle. Traditionally, the vaqueros used hobbles on a horse with closed reins. Cowboys expected their horses to ground tie with split reins.

A bridle can complement or detract from the look of your horse's head. On a delicate face, wide leather straps look out of place. You should probably avoid a rounded bridle if your horse has a large head, since the wider one helps to cover the area.

You don't want the bridle to distort the length of the head or the depth of jowls. Vertical lines of browband and throatlatch can help to shorten the look of a long head. Silver ornaments can attract the eye away from certain areas and make a short head look longer.

WESTERN PLEASURE CLASS

Western Pleasure can be the starting point in your show career. This class can even entrance you forever — the seemingly elementary routine captivates riders at all levels. It's the most popular class in most horse shows.

The judge wants to see you ride on a loose rein, sitting quietly as you perform the three gaits in both directions. He scores your horse on movement and obedience.

The Look of Western Pleasure

The horse should seem comfortable to ride. He covers ground and effortlessly changes gait. With his ears alert, he looks soft and even-tempered, and you help him by appearing to flow along with his movements.

Judges prefer good movers with definite gaits. Arizona trainer Casey Hinton believes that the better pleasure prospect starts with inborn movement. "Having the best mover is the bottom line, even though the way you train and show a horse can make a world of difference."

Texas trainer Guy Stoops has said: "Movement is Number One. Without quality, you don't have a horse you can use. Next comes that relaxed attitude, the quiet, happy individual that's pleasant to be around."

The good mover is naturally smooth and correct. He moves in a solid, cadenced gait, and he's

Dressing the Part

Your clothing meets class requirements and complements your horse. For Western shows, match your dress to the type of event. Your first shows will probably take place outdoors in a dusty pen. That doesn't mean no one cares what you wear, but your attire should match the situation.

Study the winners, and model your outfit on what they wear. You want to present a fit and trim appearance and look sharp in the pen.

Judges do have particular preferences. Some like a glamorous look of shimmering fabrics or even sequined jackets, while others prefer a more subdued turnout. AHSA judge Jim Baker says: "Try to accentuate your good points in tack and attire. I'm not against color, but riders can get the wrong colors coordinated, or have too many colors." He advises riders to avoid wearing white gloves or adding silver stirrups. Both accentuate any movement of hands or feet.

CYNTHIA MCFARLAND

WESTERN SHOW DRESS

	Pleasure, Horsemanship	Halter
SHIRT	Neat, Western or dress style Optional fitted vest or sweater	Neat, Western or dress style Jacket optional
PANTS	Wrangler jeans	Starched jeans, frontier pants, or dress slacks
CHAPS	Fitted shotgun style Leather or faux suede	Never
BOOTS	Cowboy or roper style	Cowboy or roper style
HAT	Felt or straw	Felt
NECKWEAR	Scarf, tied with square knot	Necktie optional
HAIR	Neatly pulled back into bun (ponytail acceptable at smaller shows)	Neat

Do:	Don't:
Practice around other horses, to see how your horse reacts in a crowd	Show an unsound horse
Introduce your horse to shows before you compete	Switch to a new bit right before the show
Present your horse at his best	Learn to clip your horse the day before
Maintain your composure, no matter what happens	Try to retrain your horse right before the show
Use a checklist to be sure you bring everything you need to the show	Forget to pin your entry number to your shirt
Promptly respond to the judge's announcements	Push your horse by asking him to perform beyond his ability
Appreciate the judge's opinion and applaud the winners	Jerk your horse when you think no one's looking
"Sell" yourself to the judge	Blame your horse if you don't win a ribbon
Act friendly to fellow exhibitors	Whine
Relax and enjoy yourself	Allow spectators' comments to distract you
If a mistake occurs, correct it and go on as if nothing happened	Feel devastated if you hear criticism

consistent in his rhythm throughout the class. A steady gait influences the all-important transitions. Hinton has said: "A slow walk usually means a nice transition to the lope. If your walk fluctuates, with the horse starting out slow and continually getting faster, your transition into the lope will be more than you want."

Today's pleasure horse should move flat with his front feet, especially in the lope. He raises his knees very slightly, and he "pats" the ground. A judge can spot a potential winner at the jog, where the horse briefly suspends his knees and moves with a steady cadence. The top of the croup and the rear skirts of the saddle don't bounce.

"We want the horse to lope effortlessly, and low to the ground with his feet," Hinton has said. "The horse should flow to the ground, with his left front and hind feet sweeping back and forth — not rocking up in front. The further the distance the horse can take that foot and go under his belly, the better off you are. You want your horse to go forward from his tail, with power, impulsion, and a smooth push."

Judges look for the leading hind foot to reach well forward, under your foot in the stirrup. The horse rounds his loin and flexes his back. He does not "string out" behind, or push his hind feet out past the point of the buttocks.

Stoops has described this horse as a natural athlete, moving with a soft (slight) elevation through the shoulder. "It's easy to ride. You have hang time, without the horse getting his legs off the ground too far. There's no excess hock or knee action, but you get a suspension with the front leg straightening from the shoulder and the stifle lifting. It's natural collection.

"You can tell a good pleasure horse with your ears. He goes gracefully across the ground, not beating or slapping it. He floats so you can barely hear him."

Part of the natural look of today's pleasure horse is a level topline. The horse appears fluid. From the side, he holds his neck flat so the ears and poll form one line back to the hip. His head and neck look relaxed, and he carries his head steady with his topline. Some people feel that this looks like the horse carries his head too low, but it's a comfortable, relaxed position for most Quarter Horses moving on a loose rein.

The style that Casey Hinton prefers is a horse that balances and moves from the hip rather than just dropping the head and neck. He explains that the straight topline varies according to the horse's conformation. "Some horses naturally carry the neck out of the shoulder a little lower, some a little higher. The horse with a longer neck and higher withers moves more on his hip. One that can do the balancing act is the easiest to train, because he moves better."

The pleasure horse cooperates with you. You ride him without restraint, and he's consistent in his frame and speed. He holds his nose in and he's quiet with his mouth. You should barely move your rein hand; when you do ask, he easily drops his nose and slows down, or moves into the gait as you direct.

Hinton describes this horse as "honest with his head and feet. On a loose rein, he shows off his training and the discipline that you've put into him. He's a joy to ride."

Preparing for Western Pleasure

A pleasure horse benefits from the isolation and bending maneuvers described in Chapter 6. When you can move your horse away from and back to the rail, you demonstrate flexibility. You'd use this when you need to pass another horse on the rail, or as the judge watches you reverse direction.

This Paint mare, Elegant Skip A Hit, demonstrates the qualities of today's winning pleasure horse.

For the Youngest

To introduce youngsters to the fun of showing, the leadline class requires only that the child sit in the saddle. An adult leads the horse with a lead shank, while the rider proudly holds the reins.

In a walk-trot class, the young equestrian is on her own. Through the first two gaits of a pleasure class, she guides her pony or horse on the rail.

For either class, the rider needs a trustworthy horse that she can steer. A short-legged child won't be able to influence the horse through leg aids, so the horse needs to respond to the reins.

A young rider can learn valuable lessons in self-confidence, presentation, and coping with adversity. Appearing in public scares many people, and riding a gentle partner can ease the child into performance.

Practice transitions that show no resistance. For example, the first change to the lope can move you up or down in the class. Judge Larry Gimple tries to glance at each rider during this transition. "I feel a horse will win more classes at the lope than the jog. I may go directly into the lope from the jog, depending on the quality of the class. It's harder to pick up the lope from the walk than the jog, because there's less forward motion."

When you practice, try to school your horse in the open, not on the rail. Avoid training him too much on the same routine, or he'll get bored and try evasions.

Arabian horse trainer Gary Ferguson has noted common situations that riders encounter. "They have problems not getting the horse to lope well enough behind, teaching him to stay in a frame by himself, keeping him fresh. They tend to drill the horse going around and around. When I have a problem, say getting a lead departure in a lope, I go off and do something else in a different situation. I may lope figure eights or two-track to get the horse to move off my leg. You take the problem away, fix the problem, and then put it back in the same situation. That saves your horse from being sour. He may not even know he's been fixed, because you take the problem away."

If you ride on the rail, he learns he can quit when you move to the center of the ring. Vary the location of your transitions, so he doesn't learn to anticipate. Don't always leave the schooling area the same way, or he learns that when you angle a certain direction, he can go out the gate.

Judges watch your horse's speed and direction, looking for consistency. When the horse alters his head, he changes his balance and speed. To place in this class, he should remain relaxed and move at moderately slow gaits. His speed doesn't change, unless he responds to your cue to move faster or slower.

He does need to move in a freely forward rhythm. AQHA judge Pete Wood: "I see some horses that, when you ask them to lope, they look like they need a jump start. They look like they're starting to lope, but that's the way they look all the way through the class."

Trainer Mark Taylor has noted that slow does not mean plodding. "Your horse does not have to be the slowest in the pen to win a pleasure class. Nor does he have to stay on the rail throughout, so long as he looks the same every time the judge looks at him."

If your horse lopes too fast, examine the cause. First, is he too fresh? Does he need turnout time, or longeing to become more mellow? A daily routine of steady riding can cure a horse that wants to jog or lope too fast.

Taylor recommends testing your horse. "I put the horse on the rail and ask him to work a class without my touching him [the reins]. If I've got to go ten strides and then pick him up, he's not ready to go to a horse show." You can intensify the test by riding beside a stablemate. Does your horse speed up when his companion passes him?

Slowing a horse can affect his rhythm and the quality of his gaits. Realize that he needs a certain amount of momentum to move forward. If you force him into a slow lope, he could lose cadence and start a four-beat lope. A "four-beater" (which some judges call a "trashy loper") may look as if he's loping in front and trotting behind, or vice versa.

Test your horse's rhythm by feeling the sequence of hoofbeats in each stride. A left lead begins:

1. Right rear
2. Left rear and right front
3. Left front (leading foreleg)

In a four-beat gait, the horse breaks up the second beat and the stride doesn't flow. He hits the ground too quickly with his forehand without pushing off the hindquarters. Some horses will lope correctly in some sections of the pen, then lose the rhythm when slowed too much.

Guy Stoops has noted that the athletic horse *can* lope in a slow, three-beat gait. "It's a higher degree of difficulty. Another horse that's forced to

A good place to correct a misbehaving horse is on the back rail and not in front of the judges.

go slow can't, not with an ease and presence and relaxed look. The athlete hangs back on his hocks and goes around effortlessly."

Your horse will appear smoother when you look glued to the saddle. Pete Wood: "I have seen horses that the rider made look good. Then you get on the horse's back, and he could jar your eyeteeth out." A skilled rider knows how to work with a horse's weak points to help him look his best.

A winning pleasure horse behaves honestly, treating you as you treat him. He reflects your behaviors. If you start leaning forward, your horse might accelerate. Or, he might become tense and raise his head, waiting for you to jerk his mouth.

A dishonest horse might choose specific areas of the ring to misbehave. He could speed up on the straightaway, or even start to buck when he lopes around a turn. You'll have to outsmart this character, by riding three strides ahead of him.

You can correct your horse in the show pen. Most riders use the back rail (the section behind the judge's back). Larry Gimple has advised: "Get your horse ready for the next pass. Don't have him looking good on the back rail and then leave him be in front of the judge." He adds that sometimes you need to resort to two-handing your horse. You may have lost your chance in that particular class already, but you need to school him in the pen so he learns to behave.

Reprimand the horse without pulling on him to make him nervous. For one that changes speed at the lope, Casey Hinton stops and supples the horse, and lopes again on a loose rein.

He says: "If the horse goes fast, I stop, pull his head, and again pitch the reins. So I'm not pulling on the horse so much while he's loping, which could alter the lope. Altering the movement will change the horse's balance and head position — it just snowballs. Pretty soon the horse gets to thinking, 'Hey, I don't want to do this.' He puts his head in position, saying, 'Just leave me alone.'"

Pleasure Class Strategy

When you enter the pen, find a place on the rail to space yourself. Size up the competition, and stay away from troublemakers or the best horse. (In comparison to him, your horse may appear worse than he is.)

The judge stands in the center of the pen, sometimes near one end. He'll signal the announcer to call for a gait change. When you see his cue, prepare your horse.

"Showing's not for the weak of heart," trainer Jim Porcher has said. "You have to respond quickly when the gaits are called for. You have to be thinking all the time and be aware of what your horse looks like."

Take the time to set your horse up properly. You can wait a beat, to let a spot open up ahead of you. You don't need to lope instantly, but promptly and under control. Try not to be the first rider to lope, or the last.

Larry Gimple has commented: "Do it right rather than take a chance and jump into it. I like a rider to wait till a count of three, or to go three to five strides before a transition. Sit there as if the P.A. [public address system] did not go off, then make the motion needed to move up or down."

If your horse takes the wrong lead, stop him and calmly restart. A wrong lead may not disqualify you, because other horses may have made more errors. Your horse's performance up to that point may have him in the ribbons, even with a missed lead.

Judge Whizzer Baker likes to see riders try, especially in correcting a mistake. "If you reach for a lead in a crowd and you're bumped so your horse steps off on the wrong lead, you stop and correct it and go on with complete authority in your handling of your animal. That's going to win for me. Be aware every minute of where you and your horse are, and then it's going to work."

Use a downward transition or reverse (always away from the rail) to help open space ahead of you. From the lope to the walk, halt for a second or two, then walk.

When you reverse at the walk or jog, make sure your horse doesn't "curl" his neck without bending his body. He should hold his neck straight and flat. A ring-wise horse knows that the class is half over, so don't let him display anxiety.

When the announcer requests "Everyone into the center," walk to the lineup. If a first horse

Riding in Show Ring Traffic

In a rail class, you must watch out for the other contestants. This class involves overtaking horses in front of you and spacing yourself, while you also maintain awareness of the judge's viewpoint.

Pass a rider ahead of you when she's impeding your comfortable pace. Start your passing with plenty of space, so you don't guide your horse at an abrupt angle. Go around her and move back to the rail, so you don't let her horse's speed dictate yours. If possible, avoid passing when you think the judge might call for a transition, especially at the lope. Get your horse in a good position before you lope.

If you can, pass before the judge is looking at one of you. Don't rudely place your horse between the judge and another rider.

By using the corners of the pen, you can let others pass you. Most people tend to cut across the ends. Hug the rail on the turn, looking for your spot on the straightaway. Watch for riders who inadvertently cut you off at a corner. If your horse moves faster than others in the class, stay on the rail to use more of the space in the pen.

"I appreciate riders who stay on the rail," says judge Whizzer Baker. "Be aware of your position, and know what's going on around you. Don't be foolish enough to camp on the rail while three horses cover you up. See an opening up ahead that you can ease into."

Maintain at least a horse's length (20 feet is better) from other riders. If you tailgate, the horse ahead of you could stop, buck, or collide with another entry, and you'd be part of a wreck! Spacing yourself helps your horse pay attention to you, so he doesn't speed up or break gait when others pass him.

Use the reverse as an opportunity to make space for yourself. You'll usually reverse at the walk, after you've loped. When the announcer calls for the reverse, glance behind you to check for any "tailgaters."

You'll see riders circle to try to space out. If you have to, circle only at the walk or jog. Don't circle in front of the judge, which looks like grandstanding. And because it's more difficult to ride a circle than straight, you're more likely to make a mistake!

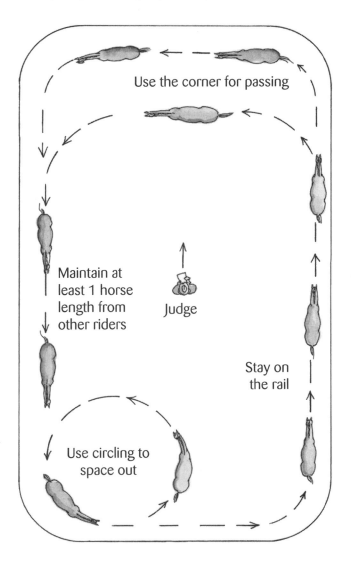

Use the corner for passing

Maintain at least 1 horse length from other riders

Judge

Stay on the rail

Use circling to space out

Judges look for an effective rider who looks "tall in the saddle" as she moves with her horse.

has already halted, that horse sets the mark. You and the others stand in alignment with the first animal, so the judge sees a straight line of horses' noses.

Try to position yourself at least six feet from your neighbors. Ten feet is even safer, in case you've "parked" beside an animal that the rider can't control.

Stand quietly, and be ready to back up only when the judge requests. You want your horse to listen to you and back easily, without looking forced. Glance behind, and back straight, without swinging your horse's hindquarters into a neighbor's space.

WESTERN HORSEMANSHIP CLASS

Whether it's called equitation or horsemanship, you can demonstrate your skill in this class. Often the event consists of two segments — an individual performance of a test and riding in a group on the rail.

These amateur and youth classes have evolved beyond a simple beauty contest that selected the most elegant "passenger." Horsemanship events challenge you to do more than just "equitate." To place in the ribbons, you must demonstrate control and a correct position while executing specific movements. Horsemanship also reflects the influence of the reining event, as you perform a precise pattern with brisk turns.

California trainer Mack Linn has explained: "Equitation means to ride and show the horse correctly, according to his individual balance. The rider has to look forward and anticipate how her own balance affects that of her horse."

Technically, the judge doesn't score the horse. What he is really looking for is an effective rider. However, the horse's way of going and his responses to your cues can boost or detract from your performance. You want a smooth-moving horse that's handy enough to collect and extend on command.

You can ride your pleasure horse in this event, but he does need to feel secure leaving the crowd to perform the individual pattern. In some shows, the group stands at one end of the pen. You move away from the other horses to work in the center, which can upset a sensitive horse.

You have to feel your horse and respond to his movements. Especially at the jog and lope, your seat should appear glued to the saddle. You refine your position and look "tall in the saddle" as you move with your horse.

Today's judges prefer the more relaxed rider over the stiff, posed look. A rigid back makes you appear artificial, and you can look as if you would topple off if the horse moved suddenly.

Position your weight evenly, and be sure your stirrups are even. Mack Linn: "The weight should be distributed equally to each side, forward and back. The object is to remain equal on both sides and to maintain a vertical posture. You want to keep your saddle in the center." He has noted that many riders tend to sit crooked, with the left hip pushed forward along with the rein hand.

To remedy this, Linn advises: "Stand up and move your right hip and right shoulder slightly forward. When you go to the right, don't forget to adjust. Most riders tend to twist the right shoulder forward when tracking right."

Hold your legs so your calves maintain contact with the horse's girth. Your horse's conformation will dictate the amount of angle, but avoid holding your legs too far out to the sides.

You sit slightly bent at the knee, but you aim for the straight look. Your heels are under you, so they line up with your shoulders and look slightly lower than your toes. Meanwhile, you try to roll your knees in and point your toes toward the horse's shoulder, heels slightly out.

Try not to carry your legs too far forward, or your lower legs back too far. This position can make you look as if you're tipping forward against the pommel, or you're perching on, not in, the saddle. The best way to correct this fault is to view photos or videos of yourself.

Stretch your leg from the hip down to maintain a correct thigh angle. Avoid bending only from the knee, which pulls your calf back instead of your thigh.

You ride from a relaxed yet secure position. Add to this the use of your upper body, your shoulders, arms, and hands. Your spine should be straight, not tilting forward or back, and your back should not be stiffly arched.

Judges want to see a steady rein hand, with a consistently horizontal line from bit to elbow. You never change hands or touch the saddle with your free hand. You ride on a short rein so your hand need move only slightly to cue your horse.

Larry Gimple has said that hands make up half the performance, with legs the other half. He looks for a quiet hand that never bounces against the horse's mouth. "In equitation, an educated hand gets the rider and horse in the best possible position for the judge to look at them. If you don't have

split reins

closed reins

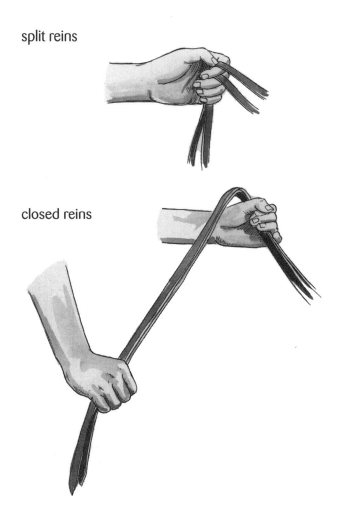

	Split Reins	Closed Reins
REIN (LEFT) HAND POSITION	Fist closed around reins 1 finger between reins Hand in front of you, 1½" over and in front of the pommel (not too close to the horn, but over and above it) Roll your hand in a little, without cocking wrist	Fist closed around reins Thumb folded over the top of fist Hand about 2" directly over the saddle horn Knuckles headed right between the horse's ears
RIGHT HAND POSITION	Elbow bent Hold hands even to help keep your shoulders square Make a fist, without clenching Hand in front of your belt, fairly close to your stomach	Holding romal Placed on your right leg Looks relaxed, without gripping
DISTANCE BETWEEN HANDS	6–10" (depends on your body size) Hands shouldn't be too far apart, but not so close to the reins that it looks like you're ready to ride two-handed.	12–15" (depends on height of saddle horn and your body size)

good hands, you don't have 50 percent of your ride — your horse will perform 50 percent under what he should be."

Western Horsemanship Exercises

Riding one-handed encourages uneven shoulders, with one shoulder higher than or ahead of the other. Straighten both shoulders by riding a circle to the right and looking over your left shoulder to see your horse's tail. Do this at every corner of the ring to check your position.

Get your position at the jog by posting for a few strides. Feel your feet under you, post or rise into two-point position, then sit gently back over your heel.

Practice holding a two-point position, to hold your lower leg in place. To test the steadiness of your legs, place jump poles, called "cavaletti," in a

Correct uneven shoulders by looking back over your outside shoulder on the circle.

row on the ground. Space them about one trot stride apart (usually about eight feet), and cross them at a slow trot.

Coach Alpha Russell has advised, "Flex your ankle, and keep your heels down. Roll your ankle in when your horse bounces over the pole."

Find your horse's "smooth spot" at the jog. Feel your horse start to jog from a hind foot, and relax your shoulders by jiggling or flopping them. Put your feet slightly forward so you can find that smooth place.

Test to see if you are braced against the stirrups, which makes you stiff. Try to ease your foot out of the stirrup as you travel at any gait. You should be able to lift your toe off the stirrup without altering your leg position, hip, or heels.

Russell explained: "Sit properly at the jog, and your horse will come back to you for a pretty jog. Sit back and sit deep, and let your weight flow down into your heels. Make your elbows heavy."

To keep your eyes up, put your neck back on your collar. When you feel your collar brushing the back of your neck, you'll establish the desirable vertical line from your ear through your shoulder, knee, and heel. Look forward with confidence, even if you're having a problem with your horse.

On a well-broke horse, you can practice a light rein hand by attaching the reins to the bit with rubber bands. Aim to ride without breaking the rubber bands.

The quality of the backup also separates the horseman from the "equitator." Russell coached: "Back your horse off your leg, not your eyeball. Take a breath, look behind you, and take contact. Don't look down at your horse.

"Your hands should not move. They stay over the saddle, and they move only when you're done. It should look like your horse reads your mind and moves from your thought."

Practicing the Pattern

Patterns give you the opportunity to show off your equestrian skills. Yes, the judge watches your equitation, but he scores you on the ease you demonstrate in solving basic questions. You show that you can control your horse's gait, speed, and direction, while maintaining a relaxed position in the saddle.

At the show, you can't predict what the judge will ask in horsemanship. Your first look at the pattern won't be till the day of the class. Prepare for any eventuality by practicing basic exercises.

Patterns can be simple or complex. Here's a sample from an AQHA show: Along the center line, trot to a certain point. Pick up the right lead, and lope five strides. Halt and perform a full turn on the haunches, either left or right. From the halt, pick up the left lead, lope five strides, halt, and back four steps.

Show officials often mark transition points with traffic cones. Make your transitions when your boot is parallel to the cone. The only exception would be in a turn on the haunches, where you halt with the horse's hind hoof at the cone. This will allow you to keep your pivot point at the cone.

Even the simplest pattern can pose difficulty. You can execute the steps, but still not score well if you don't show you're a horseman.

For practice, try these patterns below, which Alpha Russell uses to test youth and amateurs during group lessons. Ride these two-handed at first, and later use the neck rein as you will in the show pen. These do incorporate speeds at the trot, which you probably won't perform in a class. In schooling, they help you adjust your horse's responses.

Russell advises: "Use your skills to get the pattern right. Keep learning how to guide your horse, and to be a horseman. A horseman shows she has the compassion and intelligence to get her horse to perform the pattern. You show you're moderate and smart, and you don't lose your temper."

1. **Test your reinsmanship.** Line up beside another horse (or group of horses) as you would in the show ring, facing the arena fence. Tracking left, you'll walk and trot a large circle, ending up at your place in line.

From the lineup, walk in a straight line toward the fence, and start a jog trot immediately before you guide your horse into the first turn. Move him into a lively, consistent walk, so he'll flow into a steady jog when you give the aid.

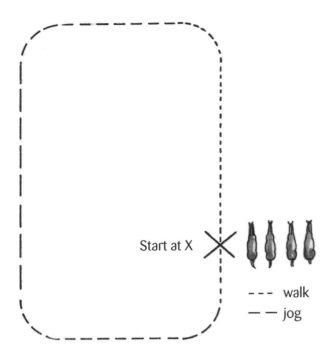

Start at X

- - - walk
— — jog

Exercise 1: Test your reinsmanship with this pattern.

Your horse will probably try to zigzag rather than walk straight. He may resist leaving the others, and he may wonder which way you'll turn as you near the fence. He'll try to outguess you, but don't "oversteer" him.

"When your horse goes by himself, he's more sensitive to your cues," coaches Russell. "Less is more when you work individually. In the pattern, he needs to relax. The judge watches you, thinking, 'Is the horse obedient to the rider, or does he have his own mind?'

"You can overcome a horse that's acting stupid by riding properly. Ride him the way you want him to be."

Here you compensate for your horse's natural tendencies. Does he wobble toward the fence? Support his inside shoulder to counteract the zigzag effect. Does he try to "dodge" on the first arc, or cut the corner? Keep him between the reins to form a smooth arc. Guide him decisively, so you tell him to listen to you.

After the second turn, speed up to a long trot. You can either sit, post, or rise into a two-point position. As you near the lineup, slow back to a

jog for the final turn. Prepare for the downward transition to the walk with a weight shift. Sit up, and cue your horse to respond to your weight so you don't have to apply pressure on the reins.

"Make your transitions right on the mark," advises Russell. "Come down deep in the downward transition. A weight shift first looks like you're kind to your horse."

On the final turn, as you near your place in the lineup, elevate your inside rein so the horse does not fall in (he probably wants to rejoin his buddies). Stop him in the lineup exactly where you started.

Know how many strides he takes between your aid and the halt. For a smooth stop, you don't want him to jolt from trot to halt in one stride, but you don't want to overshoot the mark. Aim for a slow-down to one or two jog strides, one or two walk strides, and a balanced halt. If he takes two seconds to react, you can use a quiet "Ho" under your breath about four strides from the spot.

Pay attention to how your horse positions himself in the halt. Does he stop with the off foreleg forward, and complete the stop by moving his near foreleg beside it? If so, this will help you line him up exactly.

2. Show different speeds. In another large circle, move from the walk to the long trot, and back to the jog. Track right, and pick up the trot while in the arc.

Here you demonstrate a difference in pace. Know how much leg aid you need for the upward transition. You want your horse to stride out into the new gait immediately, so you need to know how to cause your horse to "flow" upward to the next gait.

Test how your horse shifts gears by asking for the extended walk. Use your lower leg to bump, to encourage him to reach with the shoulder. Look for his head and neck to swing in front of you, in a rolling walk, and hold him at the edge between the walk and the jog.

When you have a good walk, you'll find it easier to move into a forward-moving trot. Close your leg to flow into the jog.

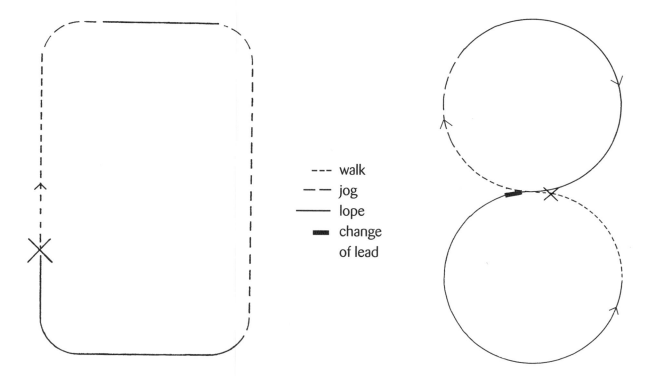

---	walk
---	jog
———	lope
▬	change of lead

Exercise 2: This exercise demonstrates a difference in pace and how well your horse makes transitions.

Exercise 3: As you lope in this exercise, pattern errors happen faster. Practice circles at slower gaits to notice where your horse drifts.

Because you'll trot on the arc, realize that the horse can fall off the pace. You might need a stronger leg aid to compensate.

After the second turn, slow to a jog. Test your horse's consistency on the corners. Many horses will fall off, or lose impulsion, when approaching a corner. Practice transitions on the arc, using both legs to bend the horse and maintain his energy.

3. Form a large figure eight. Walk, trot, lope, change leads, lope the other direction, and walk to the starting point.

As you lope, errors of the pattern happen faster. By practicing circles at slower gaits, you should have noticed where your horse tends to drift. Does he fall in when tracking left? Use your inside rein to elevate his near shoulder to counteract his tendency.

Complete the first circle of the figure eight and guide your horse across the middle. Get your seat deep, so you can change to the left lead.

In the lead change, you'll usually have the option of doing a simple change: lope, trot a few steps, and step off into the opposite lead. A flying change of lead will give you a higher score, but it would be required only in a class of advanced riders. In a novice class, the judge will probably expect a simple change.

These three patterns form large circles, with arcs that connect four straight lines. Remember to make the arcs round, bending your horse correctly. Alpha Russell has cautioned: "Make an easy arc. There are no corners in riding, only arcs."

4. Walk, jog, lope in a straight line down the center of the pen. This pattern is a common request, yet it challenges any rider. You ride a straight line, without wavering, and you change gaits at the markers. You show smooth transitions and precise control. (The judge might stand behind you to watch.)

Riding down the center can show you how much your horse depends on the rail. Without the fence line, can he track straight? Can you tell if he drifts? Test your sense of straightness by focusing on an object ahead of you, and use your legs to frame it between your horse's ears.

Watch your rein length. You want to be able to shorten contact without moving your hand more than an inch, but don't get your horse "sucked up" on a rein that is too short.

Russell has encouraged riders to "talk" to horses with soft communication, like a whisper. She compares this conversation to that of a cocktail party, where despite the hum of voices, a whisper invites the listener to focus.

"There's not one loud signal, so the horse listens and he hears you. Teach your horse to listen to things other than the hands, like your voice and legs. If you always talk with a loud hand, the horse never has to listen to your leg.

"Impression is everything. Start out with your horse relaxed, by riding with less. Give him a chance to be an angel. Don't ride on a tight rein to start. You can always add more, and it's harder to lighten."

She noted that horsemanship patterns require thinking. Show nerves can affect your performance, but solid practice develops your innate mental skills. In the show pen, you have one chance, with no rerides if you "zone out" and forget a segment. Schooling gives you the opportunity to make a mistake, and then correct it by focusing on the quality of your riding.

Russell has advised thinking about each segment while you ride it. "Each piece of the pattern has a separate score. You can have a mistake in the beginning, and then you show composure and presence of mind when you make up for it. Fix a mistake, and make the next piece better than the previous one, so you improve. And always ride ahead — where you are now is history."

Some associations include dismounting and mounting in the pattern. Practice the correct style, as described in the appropriate rule book. Usually in dismounting you should step down facing the horse's head, maintaining control with the reins. When your right foot hits the ground, slide your left foot from the stirrup. Stand facing forward a few seconds, then turn to the right, check the curb strap, and mount in a continuous, smooth movement.

Finally, refine your patterns to fit within a time limit. Some associations allow only 30 seconds for each rider.

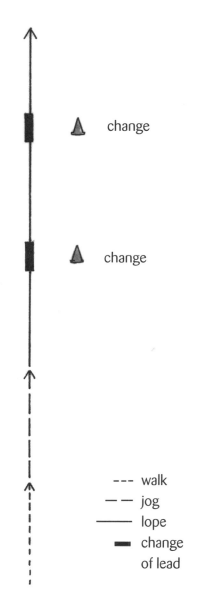

change

change

--- walk
— — jog
——— lope
━ change of lead

Exercise 4: This common exercise challenges a rider to show smooth transitions and tight control.

Western Horsemanship Strategy

Study the pattern for the individual work, as officials will post a sketch of the judge's directions near the in-gate. When the class is called, all competitors enter the ring to listen to the judge describe the routine.

Like any other show routine, avoid practicing any pattern excessively. This is where your at-home schooling pays off. Those riders who haven't "toughed it out" before the show suffer from pre-class anxiety and drill their horses in the show pattern. This can backfire, because they teach their mounts to anticipate the next gait or movement, setting themselves up to lose control.

Judges can add advanced movements, such as the flying change of lead (described in Chapter 11). The requirements of the pattern vary according to the level of the contestants. In AQHA shows, the Amateur/Novice classes would not be expected to perform a pattern as demanding as the Adult Amateurs or older Youth.

To perform a turn, you want your horse to move from his pivot foot, similar to a reining horse. You won't turn that fast, but aim for a smooth, even turn without any hesitation.

After you perform your individual work, the ring steward will direct you to wait on the rail or at the opposite end of the ring. When all exhibitors have completed the pattern, you track left and walk, jog, and lope. You then reverse and repeat the three gaits in the other direction.

Finally, everyone lines up, and you hold your best position until the steward turns in the judge's card. Whether or not the announcer calls your number, congratulate yourself for demonstrating your horsemanship skills and techniques to the best of your ability.

HALTER CLASS

In a halter class, the judge places horses by their balance, muscling, structural correctness, and breed and sex characteristics. He watches each entrant in

A halter horse is alert and balanced, with a smooth topline and muscling.

Ensure that your halter fits properly. To accent the head, the cheekpieces should line up with the jowl, and the throatlatch should fit snugly behind the curve of the jowl. The noseband should rest about halfway between the eyes and the tops of the nostrils.

motion, and he also looks for a horse that's fit and pretty.

In essence, halter is a beauty contest. To compete, your horse should match the model of the ideal Quarter Horse. Along with a smooth topline and long, thin neck, he shows muscling in the "V" of his chest, forearms, stifle, and gaskin. He also needs to project a "showy" presence through an alert expression and proud self-carriage.

Pick a halter prospect like a judge would, by conformation and type. For a small, local show, you can show your performance horse. However, you'll notice that at breed shows, many halter horses "don't ride" — they compete only in hand, not under saddle.

You'll "finish" the halter horse to perfection, with a gleaming coat. He should handle well, to walk, jog, and pose when you ask.

Show him with a chain lead, a flat leather shank with a chain attached. You thread the chain through the nearside cheek ring, under the chin, up through the offside cheek ring, and then snap it to the ring at the crownpiece. With this configuration, you can apply an even pull that releases quickly. Hold the leather part right where the chain ends.

Ensure that your halter fits properly. Place the crownpiece right behind the ears. To accent the head, the cheekpieces should line up with the jowl, and the throatlatch should fit snugly behind the curve of the jowl. The noseband should rest about halfway between the eyes and the tops of the nostrils. Most show halters feature five buckles for adjustment at crownpiece, chin strap, and connector strap.

Training for Halter

Trainers vary in how they teach a horse to pose. Some place the feet by hand. If the horse moves, they reach down and put the foot back. Others touch him with hand or boot, while applying pressure on the lead shank. The horse learns to associate the shank with moving his foot.

Casey Hinton uses a simple approach to teach a horse to set up, starting with setting the hind feet first. "I only set up three legs," he explains. "I always pick the right hind foot, wherever it is, and never move it. I only move the left hind. If the left hind is in front of the right one, I back the horse to it. If the left hind is behind the right, I move the left hind forward. So you've already eliminated one of the legs that you have to move."

Facing the horse, Hinton controls the head to direct the feet. In his method, he advises pulling down on the shank to move a back foot, because the horse's weight naturally rests more on the front feet. You move the front feet by picking up on the horse's head.

A trained horse knows to watch you as you walk and halt. He'll pose as soon as you signal him to halt. Hinton says: "As soon as they stop, they know which foot to move. They start setting the back foot before the showman has even turned around, so you end up setting only one front foot."

Reaching this point requires consistent training. When the horse makes a mistake, moving the wrong foot at the wrong time, you scold him by pulling the lead shank. Or if you pull his head up so he moves the left front foot forward, you'd discipline him if he moves the foot beyond the right one. You can back him up quickly, and then ask him to move forward again.

You don't jerk the chain, and the amount of pressure needed depends on your horse's sensitivity. As in riding, you set the habit by reprimanding for mistakes. Practice posing him so you barely move the lead shank.

Besides standing square, he must adopt a stance that enhances his appearance. You want to evaluate the spread between the forelegs and hind legs, and the vertical placement of each pair of legs. You learn to tell when all four feet are under him, and you may teach him to place his feet slightly farther apart.

Hinton tells how to use the shank to make the horse adjust the stance. Pull the head to the left for the horse to move the hindquarters to the right. Using the shank, lift the head to the right to make the left front foot move to the left to make a wider stance.

"If I want a wider set, I push the head away when I set the back feet. If I want to move the right front foot, I lift the head up and over, away from the direction I want."

Once he poses, leave him alone. Stand beside him, at a distance that's comfortable for both of you, so he holds the pose during the class. He should watch you and pay attention throughout the class. Practice moving from one side to the other, as you'll do in the class, while your horse stands immobile. With practice, your horse will learn to have more patience and stand longer.

Halter Class Strategy

Before you show, watch a previous class to see how the judge directs exhibitors. By knowing his particular method, you'll present yourself more professionally.

Showing at halter doesn't require athletic ability, but it demands patience. Halter may look easy, but you must prepare your horse by practicing the routine. Judge Peggy Jo Koll says: "Getting the horse to perform on the ground is harder than riding. It takes every day, training the horse just like you were on its back. It's not as easy as it looks."

When it's your turn to enter the pen, lead your horse toward the judge, in a straight line so the judge can see how the horse travels. Walk him with his neck reaching out in front, long and down. Usually you walk past the judge, then trot away for 30 or 40 feet. You then line up head to tail with the other contestants, while the judge "profiles" all horses. Here he compares the side views of the entrants to determine final placings.

In the lineup, stand at a safe distance from other entries. Either side by side or head to tail, maintain a horse's length on all sides. Your horse must stand still and stand square, or "set up." He stands balanced on all four feet, with front and back even. His legs are perpendicular to the ground, like the legs of a table. He holds his head and neck straight out and aligned with his spine. His stance enhances his appearance, so you teach him to pose with his feet an appropriate distance apart.

Your lead shank is your primary control. You'll see some exhibitors reach down and touch a horse's leg or foot, but judges discourage your touching the animal in the show pen. The judge expects your horse to stand attentively by himself, not by your "arranging" him.

You can let him relax slightly while the judge studies other entries away from your position. Don't release all contact with the lead shank, but try walking a small circle.

Watch the judge as he observes other entries, and have your horse ready before the judge looks at you. When he starts to profile the class, "show" your horse. This could be the most challenging segment, as some animals get bored by this time.

Pose your horse so the two of you look attentive. You want him to hold his ears up, so he looks his best, without your jerking the shank. Experiment with these methods:

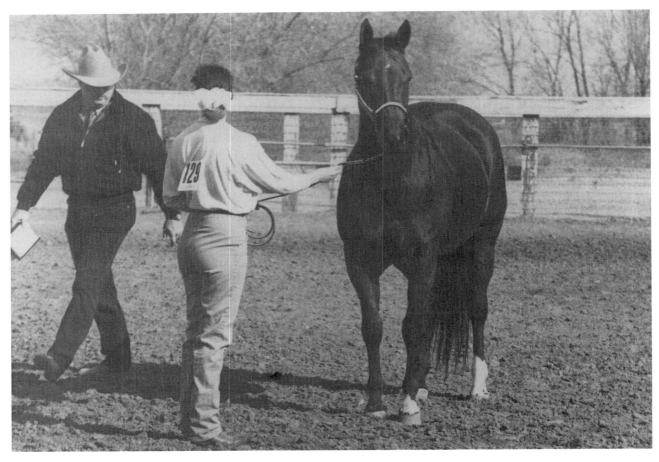

In a lineup, your horse should be balanced with all four feet square.

★ Pick up a handful of dirt; the horse will watch you sift it through your fingers.
★ Crinkle a piece of paper in your left hand.
★ Dab a strong-smelling substance on the end of the lead shank, and tap the shank end once on the horse's nose; move the shank away so the horse looks at it.

Watch your horse, but listen to the judge's instructions, too. He might direct you to move to another location in the lineup, to position horses in order of placing.

When you present your horse, look proud. Look as if you care about the animal and have pride in his quality.

Texas trainer Mike McMillian has advised, "If you project a positive attitude to the judge and your horse, you're going to do great. Horses really catch on to that, and you have his respect and control. If you stand there and look down at the dirt and don't look at the judge, your horse could run circles around you — you probably won't do well. Act professionally in the ring, because you get out of it what you put into it."

The Show Game

Equestrian competitions make up a sport that operates at various levels. You can compete without leaving town, or you can follow a circuit seeking association points, year-end awards, and megabucks in prize money. Your definition of success may be simply completing class requirements, attending a major show, or winning a silver belt buckle that proclaims you as a World Champion.

The sport may not be as well known as football or basketball, but corporate sponsorships and the impact of rodeo attract spectators and increase prestige. And like any game, you enjoy more satisfaction when you know the rules and the players.

THE WESTERN HORSE SHOW INDUSTRY

When you become serious about pursuing this activity, you'll probably join one or more national associations. These breed and show associations promote events for Western show horses:

1. **Breed Associations**
   American Quarter Horse Association
   American Paint Horse Association
   Appaloosa Horse Club, Inc.
   Pinto Horse Association of America, Inc.
   Palomino Horse Breeders of America, Inc.
   American Buckskin Registry Association
   International Buckskin Horse
      Association, Inc.

2. **Show Associations**
   American Horse Shows Association
   National Reining Horse Association
   National Reined Cow Horse Association
   National Cutting Horse Association
   National Snaffle Bit Association
   International Quarter Horse Halter
      and Pleasure Association

3. **Youth Breed Associations**
   American Junior Quarter Horse Association
   American Junior Paint Horse Association

Appaloosa Youth Association
Pinto Horse Association of America
    Youth Organization
Palomino Horse Breeders of America Youth

4. **Youth Show Associations**
    4-H
    Intercollegiate Horse Show Association

Breed associations showcase the horse to encourage more registrations and growth. Specialty breeds attract people who prefer a certain type. Shows display a breed's progress and how the animals demonstrate a standard of quality.

Each association has earned a reputation for the level of competition in its shows. Usually a smaller organization, with fewer horses eligible, would offer a less stressful introduction to showing. Youth organizations, especially 4-H and the Intercollegiate Horse Show Association, initiate beginners into a more easygoing show atmosphere. (At an IHSA show, you exhibit a provided horse, one you've never before ridden.)

The drive to win sustains today's horse industry. As in other sports, this motivation can conflict with the pursuit of sport as pure enjoyment, or even practiced as an art. California trainer Joe King has said: "I teach my riders not to care if they win at a show. The show goal is to make your horse work as good or better than at practice. The show is proof of your schooling — *that* makes the horse advance. If you win and your horse does worse than at home, you lose ground!"

In the industry, you're an amateur (also called a "non-pro") exhibitor if you don't accept payment for training horses or riders, or assist in professional training. If you're under the age of 18, you're a youth (or junior) exhibitor. Professionals often have more clout in running equine associations, as they serve on boards and committees, but amateur and youth members make up most of the show entries.

Whether amateur or professional, everyone enters the pen seeking a ribbon. To equalize competition, associations offer classes limited to riders of similar abilities. This levels the playing field on paper, but only a handful of winners emerge from any show.

After seeing the results of your first shows, you may wonder, "Are shows fair?" That depends on the judges.

AQHA

These Western Pleasure class competitors are lined up for final judging.

THE JUDGE'S ROLE

You pay your entry fee, enter the show pen, and place yourself under the judge's eye. You present your horse for her opinion, and you expect an impartial appraisal as she places the class.

Judges learn this task by participating as exhibitors, training horses and riders, and attending association seminars. High school and college students join judging teams, often sponsored by 4-H, Future Farmers of America (FFA), or breed associations. In judging competitions, they must give oral reasons for how they placed a class.

A judge represents the association that certified her as an authority. Associations award judge's cards to applicants who qualify by meeting certain standards. The approval process usually includes professional references, written or oral tests, apprenticeship programs, committee reviews, and judging competitions as described above. Judges must maintain active status by judging a minimum number of shows and attending periodic seminars.

Some associations practice rigorous testing. For example, an association might admit to its judges' school only the top 30 candidates out of 150 applicants. Of these, less than 10 may receive a judge's card.

A judge should inspire confidence, but she can't avoid controversy. Many of the losers will challenge the placings and blame the judge! Before you join the ranks of complainers, realize the demands of the task. A reputable judge meets these basic requirements:

1. Knowledge. A carded judge must possess a thorough knowledge of horses and the rules of the association. She shows an ability to compare each entrant to an ideal standard of conformation or performance and to place the horses in order. As judge Don Burt has explained: "Let everybody go the very best they can, and pick the best, the second best, and down the line."

This ranking challenges any judge, especially when a class seems to be full of what one trainer called "pickles in the pen."

Judge Brian Ellsworth has noted that the judge recognizes the horse and rider who have achieved a partnership. "It's a team effort, a belief that exists between the exhibitor and the animal. It's a oneness, an impression of an air of confidence. That team has to be finely tuned, and with the top individuals, it comes from within."

Ellsworth added that his philosophy of judging is to choose the horse he'd want to take home. This choice relates to the quality of exhibitors in a particular class. "You need a mental model of what you're looking for. You have to have a target. Judge the best of the best, or the best of the worst. It's relative that day in that class under those circumstances."

Judge Peggy Jo Koll applies a similar theory to exhibitors, such as the Showmanship at Halter events. "I try to find the person that I'd want to show my horse. You're going to pick the one who has her horse standing the best. 'Which one of you wants the job the worst?'"

Surprisingly, judging a large class, with 20 or more contestants, may be easier than judging only five entries. Horses that the judge initially picked for ribbons may make mistakes, which moves them down in the order and other horses up.

Judge Pete Wood has said that he tries to pin a small class quickly, because the top horses could make mistakes as the class goes on. "You can find first and second, and then you have to look to find the rest of the class. I'm not looking for mistakes. I look for excellence. If my best horse makes a tiny mistake, I don't knock him down too low, and I don't eliminate him."

The contemporary judge has to know a range of Western disciplines. She may specialize in a certain class and be less familiar with the trends in other events. Although your particular event may not be the judge's forte, you should still respect her opinion.

2. Integrity. Most judges gain their expertise by breeding and showing horses. They're active in the industry, so how can these experts avoid conflicts of interest?

Most complaints about judges focus on favoritism. Here's a typical situation: The judge eyes the in-gate for a halter class. Out of the 15 entrants, she recognizes two mares sired by a stallion she owned a few years ago, a horse she bred and sold as a yearling, and a famous performance champion. One exhibitor is her own ex-trainer and one is the manager of a prestigious show she'd like to judge next year.

You're an amateur, and your horse doesn't place. You hear the grumbling begin as you exit the pen: "She only likes sorrels," "She always picks the professionals," and "It's all political, anyway."

Judges themselves agree that they must maintain an open mind and high integrity. "The judge has to have an excellent knowledge of the rules, be totally apolitical, and give every horse a good look," Dr. Walter de la Brosse, a multi-carded judge, has explained. "And he has to know what he's looking for."

Judge Whizzer Baker has commented how a judges' school tests candidates through intimidation. "In classes, they slide in someone who's a World or National champion, and have that rider intentionally make a mistake to see if you're able to pick the mistake and not 'place the face.'" He mentioned another test, where judges must place contestants after watching a videotape of a class at a major show. This segment compares participants' scores to the placings by the actual show officials.

As a professional above reproach, the judge serves as a representative of the horse show industry. Hugh Williams, a former president of the Appaloosa Horse Club, once told a judges' seminar: "Understand your responsibility to the horse industry as a whole. Judges have power and should use it to improve this breed and horse sports."

Don Burt has agreed that powerful judges set trends and exert a great deal of clout. "Fifteen percent of the judges judge 90 percent of the shows. They influence the total industry."

3. Substance. Judging causes stress and physical exhaustion. Few horse shows finish quickly. The judge might stand in the ring for 10 hours a day, and stamina affects the quality of performance. "The judge has to judge every class equally," said de la Brosse. "He must be alert for the first horse and the last, whether he sees 4 or 40 in the class."

Many shows seek judges from afar, seeking objective opinions. Just getting to the show can tire the poorly conditioned judge. She must rebound quickly from the stress of travel in order to stride briskly into the ring, ready to withstand any weather. The judge should take pride in her appearance, too, as a well-dressed official inspires confidence and respect.

4. Alertness. The judge starts promptly and remains attentive. Jim Baker: "When I judge a show, it is going to start at 8 AM, even if 10 exhibitors are missing. If you wait, it snowballs. As an ex-

hibitor, I like a show like that, because I know when to be ready."

During the event, the judge keeps the show moving in a timely manner. She expedites each portion of the show day and places classes quickly, yet with sufficient time for fair evaluation of all entrants. She may have only 15 to 60 seconds to study each horse, to place it correctly. "The overall picture is very important," Baker has noted. "When you get 40 horses that are good, something has to stand out. The judge doesn't have time to analyze everyone."

The judge acts as the ring general, the person who's responsible for everything. She enlists the aid of other show officials, such as the ring steward, announcer, and ring crew.

Some shows hire two, three, four, or even five judges to score classes individually. Rules govern the averaging of scores, or the "double-judged" show could award multiple sets of prizes. Here the judges must agree how they will manage the events.

Peggy Jo Koll has explained how each judge expresses an individual opinion, without collusion. "We respect each other's opinion and realize that everybody looks at a horse differently. You may stand at a different angle and see something. Or something bothers a judge worse than it bothers me, and he scores it accordingly. We really don't care what the other one does."

By remaining alert to the action in the ring, the judge maintains a safe atmosphere. "Safety of all exhibitors is part of the judge's job," Walter de la Brosse has said. "I give an exhibitor three chances to get her horse under control. It's a value judgment, and some people get angry. But I feel they should get the disruptive horse under control *outside* the ring for everyone's safety."

5. Positive Attitude. The positive judge studies each contestant and gives everyone the same opportunity. If a horse performs poorly in one class, the judge views him impartially next time, giving him a fresh chance.

"You want to give each horse his best advantage," Don Burt has explained. "As a judge, you analyze how you will help the horses and not hinder them." The optimistic judge should not look for mistakes, such as the evasions he'd see if he concentrated on the ring's spookiest corner.

Whizzer Baker looks for riders with self-control, who demonstrate they can handle their horses whatever the situation. "I appreciate the exhibitor with a difficult-to-handle horse that's managed subtly, or the rider who is good at getting the horse right in the corner before going down the straight-away for the judge."

6. Consistency. A good judge places each class according to association rules. Appaloosa judge Bill Snyder: "A judge does not set policy or interpret the association's rules. He sees that the show follows the rules." Rules do change, and judges have to keep up with the changes.

In a breed show, the judge assumes that each entry has qualified through registration papers. She doesn't question the animal's right to be judged, and color or markings shouldn't affect the horse's placing.

Judges at open shows often confront the issue of breed favoritism. Again, the rules of the governing organization support official decisions. By accepting the judging assignment, the judge offers her opinion of the ideal animal according to the governing rulebook and the overall standards of a good horse and excellent performance.

7. Decision Making. The judge must have the courage of her convictions. In her role as ring general, she acts assertively in making confident decisions. Most association rules support her, specifying that the judge's decisions are final.

The alert judge notes as much of the ring action as possible. Obviously she cannot watch every horse at every moment, so she might miss an error that "railbirds" catch.

Judge Larry Gimple has advised show critics: "Remember that the judge doesn't see everything you see, and you don't see everything he sees. A lot of times the spectator watches only one horse and rider. They'll glance at the others, but they won't see everything, and they don't know the judge's opinion."

Occasionally the judge has to make an instant decision that might not be covered in association rules. Here she tries to be fair to all contestants. For example, Don Burt has suggested options if a trail class obstacle should break halfway through the class. "Repair it if possible. Or eliminate it from consideration. It's important for all to have the same opportunity."

Even if the audience boos her placings, the judge does not back down. She can justify her scoring by following the written rules. The class results match the standards.

Some judges post their score cards after the class. The scores and brief notes allow exhibitors to understand the placings. Comments could act as a critique, helping the entrant to improve her performance. Other judges contend that extended notes cause problems, as exhibitors protest the unseen mistakes of competitors.

8. Courtesy. Despite her role as a general, the judge should act pleasantly. She treats everyone politely, offering a warm greeting to each exhibitor.

A judge's welcome can ease your butterflies. "I try to smile and break the ice," Peggy Jo Koll has said. "Sometimes I'll say, 'Hi, how are you,' and an exhibitor will say, 'I'm scared to death. This is my first class.'"

Koll's advice to such a rider is to try to put fear aside because it interferes with thinking. She encourages exhibitors to relax at the start.

Judges need to show great tact in the ring. No matter what happens, they should never express anger or anxiety. The judge must gallantly dodge out-of-control horses and suppress astonishment when she sees outlandish or inept maneuvers.

Judges do care about exhibitors, and they want to maximize the show experience. Whizzer Baker has commented: "Part of the art of judging is the diplomacy to keep people happy when they don't win, just as much as you do when they do win."

Depending on the show rules, the judge may solicit your questions or even offer you some advice. Some judges enjoy conversing, while others frown on "giving a clinic." Extended conversations might imply unfair advantage.

The Controversy over Judging Pleasure Horses

Over the past years, a debate has ensued about the Western Pleasure class. These easy-to-ride horses sparked argument in the 1980s with their leisurely gaits, low heads, and dull expressions, when the standard shifted toward horses that critics termed "peanut rollers" and "robots."

Responding to criticism, horsemen in breed associations aimed to define the ideal performance in their rule books. As the dominant organization, the AQHA changed its class specifications. This influenced other breed associations to follow suit.

In 1990, the AQHA Executive Committee instructed judges to penalize certain faults as severely as they penalized a horse on the wrong lead, bolting, or bucking. These addressed the issue of the head carriage (no lower than level with the withers and nose in front of the vertical), light contact with a reasonably loose rein, excessive slowness, and a pained expression.

Rule changes in subsequent years helped officials recognize the good, forward-moving horse. One AQHA rule describes a "free-flowing stride of reasonable length in keeping with his conformation. He should cover a reasonable amount of ground with little effort. Ideally, he should have a balanced, flowing motion. . . . Maximum credit should be given to the flowing, balanced, and willing horse which gives the appearance of being fit and a pleasure to ride." (*Official Handbook,* 1993 edition)

Another rule stipulates that the judge is supposed to disqualify a horse with its "head carried too low (tip of ear below the withers) for more than five strides." But critics complain that these horses continue to place, and even win in pleasure classes.

Participants blame different individuals and groups for the discrepancies. Exhibitors complain that judges don't practice what they preach. But Whizzer Baker noted the challenge of current Western Pleasure requirements, where the judge must penalize a horse that carries its head so that the point of the ear is lower than the wither. This can eliminate a good performer that happens to travel well with a low head. "To determine that a horse's head cannot be a given level within a four- to eight-inch range is tough," says Baker.

In June 1993, the International Halter-Pleasure Quarter Horse Association (IHPQHA) was formed to address the discrepancies between theory and reality. Mike McMillian, IHPQHA president, explained that the organization will represent exhibitors' concerns in the pleasure classes and increase uniformity in judging. "We'd like to see standards formed, and a judges' rating system. We would like to see more guidance on style and type of modern horses."

Consistency is important to all players in the pleasure horse industry. By aiming for more consistent scores, the IHPQHA hopes to encourage more participation in pleasure classes.

This horse carries his head too low, a controversial posture that some observers call "peanut rolling."

Baker explained: "You have to be very careful about how you use that position. When I've turned in my judge's card in a class, I like to show handlers what would have made them do better."

When the judge takes the time to talk to you, respond with the same courtesy she shows you. Don't whine, "What did I do wrong?" or make excuses for a less-than-perfect showing. Listen to her opinion, and thank her.

Your Game Plan

To win at the show game, you need to set goals and follow them. Brian Ellsworth has advised: "You have to have a target. Hone in on a given area to start with, and have your goals and objectives. Do the very best you can to attain those goals. Set a goal just out of reach, then when you attain that one, set the next goal a little higher."

Your long-term goal should be satisfaction. Trainer Gill Swarbrick has said: "Horses are supposed to be fun. If it's not a pleasure, something's wrong. Maybe you need to switch horses, teachers, or goals. Don't be afraid to change your goals when you're riding. Some people set them too high, and you just can't physically achieve it. Set a goal one step at a time so you always feel good about what you're doing."

Before you decide to show, determine your motives. Most people compete to gain concrete rewards (prizes and money) or emotional achievements (satisfaction, pleasure, prestige, or ego gratification).

Every time you show, you can learn something new about your horse. Your long-term goal should be mutual satisfaction.

The way you view competition determines your approach to the sport. Do you thrive on a challenge, to seek your personal best? Or do you throw yourself into adversity, viewing sport as painful or even hazardous? Is the show ring an escape, to parade "onstage," enjoying the applause?

Every time you show, you can seize another opportunity to learn something new about your horse. Showing can become an addiction because you can get hooked on competition. Each experience leads to the anticipation of the next. •

You can enjoy the process of pursuing perfection and still be serious about the sport. "An amateur can compete with the pros, but you realize the commitment involved," Aloha Schneider has said. She is a New Mexico amateur who campaigned her Paint to national honors in Western Riding. "You have a professional attitude, and you realize it doesn't come easy. It's an exhilarating feeling to know that you've created a horse that's better than he was before. Nothing can replace that feeling of beating the best, to hold your own against people who make their living showing horses."

In all sports, today's athletes have learned the importance of reaching goals through mental rehearsal and visualization. You can program yourself by visualizing what you're going to do. You watch a rider on a video or at a clinic, and you replay a movie in your mind of what you saw. You feel positive reinforcement.

As you prepare your horse, you focus on specific requests for the actions you want. Break each action into steps of a process, and focus on what you aim to accomplish.

Sportsmanship

When you play the show game by the rules, you demonstrate that you're a good sport. You study the appropriate rule book and memorize requirements and penalties for the classes you enter. You wear correct attire and ensure that you outfit your horse in the legal bit. In the pen, you present your horse honestly, the best you can.

Many judges agree that they see a high level of sportsmanship in the show pen. Brian Ellsworth has suggested the influence of amateurs. "The amateur ranks have more of a comfort zone while showing. They don't have the pressure and can maintain a better attitude of sportsmanship.

"Any time there's money, prestige, or fame involved, people will try to cut corners somewhere. There will always have to be some type of policing mechanism to keep people within a manageable range."

As a good sport, you accept responsibility for your best effort and the risk of criticism. Under the eye of the judge and a dozen or a thousand spectators, you calmly perform the show routine.

When you win, someone else loses. Maintain your cool and accept a win or loss gracefully. Accept what you receive for your performance, and applaud the winners as the announcer calls numbers for ribbons.

A support team — your coach, family, or friends — helps you become a gracious sportsman. If a class doesn't go according to plan, you don't wilt or quit. You and your team laugh it off and use the lesson to prepare for next time. What's worse is when you win even though you made a major error that the judge somehow missed. You, and usually a certain number of spectators, know that you didn't deserve it. You recognize the fact, and still accept the ribbon.

Good sports follow a code of ethics. Treat your horse fairly, so he's on your team when the two of you compete. Let him know what you expect, and pet him, even when you lose.

Most associations cite sportsmanship in their rules. Your conduct contributes to the success of the show. If you lose your temper with your horse, fellow contestants, or show officials, you may be subject to disciplinary procedures.

You cooperate with show officials, such as for a bit check or random drug-testing. Don't feel insulted if an official requests such examinations. Such checks help equalize the competition and penalize the few dishonest exhibitors.

A veterinarian also might examine your horse for abnormal tail function. A few unscrupulous horsemen "block" their horse's tails to restrict natural tail movement. (A horse that wrings his tail indicates resistance; a quiet tail implies the horse willingly obeys.)

NOVICE PROGRAMS

First-timers may suffer anxiety attacks, but even worse can be the intimidation you suffer during your early performances. The fear of the unknown intensifies when you see the level of your competition. The classes that used to be entry level — youth and amateur — are hotly contested in today's horse shows. Fortunately, show associations have recognized the need to maintain beginners' interest in the sport.

Novice classes — where you ride against your peers — can be less intimidating. When you gain know-how and win a certain number of ribbons or amount of points, you then graduate to more demanding classes.

Trainer Alpha Russell has explained: "You eyeball everybody else at the show, and you upgrade yourself when the entry fees are low. You see what you need to do to move on — to improve your equipment or clothes, or get with a trainer."

AQHA offers novice classes limited to youth and amateurs, where you're only eligible if you've earned less than 10 performance points in AQHA–approved competition. You're considered a novice through the calendar year, regardless of the number of novice or AQHA points you earn. Once you have 25 or more novice points, you may no longer compete as a novice next year.

Brian Ellsworth has praised the classes. "Programs allow youth to make the transition into the amateur classes. They allow inexperienced youth to be competitive on a regular basis. They swim in water at their own depth, and they attain some level of success."

Sue Thomas of Gainesville, Texas, has credited the Novice Program for giving her the self-confidence to continue in AQHA shows. "We live in a small Texas town, and I have never had access to a regular trainer. I have learned primarily on my own by hauling to a lot of shows, and from what I could pick up from watching more experienced riders. The Novice Program has given me an opportunity to test what I have learned, competing with other riders who were just beginning. The Novice participants are very supportive of each other. Had it not been for this, I am sure I would have become discouraged and quit early on."

Marcia Potter of Longmont, Colorado, who earned her 25 novice points as a novice amateur, has also supported the program. "It's a way to get in and to learn a lot about ring sense, to learn how to present yourself. I'm much more aware of what judges are looking for and how to get it done.

"Without an entry-level class that you can go into and get the feeling of how it is to win, it's only the agony of defeat. Everyone gets the experience of defeat often enough, but to have it be your only experience would be terrible."

The Appaloosa Horse Club (ApHC) offers three levels in its Novice Program: Novice Youth, Novice Non-Pro, and Limited Non-Pro. Alpha Russell has considered the Limited Non-Pro class for adults aged 35 and over a "brilliant" idea. "All those parents and horse show returnees had to compete against the tough 19-year-old kids, fresh from the Youth classes. They feel a lot better about competing if they don't have to ride against 20-year-olds who have had 10 years of lessons."

Showing for Intermediate Riders

With a show season under your belt, the first-time thrills become memories. You should feel more confident about steering your horse through traffic in a pleasure class, and you can easily memorize and perform a horsemanship pattern. At the in-gate, you recognize familiar faces and greet fellow contestants in the spirit of friendly competition.

As you polish your show skills, you'll develop an aptitude for showing. You'll realize the goal of the Western horseman: to increase the degree of difficulty by striving for perfection. You also may feel the itch to launch another stage of your career and seek a change of pace in a more demanding event, or aim your horse at prestigious shows.

IMPROVING YOUR PERFORMANCE

A coach becomes invaluable as you polish your presentation. When you become serious about showing, you'll benefit from the support a coach brings.

At the bigger shows, almost all youth and amateur riders attend with a trainer.

Although you concentrate on becoming closer with your horse, a professional analyzes your performance. He should share his knowledge to instruct you in the classic concepts of horsemanship.

Arabian trainer Gary Ferguson has concentrated on empowerment, or giving his students a pride in their abilities. "At each lesson, we try to give a sense of accomplishment. We teach the rider something new that she thinks about before the next lesson, so she feels 'I am getting better, and I can do this. It's not that difficult.'"

The trainer helps you develop your commitment. As in other sports, this expert guides you through a program. The program may be achieving a certain goal, but it primarily focuses on your desire to qualify as a genuine horseman.

California trainer Art Gaytan has said: "You have to be prepared to trust the judgment of that trainer. It's up to him to find out of all the varied classes, what you're best suited for, and where you'll get the maximum benefit. Dedication will overcome obstacles."

A coach helps you keep the sport in perspective. Andy Moorman, a Florida Quarter Horse trainer, has told her students to focus on pleasing her and not care what others think. "I want them to please me. If I'm satisfied with what they did, I don't really care if the judge liked or didn't like them."

Moorman urged riders to concentrate on what happens in the show pen. "I keep working on them that when they come out of the ring, to tell me what they did, why they did it, what they felt. When they're beginners, they can't remember anything. You know you're starting to get somewhere when they can tell you what they did. Then they get to the point where they can remember what I told them, and they do it."

Project self-assurance in the ring.

SHOWING YOUR STUFF

In the pen you want to present your strengths and downplay your weaknesses. For a winning appearance, you must adopt a strong mindset. If you're timid about promoting yourself, you may find showmanship the most difficult aspect of classes.

The judge seeks a dynamic presentation, looking for the horseman who stands out from the crowd. He looks for the charisma that marks a winning horse and rider. You know the judge starts choosing his top riders immediately, and so you impress him. You play to the judge because you have only one chance to make that first impression.

When judging, Brian Ellsworth wants to see a confidence level, an air of self-assurance. "It's in the facial expression, the body language, how you carry yourself, how you address a pattern. You almost need an air of arrogance on individual patterns. That salesmanship, that desire to win, has to come from within."

You don't appear phony or brazen, but you ride as if you know you're the best. You'll watch the judge through subtle glances, so you see when he's watching you. Don't freeze into position, but ride as a contender. Also, don't stare at the judge, which can make you appear hostile.

Don't assume that the same riders always win. Judge Whizzer Baker has said: "In my own mind, I say, 'The best horse wins.' It doesn't matter that he won the class before, and he might win the class after. He might not — he might make a mistake. I actually find myself watching the one that's won, knowing that he can't be perfect every time."

Because the judge is an expert showman, he knows all the tricks and tactics. He's likely to mark you down if he suspects you're trying to bluff him or conceal unsportsmanlike behavior. Baker positions himself so he can see most of the ring. Close to the rail, he hears horses behind him. "It's amazing. You can hear a [rider] snatch if you're standing six or eight feet away. You can even hear a missed lead, from behind, mostly because very few exhibitors have the finesse to make the change smoothly. There'll be a commotion behind me, if a lead is missed or a bobble occurs. I don't even have to turn around, because the rider comes into my range of vision from the side and I pick up the number."

Showmanship involves knowing your horse. Some veteran show horses slack off in a rail class when they reverse to travel in the second direction. Watch your horse, and be ready to increase your driving leg to keep his impulsion. You could even move up in the placings, as other riders may have lost concentration as the class nears its end.

Judge Larry Gimple watches a horse's expression, mouth, and tail to see if the horse gets bored, cranky, or spooky. "I start placing the class in the second direction. That doesn't mean I won't change as the class goes on. If one horse blows, that may help another. As they lope to the right, my top three should be placed. Now I'll glance at those, but I'm looking for my four, five, and six. A judge should be conscientious about taking those extra moments for those other ribbons."

Many riders find it difficult to understand how they compare with the other contestants. A videotape will aid in analyzing the outcome of a class. Watch your video and concentrate on how you could improve your riding and your horse's appearance. Your coach will probably offer a critique after the class and while watching the video. Besides absorbing specific comments about your actions, look at your overall impression. Ask yourself: "Do I ride aggressively so my horse performs his best? Do I look like a sympathetic rider who knows when to push and when to back off? Does my body language proclaim, 'I'm a winner'? Does my horse project the accepted look in his gaits and transitions?"

Choosing a Show Horse

When you're serious about showing, the right horse can help you achieve your goals. In today's more sophisticated show industry, you need to decide if you'll concentrate on certain classes or demonstrate versatility.

As you sample the various events, you might develop specific goals. You consider your horse's abilities and your priorities to determine if you

need a different horse. Trainer Nancy Cahill has said: "You move on when your horse has limitations. Maybe he's not a great loper, or a great lead changer. You may decide you like trail or Western riding, so you don't need a pleasure horse. He may not be a '10' loper, but he's an '8' and a beautiful lead changer."

She noted that you're ready to switch horses when your riding skills exceed his ability. "Raise up a notch, and get a horse that knows more than you do. You catch up to him and step up as your money, time, and job will let you."

Another Texas trainer, Chuck Briggs, has advised that the horse can't transform you. "Some think they can buy a World Champion and they'll be a World Champion. They want to achieve the same thing that the person before them did with the horse, but they've got to have some talent to begin with — the natural ability to feel the horse and tell what he's doing."

The All-Around Horse

Trainers focus horses on the events that they have the greatest chance of winning. Some horsemen feel that this benefits the sport through attracting money and prestige. Others criticize horses that fit into only one niche.

California trainer Joe King matches a horse to a rider by first finding out which event the rider prefers, then seeing if the event fits the horse. He has commented: "Today horses have to be bred for certain divisions. There are very few all-around horses, so you look at the breeding to see what the horse is bred for. A horse can be great at one event, good at two, but not great at two. So, you train him for one division." He adds that few professional football players switch to baseball, so you can't expect a great reining horse to excel in pleasure, too.

Breed associations do offer awards for versatility. The all-around horse can show in a variety of classes, and accumulated points count toward show or year-end high-point awards. The eventual winner may win few first place ribbons against horses that specialize, but he's competitive enough to place in different classes.

If you want to compete for all-around, you'll need an exceptional equine athlete with a flexible attitude. For example, Kings Copy Cat and Texas owner Lela Kay French won the All-Around Amateur award at the 1991 and 1993 Paint World Championships. In 1993, French entered all but four Amateur performance classes and won 13 ribbons. She explains how she dedicates time to practice: "I ride every day, twice a day, in early morning and late evening. A week before the show, I roped in the morning and then in the afternoon jumped or practiced pleasure. I was pretty worn out before I got here!

"If you want to go for all-around, you've got to put out a lot of effort and have a lot of faith in your horse and confidence in yourself to be able to go on out and do something. I say, 'I'm going in this class to do the best I can, and the next class, and the next class.' You just have to go out there and do your best. You don't say, 'I blew that last class, so there's no need for me to go in this one.' You've got to say, 'That's behind me.'"

CONDITIONING YOUR SHOW HORSE

The show horse should enjoy performing, so he looks expressive and fresh. If you follow a demanding show schedule, attending three or four shows a month, your horse must hold up under the travel and strange environments.

The natural athlete that performs with an "ears forward" look can influence the judge's scores. To keep him bright for the show pen requires careful conditioning. You can modify the conditioning program described in Chapter 8, and add two fitness workouts used by many trainers.

Longeing requires only a small area and a short time span. As the horse moves around you in a circle, you can teach or reinforce basic lessons in obedience. Control the gait and speed, and limit the duration of faster gaits with a young or unfit horse. Because he works in a circle, he exerts uneven strain upon his muscles. Always longe equal periods in

Longeing can reinforce basic lessons in obedience.

both directions, to exercise all muscles both right and left. You'll protect against injury by equipping your horse with protective legwear such as splint boots. Use a line at least 25 feet long; when the horse circles at the line's end, he travels on a large, less stressful circle about 50 feet in diameter.

Every workout requires regular warm-up and cool-down periods. For example, longe at the walk for the first 10 minutes to limber up. Trot and canter 15 minutes, both directions. Ride for 45 minutes at all three gaits, performing frequent changes of directions, adding circles, turns, and figure eights or serpentines. Walk for 10 minutes to allow the horse to cool down to normal body temperature.

Many training barns rely on the mechanical hot walker. You tie your horse to one of the machine's arms, and the motor pulls the arm and the horse in a circle.

The hot walker has proven to be a real labor-saver for the busy trainer, but this motorized exerciser can also bore the horse. When forced to walk or jog in an endless circle, he learns only to follow the mechanical arm.

Keeping your horse fresh also requires an individual program. You don't want to sour him so he loses interest in performing. You'll develop a schedule that allows him to rest after show stress, and then peak him for an important competition. Rest could mean daily turnout in a paddock and trail

 PROS AND CONS OF USING A TRAINER

Advantages	Disadvantages
A professional keeps the horse polished.	The professional can limit your riding time. You don't learn as much because the trainer does the schooling.
Your horse may win more prizes when the trainer shows him. Your horse becomes more valuable.	You don't share the fun of winning. You may have to share cash prizes with the trainer.
Your horse will maintain good habits when ridden by the pro; you could "ruin" him by careless riding.	Your horse can "outgrow" you, becoming so used to the trainer that you must duplicate the trainer's moves to ride your own horse.
The pro puts in the time that you may not be able to dedicate toward practice.	Your horse could need more time at the trainer's barn, costing you more money.
You can learn more about horsemanship by watching the trainer ride. The trainer can also coach you during lessons.	The trainer may not want you to watch him schooling your horse. An excellent horse trainer could be a poor riding teacher.
The pro controls the horse's environment.	You pay increased costs of monthly board/training fees ($350–800), hauling fees to shows, and day fees at shows ($25–100). You aren't in charge of your horse, and you may need to make an appointment to visit the barn and groom or ride your own horse.
The pro directs the show season.	Do you want to compete at the shows the pro attends? If you don't, who works your horse while the pro's gone from the barn?

riding to keep him in shape. You might school him on segments of the show routine while riding on the trail.

Exhibitors will often test the horse immediately before a show, duplicating show conditions. This sharpens the horse for the imminent show. You might ride in a group lesson where you practice on the rail and perform for the "judge."

THE SHOW-HORSE TRAINER

You may decide to enlist the help of a trainer, who will prepare your horse for shows. The professional's influence can improve your chances of winning, but you'll need to weigh the pros and cons. Usually the horse boards with the trainer, but you may prefer to keep your horse at home and haul him to the trainer for lessons.

You'll need to select a trainer whose personality you trust, and who maintains an ethical reputation.

This could be your mentor or another recommended expert. As you become more serious about showing, you may progress to a specialist who has achieved prominence in the segment you prefer.

INTERMEDIATE CLASSES

In these classes, your strategy involves working order. You might want to perform the pattern first or last, to impress the judge with a dynamic go. Usually you'll end up in the middle, so you must consider how you compare with those before and after you. Competing in AQHA shows, you'll draw for the order.

Going first can favor you, because the others will have to match you. It can also be a disadvantage, because the judge might give you a conservative score when he hasn't seen the competition. If you perform last, you have the opportunity to observe others and how they handled the pattern.

TYPES OF CLASSES

	Showmanship at Halter	Trail	Western Riding
JUDGE SCORES	Handler (youth or amateur)	Horse	Horse
CLASS ROUTINE	Entries line up; handler performs a set pattern and returns to line up.	Rider aims horse to move across or through a course of 6 to 8 obstacles.	Rider guides horse through a pattern, showing all 3 gaits and the flying lead change.
IDEAL PERFORMANCE	Handler presents horse smoothly, with every detail perfect.	Rider shows precise control over horse's movements.	Horse performs with precision, consistent position, speed, and stride length.
HORSE	Pretty Clean Correct Poses well	Instantly obeys your cue Cleanly crosses obstacles	Responsive Alert Clean lead changes
RIDER/ HANDLER	Alert Poised Pleasant Courteous	Maintains a calm attitude Lets horse settle a moment after a difficult obstacle	Alert Accurate Controlled Decisive

Showmanship at Halter Class

Showmanship challenges you to show your horse to perfection. You and your horse walk in the pen turned out in your best, and you lead your horse at the walk and trot, stand him square, and turn him around. You show him so he places every foot precisely.

Just as he does under saddle, your horse follows your invisible commands. However, you must influence him without touching him directly. You ask him to respond through your use of the lead shank or your body language.

The competition is tough, as Showmanship is usually early in a day's schedule. Andrea Simons, a trainer and judge of Paints, has explained: "It's the first event that the judge sees you in. If you can get your horse to be consistent in Showmanship, and if you have the polish, it's a good first event. Showmanship is a really useful event. You can say [to the judge], 'Yes, I'm in control of this situation and I'm here for a reason.'

"It's a stage performance. I really like to see someone who likes to show me her horse. I want her performance to dictate to me that she loves this horse; therefore I will love it, because she's having a good time."

Western Pleasure, Horsemanship, and Showmanship attract the greatest number of entries. To "wow" the audience with your flair, you and your horse move in absolute harmony. The two of you then stand at attention for the judge's inspection.

Peggy Jo Koll, a judge with five associations, looks for how quickly the exhibitor sets up the horse. "You've got to get your horse square and you can't take forever to do it. You could be fast and not get your horse squared up, which is not good. We put so much emphasis on getting the horse set up quickly, that sometimes the exhibitor doesn't take the time to move the horse's foot where it should be."

Koll describes how the horse must be alert and responsive. "As you start to walk off, your horse should already be starting to move forward. It's just like the horse is your shadow, and that takes practice."

The handler must influence the horse without touching him directly.

Judges look for safe handling, watching to see how you maintain control over your horse in motion. You'll always lead from the left side, with your right hand on the lead shank. You guide the horse beside you, moving in rhythm. Walk so your shoulder is beside the horse's ear, or where his throatlatch blends into his neck.

Because you maintain all control from the lead shank, your horse must be completely broke. Any bobble counts against you, and you may not touch his foot, shoulder, neck, or head from the second you walk into the pen to the moment your judge turns in his card.

To develop fingertip control, you must get your horse to instantly obey your commands. Ideally, you'll learn Showmanship with a responsive horse.

You'll outfit him as described for a halter class, with a chain lead shank. "Used correctly, the chain keeps the horse's head up and gives you power steering," Koll noted. "It's your communication link."

Showmanship judges require a pattern. Judges usually ask novice or younger contestants for simpler maneuvers, such as trotting the horse, halting, a 180-degree turn, walking back toward the judge, and stopping to set up the horse.

Preparing the Pattern

A winning pattern combines three basics — control, timing, and placement. To develop control, practice maneuvers whenever you handle your horse. Look for him to halt with you when you say "Whoa," and walk when you start to move out. Hold the shank steady and let him punish himself

Always keep your feet at least 12 inches away from the horse's hooves. This exhibitor and her Paint horse walk in step during a halter class.

with the pressure of the tightened chain if he presses forward or lags behind you.

As you lead, face front and aim to synchronize your movements in a relaxed, natural stride. If your horse strides first with his left foot, you also start with that foot. Hold your head and eyes up, and visualize your horse moving beside you. (Glance right every few strides to check.) Keep your right hand up at a steady position, and the rest of the shank looped in your left hand about waist level.

Work on a different aspect every day. Koll: "Take your horse out of the stall, drop the lead rope, and brush him. Make him stand there for five minutes; if he moves, put him back where he's supposed to be."

Fine-tune your communication so he watches your body language and begins to move in harmony with you. He learns that your position predicts your action. When you lead, you face forward and walk. When you pose, you stand to the side facing the horse. When he stands square, you look away and toward the judge. You adjust your position — moving slightly toward him — when you want him to turn.

Turn him away from you, always to the right, so he pivots on his off hip, on an inside pivot foot. In showmanship, make a flat turn, similar to the turnaround of a reining horse. Watch the front feet — he should step his left (near) front foot across his right front foot and not move forward or back. You continue asking for the turn: 90, 180, a full 360, or occasionally a 1½ turn.

In essence, you and your horse "dance" together. Andrea Simons has noted: "You work on timing and getting the handler in sync with the horse. It's all a kind of orchestration."

She added that some exhibitors move abruptly. "I like to see the speed be fairly consistent. I don't like to see you amble out there at a walk and then zing around at a 360 and then jog out of there. The run should be consistent; a nice showmanship run is the ultimate pairing."

Practice timing at the walk, trot, and turn. Just as you do under saddle, change speeds from a slow, collected walk to a normal speed. Extend the walk, then slow and extend again.

Showmanship Strategy

Lead your horse into the pen as the judge directs. You'll enter separately from your competitors, perform the prescribed pattern, and line up, usually along the rail.

Accuracy can put you in or out of the ribbons. Memorize the posted pattern, and listen to any additional instructions.

Watch your horse and your placement in a class. While keeping your horse posed, concentrate on and show to the judge. Don't "rest" as you might in a halter class. At all times, know the judge's location and where he's looking.

Peggy Jo Koll has mentioned that exhibitors occasionally give too much attention to the judge. "Your horse needs a lot of attention. You can watch me and cut your eyes to your horse, making sure he's still standing in position. You are the shower, but you're not showing me yourself, you're showing me the horse."

The judge will examine your horse, and you must "show" in a poised, unobtrusive manner. Try to avoid obstructing the judge's view, and also "protect" the judge from your horse. With constant control, your horse won't bump, step on, kick, or bite the judge. (Yes, these things do happen in showmanship classes!)

Most association rules specify your position in relation to the judge. While the judge walks around your horse, you move from one side to the other, standing on the opposite side of the horse from the judge so you never obstruct his view. The AQHA calls this "the quarter method," dividing the area surrounding the horse into four quadrants. As you change sides, drop your shank under the horse's chin to demonstrate your constant control.

Establish your movements, and stick to your plan. Andrea Simons notes that exhibitors fail to be consistent in their actions. "With the quarter system, you need to be in place. The judge starts to walk, and you move. If you come over to one side too soon, I like to see you do it on the other side so it looks like what you meant to do. A lot of people will be correct on one side, and not on the other."

When you complete your pattern, know where the judge stands and aim your horse on a direct line to the judge. Halt and set up the horse, staying out of the judge's line of vision. If he stands to your left, you'll quickly move to the horse's off side.

You don't need a champion halter horse, but he does need to appear in the same excellent physical condition. Don't cut corners in your grooming. For example, take the time to clean your horse's hoof, before you apply hoof black. Just painting the outside doesn't impress the judge when he sees stems of straw packing the sole.

"It's an advantage to your image if you come in with immaculate turnout and your horse is spit-polish shined," says Simons. "It catches the judge's eye and gives you the confidence throughout your run."

If you consider your performance an audition, you'll concentrate on projecting yourself. Unlike other classes, you make eye contact with the judge. You display courtesy by smiling and responding to the judge's greeting and requests.

Simons explains: "I want the exhibitor to say, 'Hey, this is special. This isn't just any horse with any run!' Through her body language and her presence, it's pretty apparent which ones feel that way."

TRAIL CLASS

Trail demands a horse that's cool and calm about crossing anything in his path. He rides like a pleasure horse at the walk, jog, and lope, and he's careful with his feet as he crosses obstacles that simulate those he'd encounter on a trail ride.

One obstacle might be a space measuring five by five feet — less than half the size of a stall. Your task is to step your horse cleanly into that square formed by four wooden poles on the ground, without touching the wood, and then to perform a full turn to the right, again without touching the wood. Then you step out, still without brushing or touching the boundary.

Your goal is an effortless, graceful performance — both through each obstacle and in the transitions between them. You must ride with precision and polish to negotiate your performance.

Trail shows the trust between you. You tell the horse where to go, through obstacles that show your control and his agility. Over certain obstacles like a bridge, you allow him to perform on his own. Your guidance on course should be minimal, and the horse doesn't appear "programmed" as he picks his way over and through the obstacles.

Judge Don Burt says: "The course should test the ability of the horse while he goes from beginning to end. It should contain several types of obstacles to show his disposition. Some demonstrate calmness, such as opening the gate. Precision situations, like backing through an 'L,' show the rider's control."

Practice the sidepass to the left and right over ground rails to improve maneuverability.

Preparing for Trail

Perfect your lateral exercises, as described in Chapter 6. Before schooling over obstacles, you warm up by suppling the parts of the horse. Look for control of the shoulder, because you'll have to steer with the neck rein, holding only one finger between the reins.

Trainer Carolyn Bader has explained: "Train the horse for maneuverability, control, and obedience — not the obstacles. Before trail training begins, you must have control of the forequarter and rear quarter, and have your horse responsive in the mouth and responsive to the aids of your hands, legs, seat of the pants, and body position."

You'll also apply lateral control to the rein back, as many obstacles require backwards maneuvers. Bader noted: "Back the horse slowly for some distance, moving the hip first to the left with your right leg aid. Allow your horse to straighten, then continue backing as you apply your left leg to move the hip to the right."

Lateral exercises help you move all parts of the horse together, such as for a sidepass right or left. With this maneuverability, you can practice over specific obstacles. You'll probably face a gate, bridge, walkover, and backthrough. (Association rules describe obstacles and typical dimensions.)

When you present your horse at any obstacle, give him time to examine it. He learns to lower his head to direct his vision toward the object, with that relaxed yet alert expression that judges want to see in a horse.

Use patience while you school, and make your horse confident about simple obstacles. Point him at a pole flat on the ground, give him time to look, and cue him to walk across. In a show, you don't want him to wait too long before he moves, but in practice, you don't push him or teach him to rush.

Repeating the movements will cause the horse to develop his own caution. In a show, touching an obstacle counts against you. Your horse will probably knock his hoof against some poles while he's learning, but avoid punishing him. When he bumps a pole, he'll usually lift his feet a little higher the next time.

Be patient and allow your horse time to examine an obstacle.

As you travel over a course, concentrate on maintaining an effortless appearance. Try to sit quietly, without oversteering. You should keep your hand quiet and as low as possible, with light contact. Your weight can cue your horse where to go, as long as you move quietly so you don't overbalance him. Don't exaggerate your moves, such as pitching the reins to "showboat" through an obstacle.

You can set a practice obstacle loose or tight; if distances are close, your horse has to maneuver with precision. His responses show up as you negotiate a trail course. Let him demonstrate his weaknesses so you know what to work on. Over an easy, flat course, an experienced horse can get blasé and start touching obstacles with his hoof.

The gate, often the first obstacle on a course, gives you the opportunity to show how you and your horse work as a team. Usually you walk to the gate, pivot the horse parallel to it, sidepass to stand beside it, swing open the gate, push it away from you while you back a step or two, and walk through while holding the gate. Push the gate open

all the way. Walk through so your horse's body is on the other side, still holding the top of the gate. Reposition your horse by pivoting him and side-passing back to close the gate, wait a moment, and then continue the course.

To work the gate cleanly, keep the horse close and parallel to the gate at all times. You don't want to have to stretch to close it. Your horse should help you, by standing beside the gate before you start to shut it. Some judges may increase the challenge by requiring you to back through the gate.

Other obstacles challenge your control in tight spots. You may have to jog a serpentine course around cones or poles. Practice for these by realizing that the horse has a five-foot "wheelbase." Many courses include elevated poles, which could be parallel to the ground or with one end higher than the other.

To demonstrate, you might have to carry an object or drag an item with a rope attached to it.

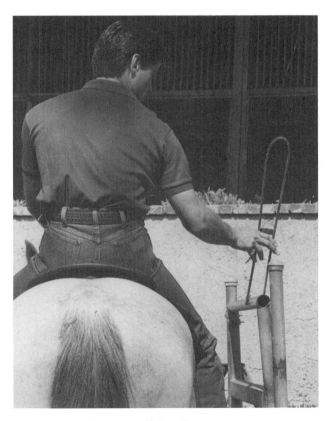

Position your horse parallel to the gate so you can grasp the latch and handle it with precision.

You may have to ground tie and leave your horse unattended for a specific period of time. Be sure to dismount first, and then drop your reins. Walk away with confidence, trusting him to stand in place for the period the judge requests.

Sidepassing in Style

The trail class usually requires the sidepass, where the horse walks left or right without moving forward. This maneuver also helps you execute the flying change of lead.

Use your outside leg and rein to cue your horse. You can practice facing into a fence, pressing your calf so your horse moves away from pressure. Make the cue definite, so he feels only your right leg when you sidepass to the left.

Trainer Casey Hinton has explained that your horse should give with the chin. "Exactly how he does the sidepass will correlate to how he'll lope and change leads. If he's pushy with his head now, he'll be pushy in the lope."

Use the sidepass in the lope transition. Sidepass facing the fence, turn, and continue your leg aid so you move the hip into the lope. The horse moves his hip over and respects your leg.

In the class, you might have to sidepass over a pole or in a "slot," a row of poles. You'll position your horse with his body over the single pole, or his front (or hind) feet in the slot. Here you move one step at a time, so your horse doesn't touch any pole. In competition, a minor bobble can put you out of the ribbons.

Trail Class Exercises

Carolyn Bader has offered the following tips on specific obstacles found on a challenging course.

OBSTACLE 1:
Jog over a circular pattern of 4 poles. "Look before you start. Create a slight arc by tipping the nose to the inside before you cross the first pole. Bend and push with your inside leg to keep the arc, and you

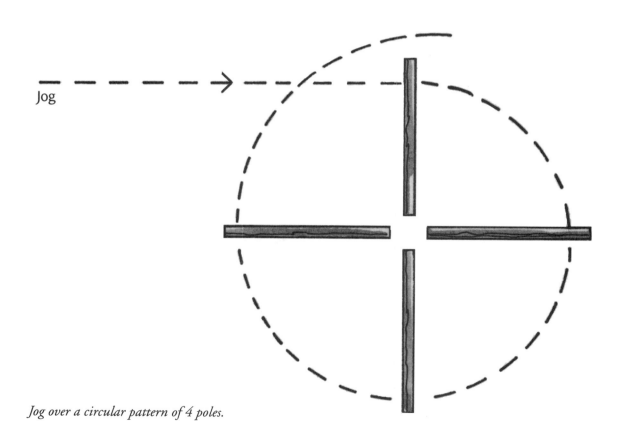

Jog over a circular pattern of 4 poles.

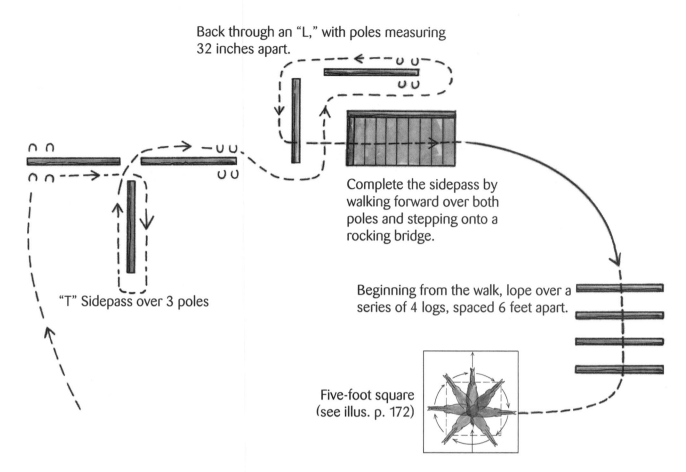

Back through an "L," with poles measuring 32 inches apart.

"T" Sidepass over 3 poles

Complete the sidepass by walking forward over both poles and stepping onto a rocking bridge.

Beginning from the walk, lope over a series of 4 logs, spaced 6 feet apart.

Five-foot square (see illus. p. 172)

may need outside leg pressure also to keep your horse moving forward at the jog."

OBSTACLE 2:

"T" Sidepass over 3 poles. "Begin the sidepass to the right, then bring the forequarter around the rearquarter through the 18-inch opening at the top of the 'T.' Proceed to sidepass right to the stem of the 'T.' Halt to settle the horse. Begin to sidepass left to the top of the 'T,' move the rearquarter to the left, and complete the last sidepass to the left. Sidepass off the 'T' until the rearquarters are lined up to enter Obstacle 3.

"Depending on the horse's length, usually you're okay if you position yourself so the pole is just behind your leg, whether your leg is hanging straight down or slightly forward. This kind of obstacle may require you to lean over somewhat to look at the pole. Leaning over too far can cause the horse to lose his balance or avoid wanting to move.

"When you turn, look on both sides so you can control the movement. Carefully move the front end in a tight spot. Try to feel the horse's body movement underneath you, and what is happening to the rear end. Most riders go years before they begin to feel where the horse's legs are."

A sharp corner like this requires you to balance caution and efficiency yet keep moving slowly in the sidepass. For precise footsteps in these confined spaces, you'll probably need to bend over and check the position of your horse's hind feet in relation to the opening in the "T."

When you signal your horse to halt, he should stop all movement immediately. One misstep can make a major difference in the final score.

OBSTACLE 3:

Part 1. Back through an "L," with poles measuring 32 inches apart. "Proceed through the 'L,' and try to avoid swinging from side to side. Choose one side or the other to watch the rail, and feel the horse's spine and rearquarter moving. Apply aids to straighten if necessary. As you approach the corner of the 'L' and the hind feet enter the corner, be conscious of the forehand. Make sure it begins to move around the corner as the rear end makes the turn."

Part 2. At the end of the "L," turn and sidepass the length of the pole. "Turn the rearquarter around the forequarter in a quarter turn to the left. As the rearquarter clears, hold the front end in and move the rearquarter one-quarter turn, putting it on the outside of the 'L.' Sidepass around the 'L' to the right. In the 'L' to the sidepass, look for no loss of forward motion. Judges like you to keep moving, even if you take tiny steps. And don't let the horse move out of the 'L' with his forefeet. You shouldn't feel him evade by dropping behind the bit or move without being told. You shouldn't sense him telling you he's uncomfortable, or 'I want to escape,' because it will show."

Part 3. Complete the sidepass by walking forward over both poles and stepping onto a rocking bridge. "This fools the horse a little. It changes his train of thought as you step into the 'L' and onto the bridge."

OBSTACLE 4:

Beginning from the walk, lope over a series of 4 logs, spaced 6 feet apart. "Depart at the lope after leaving the bridge, on the right lead at the correct arc. Approach the logs at the center. You should have some contact with the mouth, and apply your leg, to avoid a long-strided canter."

After the precision of the previous obstacles, your horse might feel too strong as he approaches the logs. In schooling, stop immediately before you cross the first log, and back far enough to correct a tendency to rush. Resume the lope from the halt.

OBSTACLE 5:

Slow to a walk to step your horse into a five-foot square, perform a full turn to the right, and step out. "Enter the square so you leave enough room to turn the forehand around the rear. Keep slight contact with the mouth and squeeze with the leg. Sit deep with your back squared."

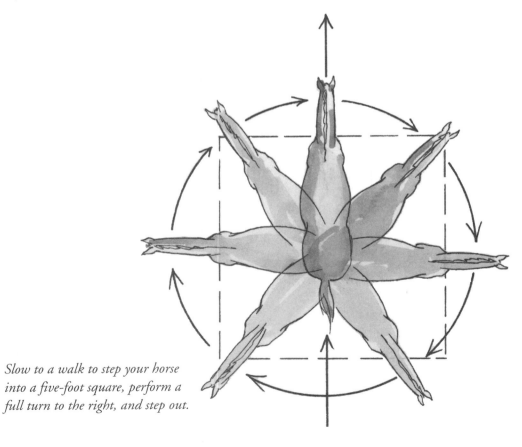

Slow to a walk to step your horse into a five-foot square, perform a full turn to the right, and step out.

Trail Strategy

In a show, you'll analyze the trail course to determine your approach. A large course may demand a flowing, brisk round. Through a more compact, well-measured layout, you'll need to move precisely.

Listen to the judge's instructions. In a brief speech to all exhibitors, he'll tell you what he expects.

Most judges want to see a prompt go. A trail class can drag on for hours, and officials appreciate riders who start when directed and crisply negotiate the course without needless hesitation. When you complete an obstacle, you look at the next one and travel right to it.

"I like promptness," Don Burt has said. "I tell riders, 'After you close the gate, jog to the walkovers and walk through promptly, without stopping and without hesitation.' That way I eliminate the rider who rides up, the horse stops, puts his nose all around, and looks at every pole. We have the horse looking at the obstacle, yes, but not stopping."

WESTERN RIDING CLASS

The Western Riding event blends the smoothness of pleasure classes with the rhythm of skilled maneuvers. You and your horse travel a specific pattern prescribed in the show association's rule book. You complete a series of transitions with accuracy and precision, as your horse gracefully performs the test.

The course includes all three gaits and the backup, with the emphasis on eight flying lead changes along a winding pattern. At the lope, you weave smoothly along the bending line and across the pen.

Appaloosa trainer and judge Dave Moore has explained: "This class is about changing leads. From the first to the second change, there's three — maybe four — strides, and not much time to judge manners, way of going, and the quality of the lope."

Rules govern where each lead change occurs, usually halfway between markers when the horse

Trail Trials

The trail trial adds natural obstacles to a short trail ride. With a more informal atmosphere, you won't need to groom your horse as intensely or wear specific attire. The ride may require you to carry certain equipment – the type you'd take on a day's ride. In addition to walkovers like ones you'd cross in a trail class, judges may score you on these areas:

* ⭐ Mounting on the offside
* ⭐ Walking over branches and tying a ribbon to a tree
* ⭐ Dismounting and cleaning all four hooves
* ⭐ Crossing a bridge (walking forward or backing up)

Local riding clubs occasionally offer these competitions. If you aren't in shape for a competitive trail ride but don't want to dress up for a show, the trail trial lets you test your horse's training.

Western Riding Class is an event combining the smoothness of pleasure classes with the rhythm of skilled maneuvers.

changes direction. Some trainers argue that this maneuver teaches the horse to change leads when he changes directions, not when the rider cues.

Moore says: "The judge has to be able to pick out the correct spot for the lead change. I like to give every rider a grace period of one stride either side of the center. The ideal change can only hap-

pen within one stride of the center — the halfway point between markers."

The change occurs when you cross the plane, or the area separating one direction from the other. If you go over the line and miss the change, the judge penalizes you for failure to change.

By knowing how your horse will respond, you can receive top scores in each segment of the pattern. The class may begin with the gate, which you open as you would in a trail class. Calmly walk over a log and move into the jog. By jogging in a straight line, you'll show the judge that your horse waits for your signals.

Because Western Riding always uses the same serpentine pattern, many riders practice the course over and over. Horses can learn to anticipate, which disturbs the flow of the pattern. Your horse should wait until you tell him to jog. You demonstrate that you're guiding him, and he's willing to listen to your light cues.

When you do practice an entire pattern, set a true lope and maintain it throughout. Trainer John Higginson has noted: "You shouldn't go through the course like a pleasure horse, moving slow and collected. I like to see a horse lope forward freely, so the changes are smoother."

At the lope, you form a "sweep" across the pen. To keep the rhythm, you might count strides, changing leads at every six. (Striding varies according to the distance between markers.)

After the final lead change, lope down the centerline, stop, and back up. You show the judge a steady pace, a smooth downward transition, and a responsive backup.

During this and every segment, the judge can add or subtract points for the horse's manners. Most judges notice the animal's expression, his eyes and ears, and how he uses his tail. A relaxed horse that moves at a consistent speed in a smooth, flowing motion will earn extra points. A resentful horse with a "helicopter" tail shows that he resists his rider, and he'll lose points. "The overall picture is taken into account in every score," explained Dave Moore. "If a horse spits the bit and wrings his tail every moment, the judge takes off points across the board."

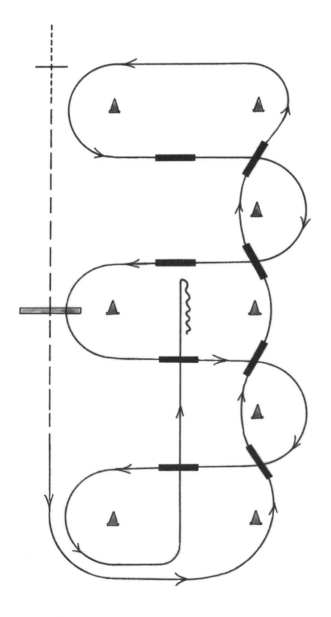

A typical Western Riding pattern: Walk. Jog over the log. Pick up the left lead, and lope through the cones performing eight lead changes, each in the wide black area indicated between cones.

The Big Show

In today's horse show industry, you know you've reached the top when you're in the running for a World Championship. Western equivalents to the Olympic games include a World Championship or National Championships.

Each Western breed has established its own pinnacle of success. Held in the summer or fall, these are invitational shows. Invitational means you qualify by earning a designated number of points.

Qualifying for the World can give you a focus for your show season. You don't even have to attend the big show, because just qualifying can satisfy your competitive aspirations. Geography, time, and finances also determine who goes and who doesn't.

The World Championship attracts thousands each year. Amateur champion Aloha Schneider explains that winning at the World may not mean first place, but maybe an eighth, ninth, or even twelfth. "It's the reward of winning at that level. Nothing can replace that exhilarating feeling of beating the best. When you wait for those final results, you say, 'I made it. I did it.' It's a personal accomplishment that you and your horse went that far." Schneider and her Paint, Bright Miracle, were ninth in the nation in Western Riding in 1990.

Many national and regional associations sponsor futurities. A futurity is an event for a specific age group of horses, usually two- or three-year-olds. Some futurities offer classes for four-year-olds, called a maturity or a derby. You pay nomination fees to maintain your horse's eligibility.

Futurities offer substantial prize money and prestige, so they attract professional horsemen. The National Reining Horse Association Futurity awards $100,000 to the winner of the Open event. Most futurities also include an amateur or non-pro division.

At breed shows, you can earn points toward lifetime performance awards. For example, your Quarter Horse could win the Register of Merit (ROM), AQHA Champion, Versatility Champion, or AQHA Superior horse in a specific event.

When qualifying for any prize, consider the effect on your horse. You'll probably work with your trainer to schedule your season. Once you've earned sufficient points to qualify, you might let your horse relax.

Realize that you increase pressure on your horse by concentrating on "the World." Decide if chasing points is worth the price you pay, and if this goal helps or hinders your development as a horseman.

Western Riding Strategy

Study the current association rulebook to review the pattern and the penalties that apply for faults. At the show, analyze the course and watch the ring crew set the markers. How close are they to the fence, and what's the distance between them? That spacing determines the number of strides between lead changes and varies from 30 to 50 feet.

Moore has noted that the judge may adjust the course to the caliber of riders. "Part of the judge's job is to make the horses look good. If four horses are entered, and you see that during the warmup not one is doing a flying lead change, spread out the markers a little. Don't set the cones at 29 feet,

11 inches if you have five kids who are just starting out. Or if you have both a junior and senior class, spread the markers for the junior class."

Because this class emphasizes the flying lead change, your horse should perform this maneuver. All association rules penalize horses that perform only a simple change of lead. You may receive a deduction for breaking gait, or be disqualified.

Be ready to start as soon as the previous entry stops and backs. To keep the show moving, expect the judge to be ready for you.

Once you start the pattern, don't rush. Aloha Schneider, whose Paint, Bright Miracle, won every Western Riding class entered in 1989: "Get right on target for your very first change. If you're one stride off, it will throw you off the entire pattern. Get your rhythm going for a smooth pattern."

The log can cause errors on course. You cross it twice, once at the jog and once at the lope. The log intimidates many contestants, as it can signal the horse to change gait, speed up for the turn, or "pop" (change) his lead.

Practice loping circles with the log, and change sizes of the log to keep your horse alert. You want to adjust his striding so he meets the log in stride.

John Higginson has advised: "Don't try to rate the horse. Let him find his place. Watch that he doesn't try to drop the shoulder and cut the log, because he knows there's a turn afterwards."

Be ready for the halt at the end of a pattern. Bring your horse to a balanced, not a sliding, stop, with his shoulders lifted and hind end underneath. He'll be prepared to back up when you give the cue.

Mastering the Flying Change of Lead

The athletic horse easily changes his leading leg when he shifts direction at the lope or gallop. In mid-air, he shifts all four legs, so he changes from left to right lead in one stride.

The flying change should appear effortless, so that the horse flies smoothly. The Western horse shouldn't leap into the air, but change flat, or close to the ground. His legs, not his body, perform the maneuver as he glides into the change. The movement occurs during suspension, and the horse appears light and airy. He doesn't scramble or bobble.

Western Riding, Reining, and Working Cow Horse classes judge this maneuver, and horses in timed events also change leads at the gallop. Changing leads reinforces the horse's respect for

Come to a balanced stop with the horse's shoulders lifted and his hind end underneath.

Cross the pole in the center, allowing the horse to meet it in stride at the lope.

the rider and encourages him to wait for your command.

Trainers stress that you change the lead, not the direction. Your horse should look straight ahead during the transition, and his body moves on a straight line. You turn in the new direction *after* you've changed the lead.

Apply diagonal aids to move the horse's body into the new lead. You'll apply your outside leg and inside flexion rein, with support from the outside brace rein. Time your leg with the stride, during the third beat of the lope. The horse's leading forefoot prepares to land, and he'll switch during the moment of suspension.

Practice for a smooth lead change by schooling the two-track at the walk. Move your horse to the right with left leg and right rein. You use your leg to move the hip, then your rein to move the shoulder. By holding up the outside (in this case, right) rein, you pick up the shoulder so the horse doesn't drop it.

Oregon trainer Tom Sorensen has explained how the horse's hips change position. "The hip should move only eight inches in most horses. Once the hip moves over, the horse will change.

Don't move the hip too much to get off center, and see how many strides it takes you to get each hip to move from your leg. Is your horse stiffer on the right? If so, you'll need to start the change sooner to the right than to the left."

Lateral control of the hip produces the lead change. At the lope, use this two-tracking movement through the transition from one lead to the other. John Higginson has instructed: "Loping to the right, as you come through to close the circle at the center, drop down to the jog. At the same time, two-track right. This picks up the inside shoulder and allows the horse to be light on the shoulder. It frees the hind end so he pushes off from the inside."

Jog a few steps, and cue for a left lead. When you achieve smooth simple changes, you can eliminate the jog steps. Your aids remain the same, moving the horse over so he switches leads in the air.

Sorensen recommends allowing more time for the loping horse to move hip and shoulder, generally about three times as long as walking. This could total 40 feet, so practice in a spacious area.

Casey Hinton teaches a similar exercise, the "circle drill," a simple change of leads performed

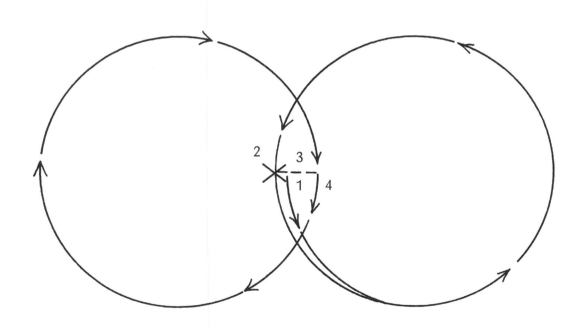

The "circle drill" exercise, described by Casey Hinton as a change of leads through the sidepass.

The Stresses of Serious Showing

When the stakes are high, the level of sport increases. Courses become more difficult, designed to test your mettle. You're surrounded by champions, and you may recognize big-name trainers in the pen. Show-ring nerves can plague anyone, even big names who often admit stage fright over riding in a huge arena with thousands of spectators watching.

At a championship, you'll cope with qualifying rounds. Here you have to make the cut, to score high enough so you compete in the finals.

Your go-round strategy varies according to the physical demands of the event. In pleasure, you show the best you can in every round. In a more demanding event like reining, you may compete to qualify, saving your horse for the final go-round. You pace yourself so your finals performance is your best.

You'll show before a group of judges at a big show like the World. Usually the rules dictate the dropping of high and low scores, so your score in a go-round reflects the average of two or three of the four or five judges. The posted score sheet indicates which judge awarded you which score.

To improve, you must overcome obstacles. Stress can help you progress when you deal with the setbacks that hinder your program. The atmosphere of the venue, the presence of prominent competitors, and the scrutiny of the media all intensify the show environment. Parental expectations may intimidate junior exhibitors.

"A lot of riders get stressed to the limit," Chuck Briggs has said. "They just choke under pressure, and make errors they wouldn't normally make, or they panic and overreact. For the good ones, it's just like another horse show."

At a show like the World, you may perform before four or five judges.

Realize that even the best riders make mistakes or have off days. Push away fear as you build your skill and confidence level.

Meet the challenge through grace under pressure. Amateur rider Jill Pennau demonstrated a champion's philosophy at the 1993 AQHA World. She went first in the Finals for Senior Western Riding, and while she watched 14 others try to beat her score, she said, "Whatever I score or place won't affect how I feel about me or my horse. I show for fun, not the awards ceremony. And it's always fun, trying to beat myself. I don't worry about others in the class." (Her score held, and she won that World Championship.)

The athlete persists, regardless of momentary setbacks. A rider continues showing, without panicking or making excuses, no matter what the disruption.

Champion amateur rider Lela Kay French has advised: "I always put forth my best effort whenever I go in a class, and I expect the best out of [my horse] Kings Copy Cat. Sometimes it works, and sometimes it doesn't. Sometimes he or I get sidetracked."

Nancy Cahill shares her philosophy: "There's another show tomorrow, and the next day, and the day after that. There's another World show next year. If it doesn't work one year, you come back and try it again. That's your goal for next year."

through the sidepass. He compares the change to the upward transition to the lope, concentrating on positioning the hip.

"The key is the start of the lopeoff, because the hip starts the lead change. Try to make your change come from the hip when you first teach it. You position the horse with your outside rein, because that rein and your leg push his body away from the pressure. You steer the head and body into position."

If you lope to the right, stop and sidepass to the right with your left rein and leg. Keep the horse's chin in during the sidepass, to maintain control during the lope.

Release the cue of your left leg, and apply pressure with your right (outside) leg and rein to put the horse into the left lead. Ensure that he lopes from the hip by emphasizing the "push" with your outside leg. You should feel the hip "jump" slightly as the horse responds.

"All you add is an extra little 'body English' on the hip when you change your leg," noted Hinton.

The horse that ducks his shoulder into the circle loses his balance. If he leans on the straightaway, he's likely to change with the forehand first. Instead of changing from the hip, he'll throw his shoulder into the change.

Correct this fault by steering with the outside rein. The outside rein positions the horse to change. Also, don't try to "help" your horse by shifting your weight. You can throw him off balance, and he may change only in front.

Some trainers teach riders to count strides to move the horse's hip over. You can count backwards, such as "4, 3, 2, 1, change." Count as the horse's front feet hit the ground, in order to form the habit of proper timing. This maneuver demands body control and coordination. Even if you are riding a seasoned horse, you will need a coach to talk you through the stages of the lead change.

How does the judge rate the smoothness of the changes? Dave Moore has advised: "If a horse is truly natural, a truly great changer going forward, the whole pattern will flow. Watch the topline — the topline will not change. The greatest lead changers that I have seen are horses that as they lope across the pen, if you put your hand over their legs and watch the topline, you won't know when the lead change happens."

He looks for a consistent cadence in the lope, before, during, and after the change. The three beats remain rhythmic, without changing pace or adding an extra "skip" to the change due to a lack of impulsion.

"Failure to change behind is one of the hardest things to see," Moore has said. "Many times it is just a half second. There are three ways a horse can change leads: hind first, front and hind at the same time, or front feet first. Some judges believe that the hind lead first is the hardest way. Therefore, they reward them. I think that some horses are more natural, and it's easier for them to change hind leads first."

12

Showing Your Working Horse

The action accelerates when you move into events that display the essence of the working horse. In reining, working cow horse, and cutting, your horse shows fancy footwork as you gallop, pivot, whirl, and stop.

In these events, your horse performs the maneuvers he'd use working stock on a ranch. Cowboys relied on skilled horses to separate cattle from the herd for branding, doctoring, or to drive to market.

These events follow a pattern and demand rhythm and grace, but at a rapid clip. Here the degree of difficulty enters the judging criteria.

These events share certain elements: a trained horse, a secure, confident rider, and the need for professional instruction. Luck also plays a part in the cattle events, as the cow acts as an unpredictable (and often unwilling) member of the performance.

To try any of these demanding events, you need a finished horse. A veteran will teach you the feel of the maneuvers. Once you've developed your ability, then you could move to a younger horse, working under a trainer's supervision.

The horse should be well muscled and stout in the hind legs. He won't be too tall, will have short cannons and hocks set low to the ground, and yet will have a long stride with "reach."

All three events require a horse with the speed and strength to stop hard. Reiner Todd Sommers finds that stopping and turning require natural ability. He has said: "A horse either has the talent to stop, or he doesn't. I can teach a horse to circle and change leads, but if he doesn't have the natural ability to stop, it's hard. It's somewhat conformation and somewhat the mind. If a horse doesn't have a strong back and strong hip, he's not able to stop."

In these events, you and your horse learn to "click," to work together with precision. When you call on him to turn sharply at a high lope, you know he'll respond to your cue. The thrill

	Reining	Working Cow Horse	Cutting
CLASS ROUTINE	Execute a set pattern, using markers set up along the fence. 9 NRHA patterns include run, sliding stop, flying change of lead, spins, rollbacks.	Perform a reining pattern. Within 2 minutes, work a single cow: "Box" the cow (hold it at one end of the pen), turn it along the fence, and drive it in circles.	Within 2½ minutes, separate cow from the herd and keep it in the middle of the pen; repeat with 1 or 2 more cows, as time permits.
IDEAL PERFORMANCE	Agile horse performs the pattern calmly, speeds up and slows on cue, without anticipating.	Horse controls the cow through the pattern.	Horse quickly separates a cow, then controls its every attempt to rejoin the herd. Horse mirrors every movement as he faces off cow, so it gives up trying.
HORSE	Quiet, yet alert and immediately responsive Shows "sting" (controlled speed with impulsion) Accepts pressure and forgives rider	Same as reiner in "dry" work In cow work, waits for you to guide him Shows courage in facing off the cow at speed	Moves just enough to control the cow Concentrates with intent expression Works on his own
RIDER	Guides horse's every move, yet sits quietly in balance	Same as reiner Thinks fast and watches the clock	Guides horse into herd Indicates cow Drops reins and lets horse work Cues horse with body and legs, mirroring cow's next movement
ASSOCIATION	National Reining Horse Association (also breed associations)	National Reined Cow Horse Association (also breed associations)	National Cutting Horse Association

of performing precise maneuvers or handling a tough cow brings you closer to your horse.

REINING

Reining is a team effort between two partners. The horse provides the athletic ability to perform the separate actions of the pattern. You not only guide him, you control his every move by setting direction and speed.

Some horsemen define reining as "cowboy dressage." Like dressage, you pursue an accurate, perfect run, yet the discipline has a unique American twist. You demand more from the horse, who performs "off" the bridle and holds his frame without rein contact. You pitch the slack to him and guide with your weight and slight movements of the outside rein.

Reiner Tim McQuay has said: "Reining started out to be the best broke horse won. Now you also

In the sliding stop, the horse gallops full out and then shifts his balance backwards. He drops his hindquarters while elevating his forehand.

need style and charisma." Winners express an elegance through the pattern, ears up and listening to the rider's every communication.

The Ideal Reining Horse

A top reining horse moves easily through the series of maneuvers. He follows a rhythm, moving from lope to gallop, gallop to lope. He maintains a steady head position and consistent balance in all phases of the pattern.

He forms round circles that match in size. He gallops the large circles with speed, then "shuts off" and gracefully lopes the small circles. Never anticipating, he shows a definite change in speed and arc.

The turnaround, also called the "spin," is a series of 360-degree turns. The horse pivots rapidly in one direction, planting one rear foot and sweep-

ing his forequarters in a circle. His outside front foot crosses over his inside front foot. Ideally he "gets in the ground" and spins flat. He "spins a hole in the ground," while his pivot foot remains stable.

As he completes a maneuver, the horse pauses. He demonstrates that he calmly waits for the next cue, and he shows obedience by a total lack of resistance.

In the spectacular sliding stop, he gallops full out and then shifts the center of his balance backwards. He drops his hindquarters under him, breaking at the loin right behind the saddle pad, while he elevates his forehand. His front legs "walk" close to the ground while his hindquarters squat and legs brace to skate "11s" in the ground. The faster he gallops, the further he'll slide. When he

Costumed
free-style rider
Shelly Reis
performs
a spin.

KATHY KADASH

Freestyle Reining

Most reining pros are men, and men also dominate the non-pro ranks. In freestyle reining, women riders shine in the difficult art of combining movements, music, and theater in a four-minute routine.

Freestyle requires technical specifications and adds choreography for artistic merit. NRHA rules state a minimum of specified reining maneuvers. Riders may ride two-handed and add additional spins, stops, and lead changes. Spectators' applause counts toward the score in freestyles run under NRHA rules.

Freestyle events reward ingenuity. At the 1993 Paint World Championships, freestyle contenders dazzled a packed house in Fort Worth. The blend of costumes, music, lighting, and drama featured characters like Batman and the Devil. A standout was "Fireman," where Shelly Reis, wearing a fireman's cape, costumed her horse completely in a red blanket. When her country music switched to "Great Balls of Fire," she removed her cape to reveal a svelte dress for spins and slides.

comes to a halt, he straightens his hocks and stands in a balanced position.

Besides style, the horse must have mettle and "sting," or the desire and willingness to take the pressure of an increased degree of difficulty.

A good reining horse wants to perform, and he'll guide easily on a loose rein. An eager performer may be hard to find, so take care of him by thoughtful riding.

Speed affects some horses. You want a horse that won't "run out of air," but not one that's "on the muscle" and won't settle. He accepts speed and discipline.

"Everything becomes more difficult the faster you go," trainer Jim McCarty has said. "Your horse has to react to your cues immediately. He doesn't say, 'Let me think about it,' so you have to cue him again, or . . . a third time. By then it's too late."

If you sour your horse — that is, push him for more speed than he can handle — he can become lazy or even crazy. He may be either too hot or he may want to quit, and so he tries to evade working the pattern in a smooth manner. Instead of that bright expression, he'll look cranky with his tail and start cheating. He could hang up in a turn or back up in a stop.

	Reining/Cow Horse	Cutting
SADDLE	Tree stays flat on horse's back in stops and turns. Close-contact seat keeps you in balance with the horse. Seat distributes your weight over your seat and feet. Seat design holds you snugly, or lets you shift your weight. Stirrups swing forward easily.	Flat, deep seat, close to horse's back Wide swells support you when horse moves abruptly. Narrow fenders swing easily. Tall (4") horn to hold for support Oxbow stirrups
BRIDLE	Grazing bit (California-style curb bit and closed reins in cow horse)	One-ear bridle Grazing bit
BOOTS	Splint boots and bell boots in front Skid boots in rear Or white boots all 4 feet	White boots, all 4 feet
ATTIRE	Shotgun chaps Spurs	Batwing chaps Spurs

Preparing for Reining

The National Reining Horse Association breaks each pattern into seven or eight separate segments, and you aim for precision in each section. Trainer Joe King has explained: "You want the horse light through your leg and through your hands. You should be able to ask, not spur, to make him turn. You pick up on the reins and ask him to move to the right by laying the rein across the neck. Or you say 'whoa' before you start to pick up on the reins, and he'll start to stop."

Practice the maneuvers, but mix them, without going through a complete pattern very often. Like the Western riding horse, a reiner can learn to anticipate your next move.

Don't drill the horse too long or too often in the same place. "Any horse's attitude will change if pressured," California trainer Mike Baker has commented. "Give him a break from the arena, and don't teach too many routines at once."

Your trainer will coach you through schooling sessions, helping you keep your horse polished

When you perform the change of lead, lope a straight line through the middle so you form smooth arcs instead of sharp turns.

and assisting you in the fine points of this demanding sport.

Circles

While schooling, you ride with two hands. Practice rating the speed, and maintain a slight arc for even circles, with your horse between the reins. Lope a straight line through the middle, where you perform the change of lead, so you form smooth arcs instead of sharp turns.

Trainer Gary Ferguson feels that circles pose difficulty for most riders. "It's easy to teach someone to stop and turn, but not to keep them slow, quiet, and relaxed in their circles. I'm a big fan of real pretty circles. In the pattern, it's the longest thing you do, and if you do it pretty you can really mark."

When performing a spin, keep an equal amount of pressure on both reins, pulling the inside rein out to the side a little. It is the neck rein that moves the shoulders as you apply some outside leg.

For the lead change, the horse has to be in position after completing one circle, ready to change and begin the next one. Ferguson said: "It's a fast thing that happens quickly, and there's a lot of room for error. You have a lot of body position and two-tracking motions, so there's four or five stages that you teach before that one simple maneuver."

Reiner Randy Paul has noted how riders lose the flow of the maneuver. "They turn the horse too hard in the lead change, rather than asking the horse to change. If the horse is trained properly, it's not a problem if you just ask. Mostly it's with the hand, as far as steering in the circle or to start a turn. If the rider doesn't wait for the horse and he moves his hand too hard, he locks up the horse."

By locking up, Paul means pulling the nose to the outside of the turn while pulling back. This abrupt neck rein ruins the bend and can affect the horse's balance.

Spinning

The spin begins with the suppling exercises that help the horse to bend his whole body. In essence, it is a turn on the haunches, or a pirouette, that you perform using the outside neck rein and inside direct rein, and then follow through with your outside leg.

Your aids keep the pivot foot (inside hind) isolated, so it remains locked down while the other three feet push the horse around it. The result is lateral control over the horse's spine.

Practice the spin by walking in a small circle and pushing the shoulder so the horse gets off his outside hind foot. Feel him rock back on his hindquarters as he rolls over his inside hind foot.

Trainer Tom Sorensen: "Any time the horse leans on your neck rein, use your outside leg. Keep an equal amount of pressure on both reins, but pull the inside rein out to the side a little. Your neck rein moves the shoulder as you apply some outside leg. Straighten the horse's body during the turn, and you have a turnaround."

The horse should step flat and maintain a steady rhythm to turn in one motion. Mike Baker has said: "You want him to relax his neck and shoulder. If they're relaxed, the rest of the body will follow."

Teach your horse to stop from leg pressure, combined with a slow, gentle pull of the reins.

He notes that the horse has to drop down into the turn, not spin halfway and then jump or fall into the move with the rest of his body. Your outside calf drives the horse into the turn, so the horse crosses over his inside front foot with the outside front foot. You feel him crouch with the hind legs, or "sit down" as he bends his hocks and turns. With your outside leg active, he stays in motion for a complete 360 degree.

Stopping

Always ask your horse to stop, without force or punishment. Practice the stop at the walk, collecting the horse so you drive the hind end far underneath his body. You feel him lock both hips in place and push his loin into the ground.

Sorensen: "The horse stops one hind leg, then the other. So you stop him one leg at a time. You want one hip, then the other, to go into the ground."

He teaches horses to stop from leg pressure, in combination with a slow, gentle pull of the reins. This encourages the horse to lighten, not pull back. Your leg encourages the horse to back off, not lean on the bridle.

Your job is to stop your horse with finesse. Saying "Whoa," you let the horse stop while you settle into the saddle with your weight in the stirrups. Look for your feet to remain steady so you don't bounce. When you're learning the stop, you can brace on the horn.

"Keep your balance stabilized," Mike Baker has advised. "You want to get the movement done and then recover. Sit right down, grip with your thighs and knees, and follow the horse in. By keeping your weight vertical or slightly back, you will avoid teaching the horse to push off his front end."

At the lope, time your request when the horse's hind legs come up under him. Ask for the stop during the third beat of the stride. Here the lead leg hits the ground, and the hind legs are in position.

Don't hold back, then burst into a run for only the last strides before you stop. This could train your horse to "scotch," or start to stop before you tell him.

Footing can help or hinder the slide. The ground should be smooth, not too damp or deep, which can hold the horse down so he has to dig into the dirt. Trainer Dolly Wallace has explained: "Ideally you want ground hard on the bottom, and soft and fluffy on top. The horse can get through the top layer and slide on the ground without sticking, as if he's wearing roller skates."

The Rollback

You could define this turn as doubling at the lope, or as a combination of the stop and turn. You lope one direction, then ask for a half-turn. You drive the horse into and through the turn, so he jumps right into the lope.

Your horse should look handy, or "catty," in this maneuver. He bends into the turn with suppleness, turning on his hocks with his front legs close to the ground to maintain his momentum. A common problem is to hang up in the rollback, or fail to push off.

Time your stop to the horse's gait. At the lope, Mike Baker has advised using a voice command as the horse starts into a stride. "He should be on the ground, so he can push with his body. He shouldn't

To practice the rollback, lope along a fence, check before you turn, and turn toward the rail.

be in mid-stride, or he'll shorten the stride." Your horse may need a second to respond, but you should feel him giving to your aids and pushing with the loin to gather himself.

The stop affects the quality of the rollback. Your horse has to be on the ground to stop and turn back, so look for his front feet to be close to the ground.

Many trainers practice the rollback along a fence line. Lope along the fence, check before you turn, and turn toward the rails. The check teaches the horse to react to your cue. The unpredictable request keeps him thinking about you and listening to you.

Your Position in the Saddle

A balanced horse works off the hindquarters and keeps his shoulders up when he turns. If he drops a shoulder when galloping, or leans his weight into it, he loses impulsion from the hindquarters and falls onto the forehand. He could resist with a counterarc (bending to the outside of a turn), get out from under you, or lose his footing.

Keep your horse bent correctly with your two reins and two legs. The position you achieve at a slower gait remains consistent in the gallop. Lift the horse with your inside rein, and push with the inside leg to keep the bend.

You need to ride aggressively and know when to signal for instant acceleration. Sit square and solid so you can stay in place. You'll change your seat slightly as you progress from the more sedate classes. A reining horse moves with a higher head position than a pleasure horse, driving forward as he extends and collects.

Gary Ferguson has explained how the reiner's vertical position differs from that of the pleasure rider's. "Reiners stay behind their horses and keep everything out in front. You sit differently, further back with your shoulders. You drop your heels more and sit your tailbone harder down into the saddle."

Reining Strategy

To remember and ride a correct, fluid pattern, focus on performing each movement without mak-

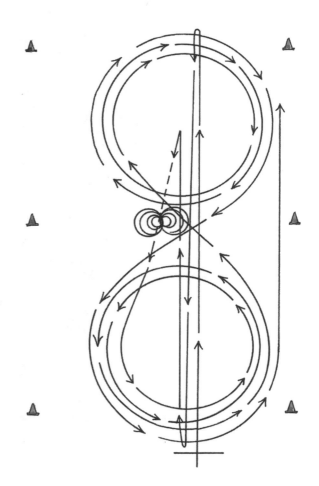

Reining patterns look confusing on paper. This one contains these maneuvers: 3 rundowns, the first two with sliding stop and rollback, the third one with a backup. Two sets of spins — 4 to the right, 4¼ to the left. Three circles on the left lead — large-fast, small-slow, and large-fast. Lead change. Three circles on the right lead — large-fast, small-slow, large-fast. Lead change, large fast circle, rundown, and sliding stop.

ing a mistake or going too fast. Rookie reiners tend to rush. "The biggest problem I see is trying to get the riders to slow their hands down, and ask the horse to do things rather than try to make it happen," Randy Paul has commented. "Especially in the show pen, the old adrenaline gets pumping, and they want to jump right in to the next maneuver after they finish one, instead of letting the horse settle."

yourself, 'Am I riding in the right position? Am I pushing hard enough?' as you ride the circles."

Keep thinking through your pattern. Count your turns in the spin, to be sure you stop at the right spot. Watch that you stop your horse past the cones set as markers.

As you perform a pattern, you gain instant appreciation for your maneuvers. You'll know you're doing well when spectators eagerly cheer good circles, rollbacks, and sliding stops. The thrill of masterful reining makes the sport fun for all participants!

WORKING COW HORSE

In the working cow horse event, you orchestrate a routine, directing the actions of a single cow (or steer) through your horse. He demonstrates his physical ability to control the animal, while he obeys your cues.

The cow adds an unpredictable element, and speed increases the challenge. Ideally you perform in synchrony, with the three of you moving as a unit through the class routine.

This class demands physical fitness and mental sharpness. When you and your horse challenge the speed and instincts of the cow, you find yourself in the toughest and most exciting contest in the horse show.

"There are very few people who have the guts to run down the fence wide open," Oklahoma trainer Carl McCuistion has said. "There's a lot that you need to know. It can be dangerous if you don't know what you're doing."

Exact requirements vary among show associations, yet basically all prescribe the following segments:

1. Perform a reining pattern, also known as "dry" work.
2. The chute crew release a cow into the show pen. You "box" the cow by holding it at the end of the arena to show that the horse can contain a cow.
3. When a buzzer sounds, you move the cow down the fence, the long side of the pen, at a

Prevent this common mistake by breaking a pattern into maneuvers. Do each one, one at a time, and hesitate in between. Give your horse a chance to fill up on air and to relax for a moment.

"You remember to slow down, to show the horse the way you trained it," Tim McQuay has said. "You're not only trying to control the brain of the horse, but you've got to control yourself. I say, 'This is the run I want to have, and I don't care what the other riders do. If it's second, it's second. I want to stick to a plan.'"

Circles give you time to think. For example, AQHA pattern 2 begins with two circles to the right. "You can get your composure and relax in those circles," Gary Ferguson has explained. "It takes a long time to run those circles — it's not like the run-around and stop, where you blink your eye and it's over. You have plenty of time to ask gallop. Nearing the opposite end, you overtake the cow and block it to make it turn to run the other way along the fence line. Again pass the cow and cause it to turn back, going in its original direction.

4. Maneuver the cow to an open area of the arena, and circle it once. Slow behind the cow, change leads, and circle the cow again in the other direction. The judge blows a whistle, signaling time. Most events allow two minutes for cow work.

McCuistion has said: "You've got to have a horse with speed, that stops hard, a horse that is really trainable so he can handle running that cow, stop on a dime, and go back the other way again. It's both mental and physical for the horse. You can have a really talented horse with no brains, so that when he gets to running he might not watch that cow."

A good cow horse responds to your guidance while "reading" the cow. He watches the cow and when you touch the rein on his neck, he knows to turn and head the cow.

Judges look for a horse that moves in balance at all times, able to shift his weight, stop with all four feet on the ground, and change directions smoothly. In the holding, they want to see the horse "settle" the cow, to control it without disturbing it and to gauge its personality.

You should feel the horse "crouch" down on a cow, as he and the cow size up each other. Trainer Bob Wallace has described this: "You want the horse to move on his hind feet, keeping his front end up. He should roll back over his hocks, 'sweeping' his forehand as he moves with the cow."

Down the fence, the horse must pace, overtake, and turn the animal. His body follows his nose, as he intently focuses on the cow's actions. He thrusts through the turns, driving his hind pivot foot well under his body, and his forequarters wheel to block the cow.

Wallace saw reining and working cow horse as complementary events. He explains: "A cow horse has to run hard, stop straight, and roll over his hocks. We like to go on and make working cow horses out of our reining horses. While the horse learns to work cattle, he stops, collects and extends, turns off his hindquarters, and changes leads. He does everything we want in reining, but it's not dry work."

You should learn from an experienced trainer, who will coach you in the basics. Your own sea-

The Non-Pro Reiner

The sport approaches art in the hands of the masters, and yet it's accessible to pros and amateurs alike. As a non-pro, you ride the same NRHA patterns as the pros, and you too can savor the thrill of a horse sliding 40 feet to a stop.

Florida non-pro Angelo Berrettini, a reiner since 1986, has explained the sport's appeal. "Riding a good reining horse is probably one notch better than driving a superior sports car. You're on the back of a living, breathing thing. When you do it, you get this rush. When you get one that turns around like a helicopter blade, the first couple times it makes you dizzy in the saddle."

NRHA non-pro classes are organized so you ride against other amateurs at your same level. And if you've earned less than $100 in NRHA, you can compete as a Rookie Non-Pro.

Berrettini speculated on why other non-pros compete at high-pressure, big-money events like the NRHA Futurity, noting that many are successful businessmen. "They're looking for some release, to be competitive in more of a one-on-one challenge. It's another vent for that drive, and they love to win."

A cutting horse should move on his hind feet, keeping his front end up and "sweeping" his forehand in movement with the cow.

soning through competition enhances your ability to work a cow successfully in the pen.

Sizing Up a Cow

Smart or dumb? Cattlemen and horsemen debate the issue of bovine intelligence, which some consider an oxymoron. Cows look dumb, and as herd animals, they opt for the security of the crowd. Yet individuals cows vary in their eternal contest with the mounted horseman. A cow can quickly learn the game, and then refuse to play. (Rules of the NCHA specify "fresh" cattle that haven't been used in cutting.)

First of all, you'll rarely encounter a "cow" in cattle events. Cow horses and cutters usually work yearling heifers or steers. Yearlings tend to be more unpredictable than mature cattle. You won't handle bulls.

The beef cattle you'll meet are semi-wild animals. They generally avoid humans. If you walk behind a cow, it will usually move away from you when you enter its "space." Most cows have learned to yield to a horse and allow him to drive them.

The horse is larger than the cow (a yearling weighs about 450 pounds, compared to your 1,100-pound horse). The horse also has a longer stride and can outrun the cow to push it in the direction you set.

The cow you work affects how you score, so you'll need to learn to "read" a cow. Usually when you and your horse approach a cow face to face, it will move backwards. From the rear, the cow will give ground and move forward.

You want a cow that's active yet controllable. In events like cutting, the cow determines the degree of difficulty and thus influences your score. You want a cow that looks lively, not a "sorry" cow or one that will charge you.

In many events, you'll draw your bovine "partner," and you're stuck with handling whatever you get. (Only in cutting do you have a choice.) You can deal with a cow by recognizing its breed and attitude.

Breeds differ in their personalities. You'll encounter docile English breeds such as the Hereford, Shorthorn, or Aberdeen Angus. Some riders feel that the Charolais is a smarter breed, with Limousin and Simmental less intelligent. In general, cattle of the Brahma lines act more feisty and high-strung. When you see long ears and a slight hump, you've met a Brahma cross. Team ropers often use Mexican cattle like the Corriente. Calf ropers may prefer Charolais and whiteface cattle, and want to avoid Longhorn calves that run full speed and won't slow down.

Cows can get "riled up" (nervous) before you meet them. When handlers move cattle to the arena, they can stress the animals by yelling at them, hitting them, or using cattle prods. Cattle may stand quietly in a holding pen waiting for the event, and then a chute crew chases them into a chute.

As herd animals, cattle like to stick together. The mood of the herd affects individuals. Dominant animals set the tone, and a wild heifer can make your job more difficult. A wild cow may run haphazardly; it could be fearful or downright cantankerous.

Weather also affects cattle. In cold temperatures cattle are more likely to run. In the heat, they may "sull" (refuse to move) or resist the horse's dominance.

You can't control what happened to a cow before you meet up, but you can observe its mood. Try to predict if it's sensible, wild, or dull. Watch the animal's eyes, ears, tail, and head angle. Do the eyes appear placid and the neck relaxed? Does it appear curious or interested? Or do you see a panicked expression and a raised tail? (That steer's ready to "high-tail" away from you!)

Champion youth cutter Kim Verville has explained: "The cow can be standing dead still, and you look at it to try to figure out which way it's going to go, so you know how to ride your horse. If the cow twitches an ear, or moves its head slightly, or flicks its tail, you know it's fixing to move."

When your horse runs eye-to-eye with the cow, watch the cow. It will tell you when it's ready to stop. "Usually there's some sign that the cow's going to slow down or stop," Carl McCuistion has commented. "Sometimes it will throw its head up, or cock an ear. You can watch the eye, and you see the eye look back at you."

In cattle events, you pay a cattle charge. This covers the rental of the livestock. Ideally the cattleman provides fresh animals, which haven't been used for this event before. The cows haven't learned how to avoid the horse, so they should play their parts.

"Cattle become aware of what the game is," Texas cutter Barbara Schulte has said. "They become desensitized to a horse. In the beginning they are intimidated by a horse, curious about him, and they respond to him."

Cow Sense

When a horse has cow sense, he demonstrates an eagerness to work cattle and the urge to control a cow's movement. He has the will to challenge a cow, and he also shows an affinity for matching wits with it. Cattle events stress a horse, as he must put forth maximum effort to block the escape of a wily cow. The horse must have the desire to drive forward and turn the cow, and the athletic ability to maintain mastery.

Your horse will tune into the cow's mind. A "cowy" horse instinctively reacts to a cow and anticipates what it will do next. Trying to figure out its next move, he stays with the cow and matches his strides to the cow's.

Dominating a cow doesn't mean attacking it. In any cattle event, the horse shouldn't touch a cow. (Contact is sometimes unavoidable during the fence work and circling of the working cow horse class but it doesn't result in the loss of points.) Cattle resent being pressured, so the horse can control a cow the same as he would another horse, through implied threats. The cowy horse knows how close to move to direct a cow, without scaring it by invading its comfort zone.

Positioning Your Horse

To practice for this event, you learn to position your horse in relation to the cow. The two of you follow the cow's movements, yet you cause the cow to go in a certain direction. Your trainer might have you first practice the basic maneuvers of fencework and circling on another rider. Learn this event on a trained horse, one that's worked cattle and

The "cowy" horse knows how to direct a cow without invading its comfort zone.

"thinks cow." He'll help you feel comfortable about learning to handle a cow. Start by driving a slow, gentle one at a walk, in a pen that's not too large. (You don't want the cow to run while you're learning.) Hold the cow a few moments along the fence, then trail it slowly down the fence. The ideal cow will move quietly, allowing your horse to follow its movements and remain in control.

Look for your horse to watch the cow, standing alertly until it moves. When the cow does turn and walk, ask the horse to step in the cow's path. (A good cow horse never "turns tail" to a cow.)

The veteran cow horse can help you learn position in relation to the cow, which is crucial in cow work. Usually you'll want to stay right with the cow, so your horse is eye-to-eye with it. Sometimes you want to be a step ahead.

Your horse shouldn't shoulder the cow, but rather intimidate it through body language. You don't want to run up on the cow or get too close, unless you need to "push" the cow to make it move.

Start the cow moving by positioning your horse near its hip. "You never want to crowd the horse to a cow," Bob Wallace has cautioned. "Just tiptoe when you go in, and very slowly enter the cow's area. Move just enough to get it moving."

Let this cow direct the action and set the speed. Place your horse beside it so the two animals move in unison along the fence line.

Wallace coached: "Get off the cow's hip so you drive it, but not enough to get your horse out of line. Stay in a straight line, head to head with your cow. As soon as you get the cow going, speed up and get around it, then turn it back against the fence."

Your horse needs to get in the ground and stop square, so he maintains position and doesn't overshoot the cow. (The cow might stop suddenly and bolt for the other side of the pen.) He can then turn around smoothly, to head the cow. He forces the cow to "switch ends." You can grab onto the horn when you turn, so you stay to the inside during

Keep your horse eye-to-eye with the cow.

the rollback. Otherwise, ride with two reins to keep your horse in position.

A common cow horse fault is incorrect position. This is your job, to rein your horse so he "rates" the cow. Place him within the controlling zone not too far or too close, too far ahead or too far back. With experience, you learn how to judge distance and rate each cow.

Guiding the cow through the circles and changing directions is probably the most difficult aspect of the routine. Here your horse really demonstrates his speed and ability to control the cow, while you determine the size and shape of the circles. You have to "hustle up" alongside some cows, or slow down to stay parallel with others.

This final sequence demands agility as the horse controls his balance while circling the cow. Where the two circles meet, slow him to drop behind the cow, change leads, and then accelerate to turn the cow in the new circle. The cow may not play along, so your horse has to speed up to get in position on the cow's opposite side.

Cow Horse Strategy

Judges look for smooth maneuvers that flow. They want to see the horse pick up the proper lead. Like reining, they penalize the horse that deviates from the ideal pattern. Don't run the cow so far that you exhaust it. You shouldn't lose control of the cow by running past it or allowing it to swerve. Crossing the cow's path or running over the cow and falling will terminate the routine.

When the cow enters the arena, let it start the action. Rein your horse two or three turnbacks to show his ability to keep the cow in one spot. Smoothly drive the cow down the fence, and demonstrate a minimum of reining.

Move the cow away from the fence for the circles. Here shoulder to shoulder is the pretty look that completes your run. You show your horse's maneuverability as he stays beside the cow and adjusts his speed if necessary.

NCHA

The National Cutting Horse Association offers cutters nine classifications:

- ★ Championship Open
- ★ Open
- ★ Championship Non-Professional
- ★ Non-Professional
- ★ Limit Amateur
- ★ Limit Non-Professional
- ★ $5,000 Limit Novice
- ★ $3,000 Limit Novice
- ★ Open Gelding

NCHA also offers classes of $2000 Limit and $5000 Novice Horse/Non-Pro. You must be a member to compete in NCHA events.

For scoring, you start with 70 points. The judge adds and subtracts points according to NCHA specifications. A good score would be around 72, with a 74 as excellent.

You gain credit for a smooth run, where your horse maintains position. Penalties accrue when you get out of position, go past the cow, or stop too soon. Your job is to know how much time to spend working a cow, and to display your boldness in mastering the cow.

Cutting is one of the richest sports, with 1,500 cuttings annually offering cash prizes that pay 17 million dollars. With rich prizes at stake, NCHA rules strictly govern competitions. NCHA videotapes all NCHA–approved classes.

The NCHA Futurity, held every December in Fort Worth, Texas, offers prize money of over one million dollars. At the Futurity and other prestigious contests, five judges score you separately. The scores are added, with the high and low discarded and the remaining three averaged.

Cutting attracts many wealthy sportsmen. When you compete in the Non-Pro division, you'll see a high quality of competition. Some of these riders have over 20 years' experience in the sport. NCHA's Amateur classification is for a non-professional who has won $20,000 or less.

CUTTING

Poise, confidence, and the desire for perfection define the successful cutter. This sport places you on stage, to take command of the cast of bovine characters in the pen. Once you set the stage, you allow the lead actor — your horse — free rein to perform on his own.

Cutting is an exercise in control. This event tests your horse's agility and cow sense. He sorts through the herd and dominates a single cow. His moves appear effortless when he maneuvers the cow to a showdown. With hard stops and fast turns, he matches every move. In the ultimate showdown, he dares the dazed cow to run but keeps it dead center in a standoff.

Cutting tests your partnership, and those smooth moves can spark an addiction for the sport. Barbara Schulte has described the appeal as "the adrenaline and the fact that you never really master it. It's the challenge of getting into harmony and synchrony, presenting a performance that's exciting that keeps us all hooked. If we experience that feeling once, we'll keep cutting for years just to get to do it again. The more you practice and learn, the more frequent those moments become."

In the pen you demonstrate your confidence and judgment. Non-pro cutter Ann Broussard, a student of Schulte's, has explained: "Most difficult, and most important, is the mental preparation. You have to work on it every time you show. If you're prepared, you'll think quickly and calmly. If you lapse, your reactions won't be as good when a situation's not perfect."

Cutting brings a cast of players on stage, with the cattle adding the degree of difficulty. In the 150 seconds you perform, you'll interact with most of the herd of two or three dozen cattle, your two herd holders, your two turnback men, and your horse. Mastering the variables and seeking a perfect run pose the challenge, and the ever-changing thrills of the pen attract thousands to this unique sport.

The action starts when you near the herd and quietly glide through them. National Cutting Horse Association (NCHA) rules require you to make at least one deep cut, to "peel out" (separate) half the cattle, and you'll probably make this cut your first time in the herd.

Driving a bunch, you focus on one particular cow. The others return to the herd until your choice remains. Gazing at this heifer, framed between your horse's ears, you commit to her and signal your choice to the judge, your helpers, and your horse by placing one hand on the horn and your rein hand flat on the horse's withers, with the reins slack. From then on you may not touch the reins, and you rely on your helpers to keep the other cows out of the way.

Now your horse takes over the drama, and you allow him to "play" the cow. It dodges left, and he mirrors the move till the cow stops. Intent on its body language, he fakes when it fakes and darts when it darts. Wherever it goes, he counters the action and gets there first, blocking any escape attempt.

"Cutting is different from other cow events because you have to put your hand down and let the horse do it," explained Schulte. "The rider has a lot of influence on how well the horse works, with seat and legs, but you still have to put your hand down. And with other events, whether it's jumping or working cow horse down the fence, you have a lot more time to plan what you're going to do. Cutting is moment to moment."

The horse's intensity captivates first-time cutters. Kim Verville has said: "On a regular horse, you just walk, trot, or lope when you show it. A cutting horse makes all these fancy moves, and it's a whole lot different. There's much more action, excitement, suspense, and challenge, because you never know what the cow's going to do next."

You know when to assert yourself and when to relinquish control to the horse. When you reach that harmony, you achieve an extreme level of sensitivity with your equine partner.

Cutting Practice

"Cutting requires concentration and the ability to respond appropriately, moment to moment," Schulte has said. Beginning cutters need to learn from experts, so you'll work with a coach. He'll help you handle the sport's unique physical and mental demands. You must have complete body control to remain upright in the saddle, no matter which direction your horse moves. Yet you ride with a supple spine, ready to flow with the horse.

You'll need a seasoned horse, one that's learned how to read cattle. Trainer Tom Lyons has explained how the horse helps a novice. "The amateur needs a good, solid, seasoned horse that has a record, that has won something, that has a lot of foundation on him and doesn't need a lot of training."

The horse influences the cow. By facing off a heifer, he mentally exerts power. He has the upper hand and brings the cow toward him. Every time he stops, he looks for the cow and guesses its next move.

You coordinate with your horse. In practice, you'll deal with the mechanics of following his moves and the techniques of herdwork. You'll ride your horse "cutting" such varied foes as a mechanical, remote-controlled cow, flags moving back and forth on a cable, goats, or people. A trained horse will work any of these, while you perfect the cutter's graceful seat.

Cutters sit loose and fluid in the saddle. As the horse shifts his weight, the cutter remains linked to the horse's pivot point. The horse moves low to the ground, sweeping his forehand to synchronize with the cow. The cutter floats with him, from one complete stop to the right to the next stop to the left. Your riding ability can help or hinder the horse. You help your horse "hold the line."

Lyons has noted how beginners unconsciously lean to the side, which upsets the horse's movement. "You need to sit straight up in the saddle. You can lean a little bit back, or a little forward, but you don't want to lean side to side. Keep your weight as centered as you can, right on top of that horse."

He adds that learning not to lean is very difficult because the momentum of the horse's movements encourages you to lean forward, or in the direction the horse is about to turn. If you're not sitting straight you can cause your horse to move incorrectly, or get out of position.

To counteract any leaning, you want to "mash down" (push) in the stirrups with toes out, heels

For a fluid seat, sit straight up in the saddle. Lean forward or back a little bit, but don't lean side to side. Keep your weight as centered as possible.

Barbara Schulte has explained: "In cutting, the picture changes from one moment to the next. You sit with your rear to get the horse to stop, and ride with your legs to get the horse to accelerate. The non-pro's biggest error is she gets out of rhythm, she doesn't use her legs at the appropriate time, or she might use her legs when she should be sitting. She has not had the practice at being quiet and mentally concentrating and being in the moment."

In cutting, you focus on your seat and aids. You shouldn't appear to cue the horse, but you may use leg pressure to help your horse start and turn.

"You get ready for the cow," said Kim Verville. "If you see the cow's going to go and your horse looks like he's not going to follow, you ride him over there with your legs."

Helpers in the Pen

Cutting is the only event where a team helps you in the pen. Your herd holders and turnback men help affect your performance. The herd holders help you get a clean cut. As you follow a bunch, they walk on each side to encourage unwanted cows to fan away and return to the herd. Once you've peeled out your cow, they keep the rest of the herd behind you, so no maverick cow tries to join the action.

Turnback men encourage the cow to face you. "They help pace the cow at a good amount of action," explained Schulte. "They keep the cow moving and as controlled in the center of the arena as possible." One of these can be your trainer, who will coach you how to approach the herd, maneuver decisively through the animals, and guide a cow away. You'll learn how to shift your position to drive a cow. Just pointing your horse to a cow won't "shape" it where you want it to be.

A herd of bunched cattle can intimidate you, if they're slow to move away from your horse. Schulte notes how self-assurance affects the cutter. "The more mastery and skill a person has, of being able to maneuver cattle and control groups as well as an individual cow, the more confidence she has in showing the horse. With time and studying and experience, there are certain ways of handling cattle that apply to different groups. Whether

down. Sit in the center of the saddle, envisioning it as a pocket. Feel your weight down in the stirrups when your horse "gets in the ground." Sitting in the pocket lets your horse pivot to turn sharply on his hindquarters. If he turns wide or incorrectly, he can lose control of the cow.

Lyons has advised to concentrate on improving basic horsemanship skills. "How you ride every day is usually how you're going to ride when you cut. You've got to do a lot of pushing back on the saddle horn instead of pulling forward in the stop." Pushing on the horn helps keep you in place.

You have to learn to let go when your horse works a cow. Leave him alone and trust his judgment, yet always remain alert. Instead of pushing a cow that tends to run, use your leg to move your horse back away from the cow. This can draw the cow toward you and the herd.

they're real slow, or really wild, or you're at the beginning of a group of cutters or at the end, that's all taken into account."

You set up a specific cow that's a clear distance away from the herd; you indicate to the judge that this is your choice; you drop your hand and commit to that animal.

Your horse keeps that cow in the middle of the pen to maintain the working advantage. While you work a cow, your herd holders and turnback men assist you in keeping control. You prevent the cow from out-maneuvering you. Cutting isn't chasing — you don't want the cow to run from wall to wall. When the "back fence" turns the cow, you lose points.

Watch for your trainer and the cow to tell you when to quit. "You have to quit legally," said Tom Lyons. "Lots of times you have to go longer than you'd like to, because the cow's not legal."

NCHA permits a quit when the cow has stopped or turned away from you. Don't lose a cow (let it run past you) or "hot quit" (turn away while it's facing you and in motion).

Cutting Strategy

What does the cutting judge look for? Barbara Schulte has listed three criteria: "Style, which is the overall grace and finesse; working time, or how long we actually spend working the cows; and degree of difficulty. How difficult was the cow cut? How much did that cow exert pressure to try to get back to the herd, and how well did you control the cow?"

At a cutting, you receive a start time in the order of draw. To prepare, you'll warm up your horse in a section of the pen, where riders wait behind the judges for their turn to cut. The judges watch the action from elevated platforms, sitting in towers or on chairs set in the beds of pickup trucks.

When a cattle change occurs between sets, riders bring in the herd and spend about 20 minutes settling them by the gate, centered between the side walls. Cutters want quiet cattle, so they can carefully separate animals for work.

At this time, you and your trainer watch the herd to pre-select the ones you want to cut. (You

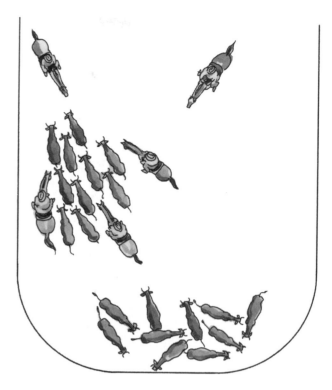

Here you "chip off" the cow you want to cut. Your herd holders guide the unwanted cattle out of the way.

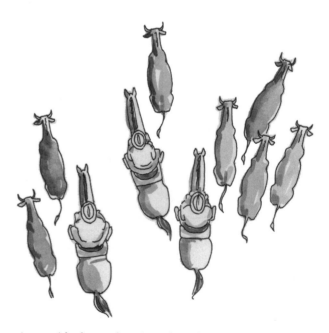

As you (the lowest horse) make a deep cut, your herd holders walk alongside the herd. The turnback men wait to assist in separating the cow you want to cut.

do have to learn to tell cows apart.) You want a cow that appears to respect a horse and lets your horse show his talents.

Schulte advised cutting a cow that shows less herd instinct than others. "That's the kind of cow we want to cut — a cow that wouldn't mind being separated and is more gentle."

If you're early in the working order, you'll be able to pick cows that no other rider has worked. NCHA rules require a herd of 2½ cows per entry. Say you're third to go out of 10, and the previous two riders cut two cows apiece. That leaves you 21 cows to choose from, ignoring the ones that already worked.

Avoid communicating anxiety to your horse. Tom Lyons has advised: "That's a big key between winning and losing, what you transmit to your horse. If you have a high-strung horse that's hanging by a thread, a professional might get him through a run and look real good but an amateur would never get through it."

Time begins when you cross an imaginary line indicated by markers on the walls. Sidle in to a herd from the left side, guiding the horse among the cows. Approach and split the herd without scattering the cattle, and move your choice a safe distance from the rest.

Judges look for the horse with expression, that displays enthusiasm and intensity as the cow "hooks up" with him. They want to see him match the cow step for step.

Maintain a positive attitude so you and your horse cope with the unpredictability of cows. Ideally the cow works for you, presenting the right amount of challenge, but it might be too wild or "soft," a lethargic type that simply tries to turn away. The turnback man on that side should push the cow back to you.

Your horse keeps his working advantage, or a correct position in response to the cow, facing head to head. He keeps his shoulders squared to the cow's, so he turns head, shoulders, rib cage with hindquarters engaged, over an outside pivot foot. If the cow dodges to the side, he moves with his head at the cow's neck. The cow turns, and the horse automatically has eye contact with it. He knows not to over- or under-estimate the cow's next move.

Work till the buzzer sounds, then proceed back across the time line before you dismount. The judge may request a bit inspection.

You should hear it when your score is announced or see it posted on the scoreboard moments after you cut. After your go, your trainer should explain how you could more effectively cut your cows. The two of you can watch your video so you understand what you could do to improve your score.

Timed Events

Dust flies as you and your horse attack the course. You sprint full out, collect to turn the first barrel, and gallop toward the next one aiming for the fastest time around the cloverleaf. This and the other timed events challenge you and your horse to run in perfect synchronization, as a single unit. Your decisive riding and your partnership with your horse shine in these fast-paced events.

In these contests, you run to and around a marker, usually a barrel or pole. The fastest time wins, yet agility contributes as much as speed: You'll be penalized if your horse gets too close to an obstacle and knocks it down. Weaving through poles and arcing around barrels requires a combination of rhythm, timing, and balance.

A horse of any breed (along with ponies and mules) can excel in timed events. You and your equine partner can start racing in play days or gymkhanas hosted by local riding clubs. If you win consistently, you can try betting your skills in a jackpot barrel race, where everyone contributes entry fees and the winners take home cash. The Josey World Champion Junior Barrel Race attracts young riders eager for a major prize.

Barrel racer Talmadge Green has mentioned a nurse who won $75,000 in one year of racing. "Even though your professionals still do well, the weekend amateur can go out and win if he has a good horse. In sports like golf or cutting, you have to pay your dues before you win."

He added that the possibilities have attracted more riders crossing over from other equestrian disciplines. "If you go out and work hard enough with a good horse, you don't need to be a big-name person to win."

Western breed associations also offer certain classes. Licensed judges oversee the action. Because Quarter Horses dominate the events, most associations follow the lead of the AQHA in their contest rules.

You might also compete in 4-H shows or rodeos, or in contests of the National Barrel Horse

Association, National Saddle Clubs Association, National Little Britches Rodeo Association, National High School Rodeo Association, or National Intercollegiate Rodeo Association. If you're ready to challenge the pros of barrel racing, you could join the Women's Professional Rodeo Association and follow the professional rodeo circuit.

Rules specify that timekeepers use electronic timers or at least two stop watches, to assure consistent clocking. Time begins and ends when the horse's nose crosses the starting line, also called the "timing line." (Most events are run down the arena and back to the start.) Riders have a running start in most events, depending on specific rules.

The typical events you'd enter are shown on the chart on the facing page.

Local clubs may offer additional races such as the sack race, boot race, and rescue race. The NSCA includes these in its pattern horse racing, called "O-Mok-See." This word, from the Blackfeet Indian tribe, can be loosely translated as "riding big."

FINE-TUNING YOUR HORSE

For speed events, you need an equine athlete that maintains both physical and mental balance. The ideal horse should instantly "shift gears." He has to leap into a gallop, collect himself to slow down, and halt willingly. He has the impulsion to gather himself and extend forward in high gear. He has to thrive on speed.

Yet just running fast won't win any events. Watch the winners; their horses turn smoothly and respond sensibly. They immediately halt at the command, "Whoa." The horse that won't stop is never ready to race at speed.

The athletic horse demonstrates agility in turns at several angles. He bends his body, giving his head and engaging his hindquarters to push himself forward. He turns fluidly at speed, combining a sliding stop with a rollback.

Riders who train their own horses for speed events note that it can take from six months to two years, depending on the horse. The athlete must

Timed events require an equine athlete that is physically and mentally balanced and thrives on speed.

refine his skills at slow gaits, to gain confidence and add finesse before running at speed.

"You can't start fast to win," Chad Crider has said, who owns Mr. Bar Easy, the four-time AQHA World Champion in Pole Bending. "You start slow, and you work at it."

Your horse must learn to rate the obstacle, to slow down and collect himself for the turn. Few horses can turn and drive at the same time — the animal has to check himself, turn, and then drive forward.

Some horses have a natural rate, once they learn the pattern. You can help your horse by approaching a barrel or pole and stopping. He learns to associate the slowdown with the obstacle.

Teach your horse to rate at a short "Ho" or a unique word like "Whup" or "Key." Don't confuse him by using the same word for slow and stop. Consistently drawl a longer "Whoooooaaaaa" for Stop, and reserve the other word for "Slow down and collect, here comes the turn." The word itself doesn't matter, as long as you regularly use the same word in the same tone and reward your horse for the correct response.

Start by walking through a pattern. Because the horse will quickly learn the routine, keep him responsive to your aids. You might trot to the first obstacle and halt. Stand for a moment, then turn at a walk and trot away. Your horse should wait for your cue but still learn to turn with light rein contact.

"The horse responds to your weight and rein," pole-bending authority Ross Carnahan has noted. "We get them real responsive to the hands, like an English rider uses a half halt. If the horse runs off a little, you sit back and he comes back to you. If he's dogging, you just lean forward and squeeze, and he'll go on."

Spurs can help reinforce your leg aid. Train your horse to leg pressure, using a touch of the spur only if he doesn't move from your leg. Practice at a lope only when he consistently responds to your aids. In the contest, you won't have time to think through each action.

TIMED EVENTS

Event	Description	Breed Associations	Show Associations
BARREL RACE	Run a cloverleaf pattern around 3 barrels.	AQHA, APHA, Appaloosa, Pinto, PHBA, IBHA	AHSA (Arabian only), NBHA, NSCA, NLBRA, NHSRA, NIRA
POLE BENDING	Run 4 times on a line of 6 poles, weaving through the line twice.	AQHA, APHA, Appaloosa, Pinto, PHBA, IBHA	AHSA (Arabian only), NBHA, NSCA, NLBRA, NHSRA
STAKE RACE	Run a figure 8 course around 2 stakes. Also called Figure 8 Stake Race.	AQHA, APHA, Appaloosa, PHBA (all for youth only), ABRA	NSCA
FLAG RACE	Grab a flag from a can, set on a barrel.	Pinto	NSCA, NLBRA
KEYHOLE	Run and turn in the "key" and run back.	Appaloosa (youth only), Pinto, ABRA	NSCA

EQUESTRIAN ABILITIES

When riding timed events, you set the pace and position the horse. Your brain connects to your horse's feet. This demands expert horsemanship and a sense of mutual trust.

When horse and rider understand one another, they form a team. Lela Kay French has described her partnership with her World Champion Paint, Kings Copy Cat. "I can relax, and he'll relax. If I tense up and my heart's pounding, he'll feel it."

To develop such a positive mental attitude, you must rely on a secure seat — a functional seat — so you can direct the horse effectively. You have to sit the abrupt jolt of acceleration, ride in rhythm to the turns, and signal for lead changes.

You ride forward, in the center of the horse, and you know when to shift your body angle upright or up over the withers. For instance, when your horse first leaps into a gallop, you lean forward and hold onto the horn.

Sit straight so your horse runs straight. If you're crooked, you influence him to run crooked. Shift your body angle at the proper moment. Don't grab the horn or brace for a turn too early, or you can throw your horse off.

Maintain your seat with strong legs. Ride with shortened stirrups so your knees are bent slightly. You should hold your balance up over the horse's center of gravity. Avoid stirrups that are too short, or you'll slow your horse by bouncing on turns and stops.

When you turn around a barrel, sit down in the saddle with your body vertical and weight steady. This influences the horse to slow for the turn. Your legs should be directly under you, never behind you. Shift your reins to one hand and use the other to grip the horn. With your rein hand high on the horse's neck, lock your elbows against your body so you can pull forward or push back. Go with the horse's arc, without leaning inward or fighting to lean the opposite direction.

Be ready for an abrupt longe as you round the third barrel or final pole — your horse will learn to run flat out for home! Galloping straight, ride low and forward, always with the horse's motion. Steer your horse with your hands about one or two inches above the withers. When you're driving the horse into a run, you can lean forward with your hands on the neck, like a jockey.

You'll see riders using a crop on this final run. Know your horse, who could resent the

When you're driving your horse into a run, lean forward with your hands on his neck, like a jockey.

GARY VORHES

SADDLE	Barrel racing style Narrow seat so you grip with your legs Tall, upright horn Wide pommel to hold you in place High, "wraparound" cantle supports you in turns. Stirrups set to keep your feet under you at all times (Rear cinch helps the saddle stay flat when the horse accelerates and turns.)
BRIDLE	Hackamore bit or gag snaffle Roping reins Adjust headstall so noseband doesn't restrict horse's breathing.
TIEDOWN	Holds horse's head in position during tight turns Snaps to ring on noseband Adjust strap to about 18 inches long, not so tight that it affects horse's balance.
BREASTCOLLAR	Keeps the saddle from slipping back
BOOTS	Neoprene splint boots protect a horse that tends to hit himself, or crossfire. Bell boots prevent overreach injuries. Skid boots on rear legs
RIDER'S DRESS	Jeans, boots, Western shirt and hat or safety helmet Whip, bat, or "over and under" quirt (attached to saddle horn) Shin guards, worn underneath jeans Gloves protect fingers from catching in mane.

pressure. A long rope-like crop called an "over and under" quirt can be effective, since even a slight movement can urge the horse forward. Rest the quirt across your leg, so you can wave it if necessary.

Riders note that horses quickly learn the pattern, and some seem to run the course on their own. But even if a pattern horse knows the routine, he can get flustered if he hits a pole or barrel. Ross Carnahan wants a horse that responds to the rider, not the props. "He can drop in to a pattern and go in a rhythm. If anything interrupts that rhythm, he's in a storm before he's done. Our horse will go exactly where you put him. If he slips or gets out of bounds a little, you can put him right back in sync and the mistake's behind you. It costs you, but it hasn't knocked you out."

Work on your timing and balance. Time your aids in the pattern, at any speed. When you approach a barrel or pole, you know when to ask for the change in arc so your horse bends in balance. Try to anticipate the moment you want the feet to extend into high gear, and signal the horse an instant before that moment. He has to process your signal and then move forward.

When you're learning, ride the pattern once or twice a week, varying the course between trot and lope. Avoid souring him by practicing the pattern too much. A sour horse can sull up and begin to resent the work.

Keep your horse fresh through pleasure rides, or by showing in some rail classes. The horse will learn that entering the arena doesn't always mean having to run. This equine athlete needs to be in good condition, so ride him every day. You might exercise him at a long trot, for 20 or 30 minutes, interspersing this gait with the walk and lope.

Famous racers can help you improve your runs through clinics and barrel racing schools. A horse might develop a bad habit like slicing (brushing) a barrel, hitting it, charging, or hanging (losing speed) on turns. The horse could just quit, and refuse to turn or run. A trainer can advise you how to correct such problems.

TACK AND DRESS

Speed increases the hazards in any riding discipline, so plan ahead to prevent accidents. Use well-fitted, humane equipment, especially a saddle that fits correctly on withers and back.

At a show, your tack and attire must meet the rulebook's specifications. Following the lead of professional barrel racers, you can dress in a colorful long-sleeved Western shirt and jeans, with a Western hat and boots. Barrel racers often wear color-coordinated outfits, with pants, shirt, and hat matching the horse's saddle pad, boots, and even breastcollar.

Be sure your hat stays in place, as some rules penalize you if it falls off. Add a stampede string, threaded through the brim and knotted under your chin so it won't fall off even if it blows off your head. A safety helmet offers better protection, and its chin strap secures the headgear.

BARREL RACING

Across North America, close to 200,000 barrel racers compete in the sport. Barrel racing has a high audience appeal, with rodeo spectators rating it second favorite (bull-riding is ranked first).

Barrel racing demands stamina and concentration. Horse and rider carve figure eights around a triangular course of three barrels, forming a clover-leaf pattern. AQHA rules specify 30 yards between the first two barrels, and 35 yards between the second and third.

Barrel racing is a contest of three turns of almost 360 degrees, where tight, fast turns can shave seconds from the time. The horse performs as in a rollback; he arcs his body to curve around a barrel and maintains his balance on the inside hind leg.

You may start on either of the two barrels (55-gallon steel drums) closest to the starting line. Most "can chasers" begin by circling the barrel on the right, so their horses can switch to the left lead for the second barrel.

After circling the third barrel, you "run for home" at full speed toward the timers. The arena size determines your time. Good times range from 13 seconds (in a smaller arena) to 18 seconds.

Barrel Racing Strategy

Ride with two hands and supple the horse to yield to leg pressure. In a turn, he should move away from your leg and bend his neck.

"You want tight turns," Stephanie Essman has explained, AQHA Amateur World Champion in barrel racing and pole bending. "You don't want to have to yank him around. Ideally you pick him up before the barrel, and he does the turn on his own. Then he comes out on his own."

Watch the horse's body position. An athletic horse shifts his shoulders to the side without dropping the inside shoulder. Even at speed, he keeps the inside shoulder up to maintain his balance.

When you study the experts on video or at events, you'll see that the horse turns by engaging the hindquarters. He readies himself and willingly pivots closely around the barrel. He completes the maneuver by moving out, resuming his gallop.

"It's one big motion," said Champion All-Around rider Elaina Chavez. "Your horse has to flow into the turn, not stop, turn, and run. You make everything as smooth as you can."

The horse bends his forehand without swinging his hindquarters to the outside. You can school him to bend around your inside leg at the girth.

With your reins, tuck the nose to the inside. Avoid pulling back in a turn, which can affect the horse's balance. You shouldn't feel the hindquarters fall to the outside of a turn or feel him swing so wide that he loses momentum.

"You can cue him with your body," Tona Wright, high school rodeo champion, has explained. "Sit down and cue. With your hands and feet, ask him to move over or come closer. It's not that hard, and you can pick up your horse fast if you need to move over."

Many barrel racers envision a "pocket" in front of each barrel, the area before the barrel where the horse "gears down" and collects his forward motion to begin the turn. A pocket helps you come out of the turn faster. You check your horse's speed at the right moment, for minimum loss of forward motion. This can be 12 to 18 feet away from the barrel, depending on how straight and wide your horse turns, and the dimensions of the arena.

Jeff Barnes/NBHA

Envision a "pocket" in front of the barrel.

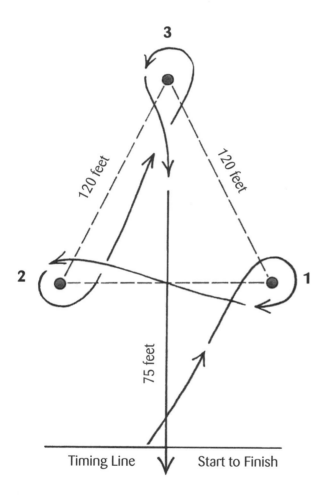

You can run the pattern from right to left, or left to right. Most riders choose the right-side barrel as barrel number 1. You cross the starting line, circle number 1, run 30 yards to circle number 2, and run to number 3. Circle 3 and run for home.

Improving the Sport

Through earning National Barrel Horse Association points, you can qualify for the World's Largest Barrel Race, the National Finals in the NBHA's hometown, Augusta, Georgia. In its first year, 1,347 riders competed for championships and over $200,000 in prize money. This one show attracted the greatest number of barrel racers in history.

One of NBHA's goals is setting standards through rules and conditions. The National Finals has a dress code that is not required in local events. NBHA's District Directors sanction events only in safe arenas that use electronic timers.

Barrel racer Talmadge Green notes that the NBHA has improved the sport's image. "NBHA gives us a lot of credibility," he says. "People are starting to pay attention to barrel racing. It used to be wild and 'ya-hoo,' but now we've passed any other organization started in such a short time, in the total number of members and states participating."

NBHA Levels the Playing Field

The National Barrel Horse Association unites barrel racers and gives many riders the opportunity to gain their share of the glory. Formed in 1992, NBHA addresses the disparity between winners and losers.

Every level of the sport includes fast and not-so-fast contestants. If you and your horse don't turn fast enough, the stars will always reap the glory of prizes and money. You don't gain any encouragement, and you might give up trying. It doesn't work that way in NBHA's sanctioned shows, where you compete in a 3-division (3-D) format. This equalizes the competition, because everyone runs in the same barrel race. The resulting time brackets determine the three divisions.

At each show, seconds divide the brackets. If the fastest time is 15.200 seconds, every rider within one second of that time becomes a 1st Division contestant. The 2nd Division begins with the competitors running one second or up to two seconds slower than the fastest time overall. The 3rd Division begins with those who ran two seconds or slower than the fastest time overall.

This means that if your horse runs one second slower than the winner, you're the first place rider in the 2-D (the person behind you is slightly slower than you and wins second place in the 2-D). In each time bracket, the fastest five win NBHA points. So you could win points, while a rider faster than you may not, if she doesn't run in the top five of her division.

"The 3-D format levels the playing field," NBHA Director Rick Sykes has explained. "This format is a natural handicapping program. It gives everyone the same chance to compete, based on the time they actually run."

He notes that this system encourages the majority of riders, the ones who don't have fast horses. Instead of "making their weekly donation to the jackpot" and supporting the usual winners, they have the opportunity to reap the glory. They've been at the bottom of a pyramid, topped by the superstars, and now average runners can compete against their peers.

Sykes comments: "Now, people who have never won can get a check. It could be only $10, but they're totally thrilled."

The contest is open to all, not segmented into open, amateur, or novice. The only distinction is by age. Youth and Junior riders compete among contestants in their age groups, and Seniors ride against other 50-plus participants. (Seniors don't run in the 3-D format.)

"The 3-D format unifies your numbers," says barrel racer Talmadge Green. "What hurts when you split your numbers into novice and amateur is that you don't get growth. In the 3-D, the more who enter, the bigger the numbers in the jackpot. That's helped the 3-D get bigger and better."

Barrel racer Elisha Aker has said that: "hitting the pockets is crucial. It's how far away you start turning. The distance depends on your horse, and how he responds to your rein and weight." Yet not all horses make pockets. An exceptionally agile one can turn more tightly. "My horse goes in right next to the barrel, and he goes out next to it," said one rider.

Once you've circled half the barrel, so your horse's shoulder is just past it, switch to a driving motion. Grab the horn and use your outside leg behind the girth to drive forward.

The first barrel is crucial to a good run. "The first barrel is the money barrel," said Tona Wright. "If you don't get that one turned, it affects your run. If you're out of position, coming out of the first barrel, you get wide for the others." Once you're running wide, then you have to correct your horse and you can affect his run."

Before you start, plan how you'll angle your approach to the first barrel. At breed shows and many club shows, you'll start running after entering the arena, with the gate closed. In an indoor arena or stadium, you may enter at a run, galloping down an alleyway to burst into the arena.

Most riders start on the right lead, first turning the barrel on the right side of the arena. This establishes a good pattern, with the horse turning the second barrel to the left.

Stephanie Essman: "You have to trust the horse, that he will turn the first barrel. My horse can do the pattern by himself, and we depend on each other. He looks and I guide."

With a good turn at the first barrel, you can get a straight approach to the second. The athletic horse learns to switch leads on the pattern, going into the second barrel. Some horses switch two strides before the barrel, while others switch right before the turn.

Your horse might shoulder the second barrel, as he makes the abrupt turn toward the third. At the third barrel, you do a rollback to longe into the final sprint.

Other variations of barrel racing include speed barrels and straight barrels. In both, you run around three barrels set in a straight line, from 50 to 55 feet apart. Speed barrels require you to weave along the line, down and back. In straight barrels, you circle each one, then reverse direction to circle all again on your way back.

POLE BENDING

Pole bending is a contest of 11 turns, around a line of six poles that your horse "bends" twice during the run. White poles stand six feet tall, set 20 to 21 feet apart with the first one 21 feet from the starting line. Most shows use poles of 1½-inch plastic pipe, fitted into molded rubber bases for safety. Measuring 14 inches in diameter, the base secures the pole to hold it steady and upright.

Galloping across the starting line, you run past the line of poles, turn at the farthest one, and then weave back down the remaining five. You want your horse to arc his body close to each pole, without

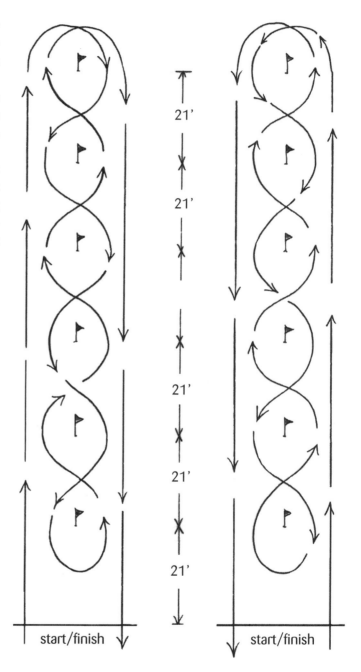

Galloping across the starting line, you run past all the poles, turn at the farthest, and then weave back down the remaining five.

Caring for Your Racer

The excitement of the contest affects both you and your horse. Many event horses appear out of control as they anticipate the pattern. You want your horse to "rev up" for a good running start, but you don't want him to dread competing.

At any timed event, you'll see at least one gate-sour horse that refuses to enter the ring. This animal endangers itself and others, as the rider has to ask a gate-person to lead her through the gate.

A breed show judge can disqualify a horse that won't walk into the arena. A few outstanding competitors demonstrate the ideal. They walk in, explode full blast on command, perform flawlessly, halt, and walk out the gate.

"A good mind is most important," says barrel racing and pole bending champion Stephanie Essman. "My horse, The Flying Bug, doesn't get hot or hyper. He looks forward to work, and what he likes best is to run down the ramp."

Aim for such control by teaching your horse a routine. With your body language, you say, "Calm down — no running now." While waiting or walking in large, slow circles near the gate, sit quietly, breathe, and relax with loosened reins.

If your horse nervously jigs and you restrict him with tight reins, you are telling him, "Stay antsy! Something's going to happen!" When you remain calm and detached, a sensible horse will assume your attitude.

As the announcer calls your number, you guide your horse through the in-gate. You pick up the reins when it's time to compete, to collect him for the first stride of the gallop. He runs and then relaxes as you reward him with the release of pressure. You resume a calm attitude while leaving the arena.

Ride aggressively yet responsibly, without resorting to spur or whip at every stride. You'll discourage your horse from trying his best if you use excessive force.

Care for him after the event. These horses do tend to undergo leg injuries, especially to the hocks, knees, and tendons. They also develop back problems.

Essman advises: "Wrap the legs well before you ride, and warm up and cool out. If he runs real hard, I rub him with liniment and apply standing leg wraps."

---

touching it. He does a flying lead change at the gallop, usually as he passes each pole. "You just flow through there real smooth," Ross Carnahan has commented. "There's no feeling like it."

Rounding the last pole in the line, you weave back through. After circling the final pole, you gallop back past the starting point.

Average times run from 20 to 25 seconds. A 19-second run is exceptionally fast.

The Appaloosa Horse Club has the Nez Perce Stake Race and the Camas Prairie Stump Race. Following the Nez Perce traditions, two horses run side-by-side pole bending or barrel racing patterns (in arenas wide enough for the two-horse race). The winner of each time-trial elimination then races against another winner, progressing to the two fastest horses running against each other.

ApHC rules regulate behavior more specifically than other breed associations. The judge can disqualify you for touching a stake with the hand, striking the horse forward of the cinch, or failing to get behind the starting line in time.

NSCA runs many of its races on a course of four lanes, 30 feet wide and 165 feet long. Each horse must stay within his lane.

Pole Bending Strategy

Many riders compete in both barrels and poles, with horses recognizing the pattern by the obstacles. To win in pole bending, you need a light-footed horse that runs on top of the ground. Carnahan, who has trained several AQHA World Champions in pole bending, has said: "It takes a special horse. He can't just run in there and make one lead change like a barrel horse, but he has to be that fast. It's very demanding. When he makes that first turn, then he has to settle down and work.

"Pole bending horses are versatile. They have to possess the athletic ability of a cutting horse, the speed of a race horse, the handling of a reining horse, and the disposition of a pleasure horse. Today's pole bending horses are doing this and making pole bending an exciting sport for all."

In the middle poles of pole bending, aim for your horse to flex around each one in a smooth, continuous arc. The pole acts as a visual cue for the horse to move its body over.

Pole bending involves speed and rhythmic lead changes.

The last pole can make or break your run. Keep your rollback tight and smooth. Take off again at the center of the pole and resume speed as fast as you can.

You have to guide your horse and sit up straight. "A lot of riders lean," Carnahan said. "When you see a pole coming at you, the natural instinct is to lean your body forward and try to miss it. You should sit back and guide your horse away from it, because the horse is what's going to hit the pole."

When you watch winning runs, you'll notice that many riders use voice commands. Besides stopping at "Whoa," a horse can respond to other spoken messages.

Teach your horse to change leads with your legs or voice. An instant before you cue, speak to it. You could say, "Change," or use a kiss or a "ssshhh." Again, choose and stick to a unique sound.

Many riders consider pole bending the most challenging event, with its rhythmic lead changes. The gap between poles equals about two strides. You can change leads halfway between poles, or when the horse has "bent" the previous pole and

started its next stride. Cue for the change when you go by a pole.

Pole bender Koell Wright explains: "I use my inside leg on each pole to cue my horse to change leads. I check her at the end pole to sit down and turn. It's hardest to keep her off the poles, because she goes so fast through them. I use my leg to move her over."

The last pole, the one near the gate, can make or break your run. You have to go all the way to that pole, then make a rollback without swerving wide. You don't want to lose time trying to shut down and turn.

Champion youth rider Alegra Padilla has explained: "You make a half-pivot, keeping the horse moving as fast as you can. At the center point when you're going around a pole, the horse slides on his rear and walks in front. He takes off again when the pole is at the center of his body, and he resumes the same speed."

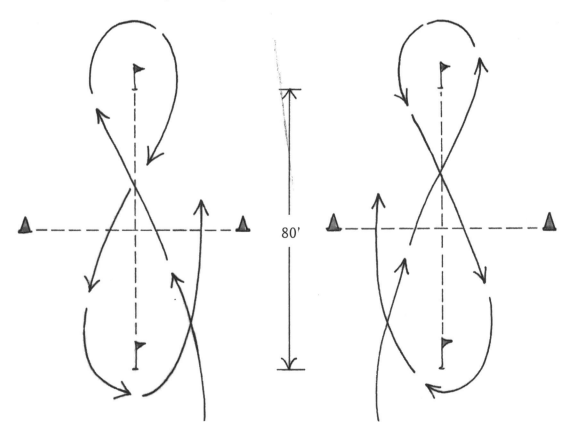

80'

AQHA uses this pattern for the stake race. From a running start, you may begin your run on either the right or left of the pole closest to the starting line.

Stake Race

This pattern requires only two tight turns around two poles set 80 feet apart. Also called the "figure eight" stake race, its pattern forms a figure eight.

You run past the center starting line, indicated by markers set apart across the halfway point between the two stakes. You round the second stake, again cross over the center line between the markers, turn the first stake, and run back past the starting point. Average times measure 10 seconds, with the fastest riders clocking under 8 seconds.

Flag Race

Associations specify different courses in this race. Whatever the course, avoid penalties by pulling the flag straight up from the can or bucket, not from the side.

Pattern 1

The simplest pattern uses a single barrel, set on end with a coffee can or bucket placed on top. Inside the can is a flag, with its staff positioned in sand to remain upright.

You cross the starting line, run around the barrel, and grab the flag from the can. Holding the flag, you dash back over the line to complete the pattern.

You can earn a five-second penalty if you tip over the can when you grab the flag. If you or your horse knock over the barrel, that's a ten-second penalty.

Pattern 2

Three barrels are set in a triangular pattern, similar to that of a barrel race. Here you grab a flag from the first barrel, run around the second barrel, and deposit the flag at the third barrel. Rules vary as to the exact course and penalties.

Pattern 3

This course uses two barrels, set beside one another 25 to 40 feet apart. Each barrel has a bucket, and one has a flag.

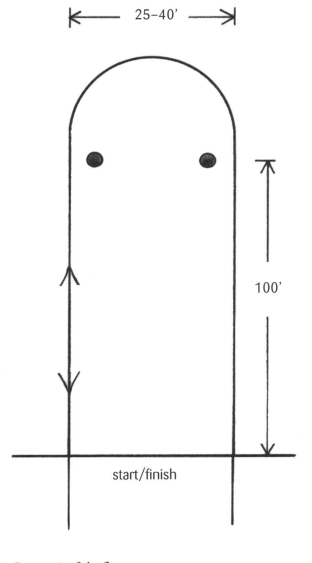

Pattern 3 of the flag race.

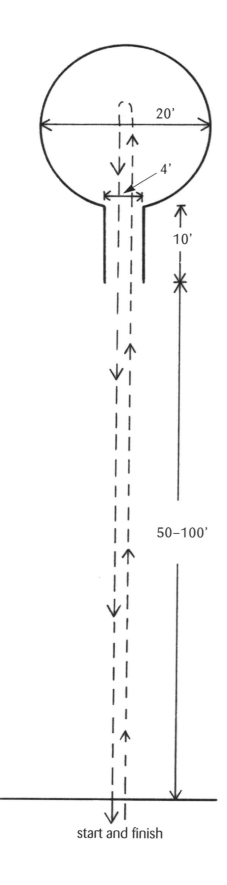

20'

4'

10'

50–100'

start and finish

You run in a U-shaped pattern. Go to the barrel with the flag, pick it up, and run to the second barrel. Place the flag in that bucket, and run for home.

KEYHOLE RACE

You follow a limed keyhole, which marks the course. Run your horse across the starting line down the lane, turn around in the circle, and run back. If your horse sets a foot outside the boundary, you're disqualified.

Gallop through the throat of the keyhole and turn in either direction. A horse that can quickly rollback excels in this race.

Arena Contests

A horse and a rope are the cowboy's traditional tools. Mounted on a good cow horse, he could use his catch rope to immobilize a calf, cow, or steer. Then the crew could brand or doctor the cow.

Roping began in the 1700s, with the vaqueros developing the art in order to handle range cattle. (Before they used ropes, they would capture wily animals with a hocking knife, which sliced the tendon above the hock and crippled the captive.)

Derived from this ranching skill, contemporary events pit ropers against cattle in the eternal battle of wills. The cow seeks to escape the horseman, and the horseman throws his loop and jerks the slack into a noose to capture the critter.

Another cattle event, team penning, captures cattle without any physical contact. This involves maneuvers similar to those of the working cow horse and the roping horse, to drive three cattle into a pen. See a complete description later in this chapter.

Cattle events demand skill as a horseman and a roper. Here you combine your equestrian know-how with cow sense and physical ability, so you contain your cow(s) in the shortest period of time. In the arena, fractions of a second determine those who win trophies and cash.

This chapter covers the events aimed at youth and non-professional riders, who ride their own horses. Roping events also occur at professional rodeos, which are open only to riders who hold a card that certifies them as pros on the circuit.

Today's events reflect Western methods, following two cowboy cultures. In the Plains region, cowhands tied "hard and fast," where you knotted the end of your grass rope (originally fashioned from twisted fibers of the maguey, hechuguilla, or hemp plants) around your saddle horn. When you caught a critter, your horse jerked it to a sudden stop. He controlled it to drag it where you wanted. Or, if the critter used its weight or gravity, your horse was pulled.

Cowboys who followed the traditions of the Mexican vaquero used the dally method, from the Spanish "dar la vuelta," meaning "take a turn." The vaquero roped with a braided rawhide reata, often over 60 feet long, that could break instead of absorbing the jerk of the roped steer. With the dally, you turned the rope once or twice around your saddle horn so you could release slack to "play" the steer. Dallying is easier on the cow, and your horse, than a rope tied hard and fast. However, you must learn to dally properly to avoid catching a finger under the rope.

These events occur in two sites: the show pen at a breed show (judged event), and the arena in a contest or rodeo (timed event). You'll probably compete in events held by local roping or penning clubs (open to the public or limited to members only), local rodeos, or semi-professional rodeos. National associations for non-professional riders include the U.S. Team Roping Championships and the U.S. Team Penning Association.

See "Youth Roping Events" later in this chapter for more details on various types of roping events. Both 4-H and FFA members also participate in

CATTLE ROPING EVENTS

	Team	Calf	Steer Stopping
USUAL ROUTINE	2 riders rope 1 steer. The header catches the steer's horns, while the heeler ropes the hind legs.	Rider chases calf, swings rope at slight downward angle so loop settles around calf's neck.	Rider chases 1 steer, ropes its horns, and stops the steer.
IDEAL PERFORMANCE	Smoothly choreographed Both header and heeler easily rope the steer and stretch it between the 2 horses.	Horse rapidly overtakes calf, with his nose almost on calf's tail. Rider quickly ties calf with piggin string.	Easily ropes steer Pulls slack so steer faces horse
HORSE	Heading horse quickly positions rider for an easy catch and positions steer for heeling. Heeling horse moves into position behind steer for the throw. Both horses face the roped steer.	Positions rider straight behind calf Stops hard so calf loses its footing Holds rope taut so roper can tie calf	Same as heading horse in team event
RIDER	Header makes catch and dallies; watches steer as heeler ropes heels.	Standing in stirrups, throws rope when close to calf and dismounts to tie 3 of its legs	Same as header in team event
GOOD TIMES	9–10 seconds	8–12 seconds	
PENALTIES	10 seconds for breaking barrier; 5 seconds for catching only 1 hind leg	10 seconds for breaking barrier; no score if tied calf stands up before 6 seconds after completion of tie	No penalties listed in rule book.

youth events, including local, regional, and statewide competitions. Young riders can compete for rodeo scholarships through many Western colleges.

ROPING BASICS

In roping, both you and the cow start running from one end of the arena. The cow receives a head start to get a certain distance ahead of you.

You wait in a roper's box, behind a barrier. The box is a three-sided pen, about the size of a horse's stall. The barrier across the front, facing the arena, functions like a starting gate at a racetrack.

The barrier is a rope or cord, stretched across the front of the box and secured with a string. A flag hanging from the string, the pigtail, indicates if the barrier's secured or released. For safety, the barrier releases (springs open) if your horse pushes against it. If you break the barrier — push against it too soon, before the cow has his obligatory head start — the string breaks and the barrier releases, and you earn a penalty that's added to your time.

The calves or steers line up in the chute, head to tail. The chute crew funnels cattle from the holding pen into the chute. A gate separates the current cow from the one behind it, and a headgate holds it in place, beside the roping box.

You build your loop and nod your head to signal when you're ready to rope. You hear a bang when the crew opens the headgate to release the animal.

The cow crosses the score line, or the designated head start distance, before your barrier springs open. A crew member can release your barrier, or the cow itself can regulate the barrier rope by use of a neck rope that pulls a pin. (A string or rubber band connects the cow's rope to the barrier.) With either method, the barrier opens and you take off after your cow.

Time begins when the flag drops at the barrier, and time ends when a mounted flagman (also called the "flagger") signals a successful catch. This field judge rides near you, watching you rope while he holds a flag high. He drops his arm and the flag the instant you complete your rope or tie. If you receive any penalties, he signals the amount (usually by holding up 5 or 10 fingers). A timekeeper, who

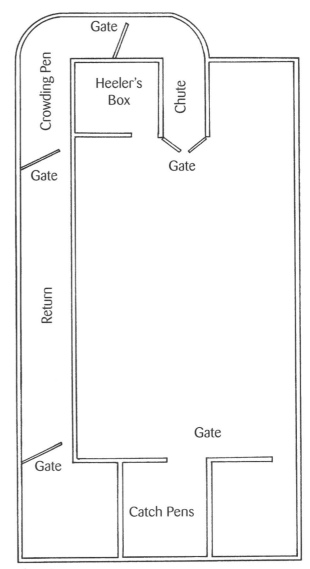

A roping arena.

most often observes the action while perched in a tower, records your time, and the announcer calls the result.

For adults, roping remains primarily a man's sport, although women aren't barred from competing. The activity demands a certain amount of physical strength, especially tiedown calf roping. A few women compete in team roping, usually paired with a male partner. Women dominate breakaway roping (see under "Calf Roping" later in this chapter). Youth compete equally in roping events, with fewer girls competing in the older age groups.

The Roper's Horse

A good roping horse enjoys his work. He's correct and quick in helping to place you in the proper position to throw your rope.

You need a steady horse trained for roping — not one who's new to the sport while you're learning. On a seasoned mount, you can concentrate on handling the rope while the horse automatically follows the cow. He acts as your "legs," carrying you into position to rope the animal.

A veteran increases your chances of catching the cow and winning trophies or money. With substantial entry fees in many ropings, you're smart to start your career on a horse that works for you. Expect to pay at least $2,500 to 5,000 for a reliable mount.

Roper Wes Hough trains horses, testing their mental attitude for the sport. "It's mainly disposition. If he has a nice mind and a minimum of athletic ability, you can do something with him. It takes 90 days trial to test a pleasure horse, to get him ready to be asked to rope. I play with him in the gate and follow a slow steer to get his mind soft. Then I spend a year, two years, or more, to make a horse that anyone can compete on."

You want a horse that stands quietly in the box, waiting for your cue to go. He "busts wide open" from the box, judges the cow's speed, and rates the cow, or holds his position so you can throw from a sure distance. A horse with cow sense usually takes to the sport, as he wants to reach the cow and knows how fast to run to keep pace with it. He doesn't outrun the cow or hang back so you have to throw a long loop. He can anticipate the cow's direction and track the ones that don't run straight down the center of the arena.

A good rope horse has the speed to sprint into action from a standing start. He shoots from the box to accelerate to 30 miles per hour in a few seconds, demonstrating that roping can be the fastest equine sport.

He has the strength to absorb the jerk of a roped calf or steer. When you throw the rope, he braces himself by lowering his hindquarters and rocking back to take up the slack. With the critter caught, he works the rope to keep the rope taut. He holds the cow in one spot, so you can tie it (if you're calf roping) or your partner can rope it (if you're the header in team roping).

A good rope horse is also sensible about the rope. He doesn't flick an ear while you swing your loop over his head. If you miss your throw, you'll recoil your loop for another shot. Your horse won't get tangled in the rope, or if he does step inside a coil, he'll wait while you maneuver the rope free of his foot.

When you're learning, you won't need a superfast horse, or a big stout horse. "Heart is what matters," says team roper Andy Luna. "A little horse with a big heart won't quit."

This horse stops at the proper moment, not too soon and not too late. He executes your cue when you barely indicate your desire. When you give the aid, he readily reins, stops, or turns.

You'll want to avoid roping on a horse that cheats, or has learned evasions that hinder your skills. In the box, he should stand with all four feet on the ground as he waits for your cue to sprint after the cow. He should wait alertly, ready to go but listening for the signal. A trained horse will "score," leaping ahead when you drop your rein hand on his neck or the saddle horn.

A horse that anticipates can act up in the box, even rearing. When he doesn't concentrate on your signal, you'll waste time controlling him before the two of you get to the cow. That horse also can break the barrier. You can retrain him by standing in the box while a helper lets cows out of the chute. You school him not to chase every cow.

Your horse serves as a true partner in roping, so treat him fairly. You'll see ropers lose their tempers and punish the horse for their mistakes. Jerking a horse in the box or hitting him with a rope sours him.

Outsmarting the Cow

Most jackpot ropings run the cattle through chutes, so you get the luck of the draw. Rodeos usually draw for cattle, and you can spot your steer or calf by the number painted on the hip or stamped on an ear tag. You check him out, eyeing him in the pen or asking other ropers about him. Is he good to rope, or is he a "sorry" steer? Does that calf swerve back and forth?

Ropers find that a higher-headed calf is easier to catch, while one that's wild in the pen can be feisty at the end of a rope.

He might be a strong runner, who launches from the chute. Andy Luna has said: "If you get one that runs real fast, you're going to be 10 or 12 seconds on him. You can't catch him quick enough to be 6. If you get one who barely gets to the line and doesn't try to outrun you, you can rope him real fast."

Cattle can become rope-wise and begin to duck their heads to avoid the rope or run to the right or left. Some will "drag," or freeze, when the header catches them. When cattle plant all four feet, the heeler has trouble catching the hind legs.

"You must be able to adjust your swing and delivery if you draw a ducker or a dragger," said Luna. "Cattle get smart and they learn little tricks. They probably learn quicker than a horse."

Fresh steers won't know those tricks, but they can run harder and be more difficult to catch. Calves should be fresh, but even one round can teach a calf to swerve from side to side to avoid the rope. In team roping, you may rope the same steer over and over. The arena could keep him in the herd for months at a time.

"You have to be a horseman and on top of that be able to read cattle," Texas roping coach Terry McCutcheon has commented. "Understand that not all cattle break and run really nice down the middle of the pen."

Roping Practice

A rope is a tool that you must learn to master. To catch a cow, you develop rope-handling techniques using your hand-eye coordination, like

Roping requires hours of practice and should become so automatic and quick that you can't separate the moves by watching.

Choosing a Rope

A catch rope consists of a length of twisted synthetic strands that ends in the hondo (pronounced "hon-doo"). The hondo forms the loop, and it slides to reduce or increase the loop's size. On the hondo is a burner, a piece of rawhide that covers the eye of the hondo, where the rope slides through. This protects the rope from wear and extends its useful life.

A rope is an amazing device that extends your reach. Instead of grabbing a cow or haltering its head, a rope lets you control an animal without touching it. In the hands of an expert, the rope transforms itself from a length of twisted strands into a living, mobile loop that easily settles over a cow's head.

Every rope feels different, and ropers develop preferences. Choose a rope that feels comfortable and that you can control, so you feel confident about catching a cow. It should swing with an even feel, without any hard or soft spots.

"Feel is the main reason to choose a rope," according to Cole Smith of Smith Brothers Ropes. "A header swings a softer rope, with a smaller loop. A hard rope can swing off the horns before you pull the slack. A softer one will pull down, not off, the horns. A heeler throws a bigger loop, because he wants it to stand up between the steer's legs."

The exact length of a rope depends on the roper's judgment. A shorter rope might stop a cow quicker, but it does limit the margin of error. Once the loop settles onto a cow, you then have to tighten the rope's length by jerking the slack, while you hold onto the end by dallying.

Nylon ropes will stretch. Poly and poly grass won't, as calf ropers want a quick stop.

Weather can affect a rope's feel. On a breezy day outdoors, you'll have to adjust for wind speed and direction. With a grass rope, moist air makes the fibers stiff. Ropers deal with humidity by rubbing powder on the rope for a slicker, softer feel. Rub baby powder three or four feet behind the hondo, and where you place your hand when you jerk the slack.

CYNTHIA McFARLAND

forming a loop, swinging, throwing, and jerking the slack. You work through a progression of actions first on the ground, and later on your horse.

McCutcheon explained: "Understand your basics in how a rope moves. That involves how you use the physics of a rope being swung around your head, how you develop loop speed, how you develop a release and a follow through. Then, where is that loop going? If you understand those basics, then you can direct where that rope goes. When you control direction, then you can learn to catch pretty quick, on the ground."

To get the feel of throwing, you'll learn to rope a dummy — a plastic calf or steer head, stuck on a bale of hay or strapped onto a sawhorse. If possible, take lessons from an experienced roper, or attend roping schools sponsored by local clubs or clinics presented at a champion's ranch.

"The best way to learn is to go to a roping school," said Andy Luna. "You spend $300 or $400 to learn from a World Champion. Spend the money and get the basics, so you progress. They work with you on different swings, and they fit your swing to you, rather than try to alter your swing."

Roping becomes so automatic and rapid in motion that it's hard to follow the sequence of separate moves by watching. Many experts can't break the actions into words. Fortunately, it takes most ropers only an hour to learn the maneuver of windup, swing, and throw. Then you practice for months to refine the basics, and you can spend the rest of your roping career seeking that "perfect loop."

When you learn on the dummy, you practice these basics of handling the rope and catching the target. Start by folding the rope into three or four coils. Coils should be open, with no twists, kinks, or waves, and lined up so you can feed the rope through your hands when you throw the loop.

Hold the coils in your left hand. Grasp them with your thumb up — your thumb releases or holds the rope. The hondo faces forward and down, about halfway down the loop from your hand.

With your right hand, build a loop about three feet across by shaking it out. Place your thumb up, on the top of the loop. The section between coils and loop forms a straight line, the "spoke."

Raise your arm high, elbow level with your chin, to swing the loop over your head. Feed more line to the loop, so it's about four feet in diameter. Swing two, three, or four times before you throw. Swing with determination for a broad, open loop that forms a square shape. A "soft" loop can lose its force before it reaches the cow.

Concentrate on your target, and look at what you plan to rope. Your hand delivers the rope where your eye focuses, usually at an angle so it lands on the target.

Hold your wrist steady when you throw the loop hard, and make a definite release. Maintain momentum by following through with your entire arm. You want the loop to stay flat and open, with only a little slack while it flies straight and flat toward the target. At the same time, you feed the line through your left hand by lifting your thumb.

ERIC SINES

A young roper throwing a loop at a "dummy."

	Team Roping and Steer Stopping	Calf
SADDLE	Stout, double-rigged with sturdy tree (wood, rawhide-covered) Dally horn, 3 to 3½" high Well-padded (two saddle pads) Wide front cinch Wide rear cinch to hold saddle down Deep stirrups	Saddle same as team roper's Some calf ropers prefer a lower cantle for a quick dismount. Large, heavy stirrups
BRIDLE	Grazing bit or hackamore bit Roping reins	Same as team roper's Add neck rope of nylon or cotton rope, and thread your catch rope through the neck rope on the off side.
TIEDOWN	Connected to a noseband Fairly snug, so horse can brace against it as sets steer	Same as team roper's
BREASTCOLLAR	Wide leather or nylon web padded with fleece and connected to cinch	Same as team roper's
BOOTS	Neoprene splint boots and vinyl bell boots in front Skid boots in rear	Skid boots in rear
RIDER'S	Jeans, boots, Western shirt and hat (Required by USTRC) Cotton glove to protect your roping hand, close-fitting for a feel of the rope	

Close your hands when the loop lands, and keep those thumbs up. With your right hand, jerk the slack to tighten the loop around the dummy's horn or head, yanking the rope firmly back. Aim for a smooth motion, with release flowing into the pull when you get the slack back.

When you practice roping from the horse, you'll either dally (for steers) or use a breakaway rope (for calves.) To dally, you reach for the slack, pull, and bring the rope back to the saddle horn while turning your hand palm side down. Dally with your thumb up, to wrap the rope once or twice counterclockwise, from right to left.

Move your hand down the rope, toward your hip, as you hold the dally. Adjust the rope length by lifting your thumb to let the rope slide, and press your thumb to stop it. (Wearing a glove helps protect against rope burns.)

You can rope left-handed, but few southpaws rope that way. You'd need a special rope, spun to the left. You won't be able to head, because you and the heeler would have to switch places after leaving the box.

While you're learning, study ropers at contests. Try to analyze particular actions, and compare the results. Watch videotapes, where you can play a

A well-equipped calf-roping horse

10-second run in slow motion. When you can catch regularly on the ground, start to put it all together. Try roping the plastic head from the back of your horse. (You might raise the target to the height of a cow.) Walk to the target and rope from a standstill at first.

"You need to be patient with yourself and know it takes time to learn," Terry McCutcheon has noted. "In order to develop those 100 catches in a row on the ground, and then progress to a horse, some people may be very successful on the ground and not catch anything on a horse. You have to adjust to a particular horse. Some will track better than others, and you don't have to do too much; others you have to help a lot."

In roping, you control both the horse and the rope. You have to move into a position that in-

creases your chance of catching the cow. Horsemanship skills come first, because you pilot your horse to that spot. You feel comfortable and secure in the saddle while you learn to handle the rope.

Leona Wright, a champion 4-H roper who now rides in National Intercollegiate Rodeos, has said, "What's hardest about roping is trying to stay consistent. You try to make every run the same, while there are so many variables that come into play."

Improve your odds by guiding your horse with confidence. With roping reins of one continuous length, you don't have to worry about losing the reins. The short length won't get in your way, and your horse should neck rein and stop on cue.

Hold the reins with two fingers, with the coils also in your rein (left) hand. When you're pursu-

Caution: Roper at Work

Roping can be dangerous. Many a cowboy has lost a finger or thumb to a rope tightened at the wrong time.

"You need to learn how to use that rascal," roper Terry McCutcheon has advised. "You have to understand that a rope can get you in a lot of trouble." In his roping classes at Cooke County College, he teaches the cautions of using this piece of equipment.

"Roping can be an awful lot of fun. On the other hand, it can cause damage if it's not used correctly. We push the safety factor. Ninety-five percent of the time, it's controllable."

When you rope, keep your thumbs up, on top of the rope, so you can release coils without getting tangled in them. Don't play with unwilling targets. Don't play Monte Montana and rope a person, because a joke could cause a tragic accident.

Be sure to cinch up tight, so your saddle won't twist from the impact. Secure the rear cinch to hold the saddle in place. If it's too loose, the rear of the saddle can fly up and pitch you forward.

ing a cow, you stand in the stirrups with your rein hand ahead of the horn. Swing the loop with your right hand, just as you did on the ground.

You'll also practice leaving the box, without a cow. Ride in and rein your horse around so he stands at the back of the box. Turn him at a slight angle, so you can watch the cow in the chute beside you, on your right. (If you're a heeler, you'd normally start from the box on the opposite side of the cow, so you'd look to your left.)

Hold the reins just above the saddle horn. Build your loop and tuck it under your right arm. When you cue your horse to go, lean forward, grip with your knees, and stand in the stirrups while you pull yourself up with the horn. You'll be secure when he launches himself into a gallop.

TEAM ROPING

With thousands of ropers in competition, team roping is one of the most popular sports, equestrian or otherwise, in certain areas of the Southwest. A team of four — two riders and two horses — cooperates, with both riders roping the steer. When the ropes stretch the steer between heading and heeling horses, it's helpless to charge either animal.

In team roping, timing is crucial. Aim for consistency before you develop speed.

The event starts with a steer in the chute, and each horse entering a roper's box, one on each side of the chute that confines the steer. The header stands in the box to the left of the steer, the heeler to the steer's right. The header's horse, which always starts first, stands behind a barrier. (A few ropings also place a barrier in front of the heeler.)

Once out of the chute, the steer has a head start, or a score line of 10 to 25 feet. A short score line gives the animal less of a head start.

The header sees the steer is ready, and he nods for the gate to open. Both header and heeler leave the boxes simultaneously, with the heading horse galloping first to the steer's left hip. The header ropes the horns of the steer. (Most steers wear horn wraps, or pads that fit around the base of the horns and over the ears. This cushions the jerk of the rope, so repeated ropings don't cause burns against the ears or skull.) He turns the steer away, pulling the slack of his rope, to set it up for the heeler.

The heeler ropes both hind legs. "Timing is crucial," Andy Luna has said. "The header does his job and the steer hops. You hold the loop back when his feet are off the ground. If the steer is hopping, you time his back feet. When his feet start to come forward, you deliver your loop in front of them. When your timing's perfect, you get a curl in the rope."

The heeler makes the catch, dallies, and holds the slack. The header turns his horse so both face the roped steer, and the flagman signals time.

The heeler loosens his slack, and usually the steer hops out of the loop. The header follows the steer to the catch pen, where a crew member removes his rope from the steer's head (and the heel rope, if it dragged behind the steer).

Team Roping Practice

Each partner develops skill in his part of the action. Headers and heelers don't always pair up the same way, as some ropings match them right before their runs.

Improve your technique by aiming for consistency before you develop speed. If one of you misses, that ruins your time or even earns a no-time in some contests.

Practice your timing, so you pull slack at the exact moment you catch. Don't "pull it out" too soon, because the steer could stumble or duck his head.

Watch the steer every moment, even as you dally. Your horse may have to speed up if the steer charges him.

Wrap your saddle horn with a piece of inner tube so the nylon rope will grab to the rubber when you dally. Cut a doughnut shape from the tube, with the width about two inches across. Twist and wrap it in a figure eight.

Heading

You'll throw your loop to sweep counterclockwise, from right to left. Most good headers swing twice and throw, aiming to catch both horns. With the rope on the horns, you can turn your horse away from the steer while dallying.

The header has three legal catches:

1. Around both horns
2. Half a head (one horn and around the neck)
3. Around the neck

Target the left horn. With a good horse, you'll automatically be a foot or two behind the steer's left hip, the proper spot to throw your loop. He'll space himself and rate the steer, waiting for you to throw to the right.

If your horse is less than perfect, you may have to cue him. Move him into position with your legs or body weight rather than the rein, so you can concentrate on your rope. Try not to rein him while you rope, or you might teach him to duck out, or turn away from the steer too soon. He must wait for you to rein him after you start to dally.

Throw the rope toward the base of the left horn, and let the slack float down the steer's left side. As you pull the slack, you'll see the steer's head start to turn left.

Dally at least one wrap, and hold the rope with no slack. With the steer caught, turn your horse left. You'll feel him plant his left hind leg and pivot to lead the steer. You should be able to dally by

The Contest and Classifications

You can enter a variety of roping events. In a jackpot roping, everyone contributes part of their entry fees into the jackpot, split by the fastest ropers. The draw-pot pairs ropers in a draw, so you don't know who will be your roping partner, or even if you'll head or heel. A round robin rotates ropers through a list, pairing different headers and heelers every steer. In a calcutta, spectators bet on ropers and share the winnings of a team.

You might win money by go-round (a preliminary round), fast time, or average (a total of all your times). In a progressive roping, you continue to rope only after you've successfully roped your first steer. If you miss, you drop out of the progressive.

To level the playing field, the U.S. Team Roping Championships (USTRC) classifies every roper with a number that describes ability.

Your classification number reflects the evaluation of a number of observers who are your peers in the roping sport. The higher the number, the better roper you are. You pair with a partner whose number combines with yours, and the two of you compete in designated roping divisions.

Ropings typically offer #5 through #11 divisions. Say you're a class 2. You can pair with a class 4 for a #7 roping, or a class 6 for a #8. (That's assuming a class 6 chooses to take the chance — if you're the header and you miss, he won't get to show his stuff!)

An arena operator can assign you a temporary, unofficial number good for only that roping. US-TRC suggests that the operator give you a number 5. If the operator sees immediately that you should have a lower number, he may adjust it right after the first time you rope. He'll contact the USTRC Classification Office, who will issue you a free, six-month card. You may also call the USTRC directly for a card. Officials will survey USTRC directors in your area (chosen by a random computer selection) to assign you a Temporary First-Time Number. Or you can participate in a telephone interview, where you answer a battery of questions to determine your level of skill.

When you join the USTRC, you receive a Gold Spur card, good for the entire year. The USTRC currently manages about 60,000 ropers across the United States. You need this card in order to compete in almost any adult event except practice ropings or small, local jackpot ropings. Only as a USTRC cardholder will you receive your winnings.

Classifications can change from year to year, as a roper's ability improves (or drops) with experience, age, or injury. Directors annually vote on the classifications of all the ropers. If you don't agree with your classification, your number appears on a mid-year "short" ballot sent to your area's directors. A director or other USTRC individual can also place your name on this ballot. You can also appeal to change your classification.

Roping is an honor system, in the spirit of the West. Obviously you want to keep a low number to better your chances. If you claim you're a #1, and you can catch in a reasonable time, maybe you should really be a #3. Your fellow ropers will surely protest if they suspect you have a "bad number," and you'll move up in class.

FRAN D. SMITH

feel, and don't look at your horse or saddle horn as you play the steer.

Lope your horse slowly forward so the steer is in tow for the heeler. Look back to see that you're getting the steer lined out, moving straight and hopping slowly for an easy catch by the heeler.

If your loop misses, slow the horse and recoil your rope to build a second loop. In competition, breed associations allow a second loop; the U.S. Team Roping Championships (USTRC) do not.

Heeling

To learn heeling, you usually start roping as a header. Practice on a dummy that simulates the steer's hind legs, such as a sawhorse. The legal catch is both hind legs. One hind leg earns you a five-second penalty, but it does complete the run.

Leaving the box, you run to the right. The header catches the head and turns the steer, so you're facing the steer's left hip. Stay at the side and move a few feet behind.

Throw your loop when the heels are off the ground. You want to deliver your loop so it floats over the steer's back and stands up, at a right angle with the steer's body. With perfect timing, the steer hops into the loop. "The rope won't even hit the ground when you do it just right," Andy Luna has said. "That's what they call roping them out of the air."

Heelers used to "set a trap," or throw the loop on the ground ahead of the steer so he stepped in the loop. Timing the loop with the hop is faster.

Luna said: "You watch the whole time. You don't just throw and pull. A steer could stumble or the header slow down, so instead of hopping off he shuffles his feet. Then the rope will hit instead of just roping him out of the air, and you have to just let the rope lie there."

Trainer Bobby Lewis ropes a calf at the AQHA World. Reserve for the Leading Exhibitor award, he won the World Championship in Junior Heading and was Reserve in Junior Heeling. Riding in ten classes, he placed in each one.

USTRC CLASSIFICATIONS

Number	Ability
1	True beginner
2	Novice
3	Upper Novice
4	Heeler: lower ⅓ of intermediate ropers Header: outstanding novice
5	Heeler: intermediate or mid-level roper Header: good
6	Heeler: upper intermediate Header: top non-professional
7	Heeler: lower ½ open professional Header: top professional
8	Upper ½ open or professional heeler
9	Top 20 open or professional heeler

Aim the hondo at the right hock and look for the top of the loop to settle in place. The wrap should close just below the hocks. Dally without letting the rope slide off the horn, while your horse sets up (stops). He shouldn't set up too early, or you could lose your rope before you can dally.

Your horse stays in the ground, immobile, while the header reins his horse to the right. You both face the steer to complete the run.

CALF ROPING

Standing in the box, with the calf on your right, you nod at the gateman. The calf streaks out, the barrier springs open, and your horse scores the calf. He rates it while you swing your rope and see the loop settle around the calf's neck.

Up to now, the action resembled team roping. From this point on, you follow different techniques.

As you jerk your slack, you then pitch the slack while your horse stops hard to brace himself. He comes to a sudden stop, and you dismount and sprint down the rope to the calf.

While your horse stands to keep the rope taut, you "flank" the calf, or pick it up and lie it on its side. Holding the calf flat, you tie three legs together with your piggin string. Raise both hands and stand up when you're done, and the timer signals you've completed your run. A tie judge makes sure that the calf remains down for six seconds, for your time to count.

In breakaway roping, you tie the rope to your saddle horn with a piece of string. You swing your rope, catch the calf, and stop your horse while you pull the slack. The string breaks and releases your rope when the slack tightens. In competition, the flagman signals time when the rope breaks loose from your saddle horn. (Some associations require that you tie a white flag at the junction of rope and string. The flag's movement signals the breaking of the string.)

Catch That Calf

Prepare by coiling one or two ropes and tying them to the saddle horn in a figure eight knot. Tuck one end of your piggin string under your belt, on your right side, and coil the rest to hold it in your teeth. Ride into the box and get your rope up so you're in position for a quick catch. Stand up in your stirrups for the entire run.

You and your horse focus on the calf when you wait in the box. When you see the calf standing straight in the chute, ready to run, nod your head at the gateman.

Chasing the calf, your horse should run full out to move directly behind the calf. Then he should rate the calf, staying on its tail about two or three feet behind, with his head down as he watches the calf. He follows every turn to keep you in position — you shouldn't have to rein him.

Throw your rope quickly, when you're in place to catch. (Some calves duck from side to side.)

A calf's head presents a smaller target than a steer's. You want your loop to fit neatly around the calf's neck, not so small that it encircles only the ears, or so large that it slides to the body. Standing in your stirrups, you'll aim the rope downward, at a steeper angle than a header would for a steer.

"It's a little harder to rope a calf than a steer," Terry McCutcheon has said. "We start our students learning to rope a calf first. If they get the basics of that, they'll be able to adapt to the heading aspect pretty quick."

Learn to pull the slack. When the rope settles around the neck, pull straight back to tighten the loop so the calf won't run through it. Wave the rope straight down the calf's back.

You can practice your roping skills with a breakaway rope. Fit a breakaway hondo on your loop, connecting the regular hondo to the main part of the rope. When your loop tightens around the calf's neck, the hondo separates and the calf continues running.

A good breakaway roper can catch a calf in three seconds. A good horse starts to stop when he hears the rope and sees it settle on the calf. World Champion calf ropers take between eight and twelve seconds for a run, so the dismount and tie take longer than the actual roping.

To shorten the time, you can practice dismounting as your slack tightens. Rope from directly behind the calf, so your horse won't duck off (swing to the side) as you dismount. Most calf ropers dismount on the off side so they can grab the calf from the right.

When you start to the ground, your horse stops on his haunches without bouncing, all four feet on the ground. He must set back to tighten the rope and hold the calf in place. He should plant himself, push back in his stop, back up, and lean into the tiedown to prevent any slack in the rope. He then intently watches the calf to hold it in place for you.

The calf roping horse wears a neck rope, through which you run your catch rope before tying it to the saddle horn. This helps the horse maintain control over the calf while the horse faces it during the tie.

Your horse should follow directly behind the calf, about two or three feet behind. You shouldn't have to rein him.

While the horse does his job, you run down the rope to the calf. The faster you restrain the calf, the less it can fight you. Usually the calf will be standing up. (If the horse jerked it to the ground and it's still on its side, you must lift it to get all four feet under it.) Rodeos and some other associations enforce a "no jerkdown" rule, where your horse must not jerk the calf so hard that the animal flips over backwards. In this case, you have to control the rope to soften the impact as the horse stops.

If the calf is up and moving, you block its motion (the horse helps by keeping the rope taut) and flank it. You can practice tying on a calf without your horse. With a neck rope on the calf, tie the calf to the fence, or have an assistant hold the rope. Flank the calf by grabbing its right foreleg and the loose skin of its flank, and flip it down on its side with your hands and legs. Use momentum and leverage to control the calf, and straddle it so you can hog-tie it with "two wraps and a hooey."

Ropers vary in their tying styles. Generally you grab the coiled end of the piggin string from your mouth and place it over the foreleg closest to you. Tighten the string and pull the rest free from your belt. Pick up both hind legs and cross them over the foreleg. You pull the foreleg back and hind legs forward.

You might hold legs close to the ground so the calf won't kick, or hold them higher to maintain control. Wrap clockwise, twice, around all three legs, and tie a half-hitch (the hooey) around the hind legs.

You walk back to your horse, who's still working the rope to hold it tight, and remount. After the six-second wait, the crew unties your wraps and hands you your rope.

For a fast time, you want to tie quickly. As in all roping movements, first learn the correct sequence. Then refine your speed by repeating the actions hundreds of times. Experts develop the most

Your horse works with you by holding the rope tight, but not pulling the calf.

efficient techniques by analyzing each specific motion and angle of arms, wrists, hands, and fingers.

Your horse has to help you. One wrong move can add to your time, put you out of the money, or cause a wreck. He shouldn't shut you out or keep going instead of slowing when you rope. You don't want him to "quarter," or stop angled to the side, so he pulls the calf over to the side. When you tie and he holds the rope tight, he shouldn't pull to drag the calf or choke it.

YOUTH ROPING EVENTS

Young ropers also rope calves and team rope steers. They develop their skills in simpler events, offered through youth organizations.

Two contestants compete in ribbon roping, a runner and a roper. The calf has a ribbon tied to its tail. You leave the box and rope the calf. The runner (sometimes called a "mugger") holds the calf while you dismount and grab the ribbon from the calf's tail. You then run back across a finish line to complete the time.

In goat tying, you tie a goat, as you would a calf. The goat is staked in the arena, with a collar around its neck. You gallop your horse across a starting line, aiming toward the goat, and halt as close as you can before you dismount. You flip the goat on its side and cross and tie any three legs with a leather thong or braided nylon goat string. Time ends when you signal completion of the tie. As in calf roping, the tie must hold for six seconds.

Other youth events prepare the youngest ropers: Step-down roping requires only roping the calf and dismounting from the horse. In calf touching, the roper runs alongside the rope and touches the calf to signal time.

National Little Britches Rodeo Association groups youth aged 8 through 13 as Juniors, and 14 through 18 as Seniors. High school students may join the National High School Rodeo Association, and the National Intercollegiate Rodeo Association is open to enrolled college students. 4-H rodeos offer events by age group and generally permit boys and girls to compete equally in all events.

SINGLE STEER EVENTS

You can also compete as a single steer roper, or steer dauber. In steer stopping, offered by some breed associations, you head a steer. You rope the horns, stop your horse, and dally. Time ends when the steer faces you, thus demonstrating that your horse can stop the steer.

In another timed event, steer daubing, you use a lance to paint a whitewash mark on the steer.

YOUTH RODEO ASSOCIATION EVENTS

	Little Britches	High School	Intercollegiate
CALF ROPING	Senior boys	Men	Men
RIBBON ROPING	Junior boys, junior girls		
GOAT TYING	Senior girls, junior girls	Women	Women
TEAM ROPING	Senior boys, senior girls	Both	Both
BREAKAWAY ROPING	Senior girls, junior boys, junior girls	Women	Women

The steer has two large circles painted on its hips, one on each side. You break from the box and overtake the steer. With the wet tip of your lance, you daub within the circle.

The final variation, steer roping, is reserved for rodeo cowboys. This event is legal in only a few Western states. Also called "steer tripping," the rider ropes a steer's horns from the left side and sets the trip by tossing the slack over the steer's right hip. He reins the horse to the left to trip the steer's hind legs. In another version of this event, the roper then ties three of the steer's legs after tripping the animal.

TEAM PENNING

Poised in their saddles, the riders wait for the signal. When the announcer alerts, "Your cattle are ready,"

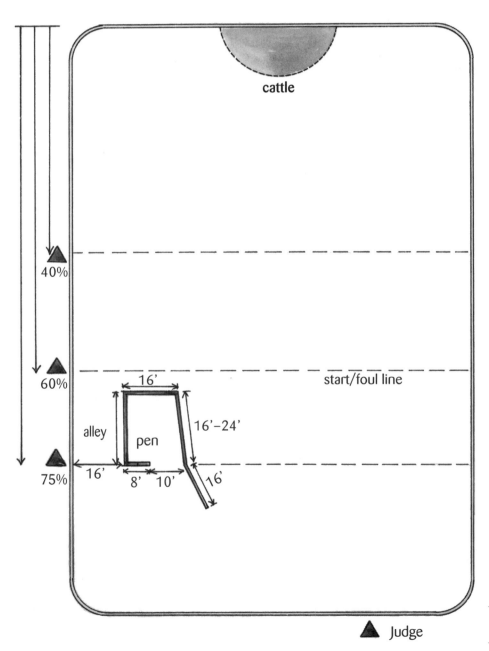

Arena layout for the U.S. Team Penning Association, Inc.

they explode into a gallop and plunge toward a herd of 30 suspicious cattle.

Team penning requires a three-rider team to sort three specific cattle from the herd and corral them in a portable pen set up in the arena as quickly as possible. The event demands handy horses, alert riders, and a team spirit. Cattle occasionally cooperate, and luck plays a part.

This contest attracts a wide variety of riders, making team penning one of the fastest growing Western sports. The action resembles polo, with riders showing off their skill at maneuvering cattle instead of a ball. Derived from ranchwork, the sport means penning cattle in a fast time.

Team penning uses a large arena, with cattle in one end and the pen near the opposite end. The pen is set at a distance 75 percent of the arena's length, measured from the fence at the cattle end. U.S. Team Penning Association (USTPA) rules specify a pen of the measurements and placement as illustrated here. Two judges observe the action,

one at the start/foul line (marked at 60 percent of the arena's length from the cattle end), and the other beside the pen. Two timekeepers clock every go-round.

To keep the contest fair, riders known as "settlers" bunch the cattle closely before each team's run. They also assure that each herd includes 30 cattle, with 10 groups of three, each wearing an assigned number from 0 to 9. Settlers herd the cattle out of the arena after 10 runs, to bring in a fresh bunch for the next 10 teams.

Penners usually work with cows from 450 to 750 pounds, with a herd of uniform size and possibly the same color. Bovine personalities come into play, with the Brahmans just as fast and feisty as in cutting, and the English breeds slower and more docile. Penners may have to work with roping stock, which might resist moving as they wait for the rope.

Time begins when the first horse's nose crosses the start line. It ends when the team has corraled

Team penning requires handy horses, alert riders, team spirit, and luck.

at least one cow (a team can call time with a single cow, or two cows, instead of the desired three), and a rider halts his horse so the horse's nose is in the pen and holds up a hand. All undesignated cattle must be on the cattle side of the start line before time ends.

How the riders read — or misread — cattle makes the sport entertaining to spectators. When a cow switches direction and darts away from a surprised penner, the audience whoops and cheers. Unlike other Western cattle events, when you're penning you may not touch the cattle with ropes, hats, or any equipment. No cattle are injured. If your horse shoves a cow and knocks it down, instead of waiting for it to move out of the way, the judges may disqualify you.

Cattle occasionally decide not to participate at all. If you or your partners "chouse" cattle too much, a tired Hereford might lie down and refuse to move. This puts your team at a real disadvantage, and you'll probably end up with a "no time."

The penning atmosphere is casual, with riders outfitted in working gear. You won't see any polished hooves or braided tails at a penning. Unlike horse shows, you also won't see or hear any trainers coaching their students.

The Team Penning Horse

Team penning doesn't require any special type of horse. Your horse does have to have quick reactions, speed, and cow sense. To handle the intensity of the action, he also needs endurance. A good handle is crucial, especially a horse that stops exactly where you ask him. When you signal for time, your horse earns you a ten-second penalty if he stops with his entire body within the pen!

Your horse should be used to cattle and willing to haze a feisty steer. A steer might turn to challenge him, and he has to go head to head to make the animal move forward or turn. He has to gauge the limits of a cow's personal space, to know how close to crowd it to make it move or when to back off to keep it in place. He knows not to get "right in the cow's face."

Bob Hyatt of the New Mexico Team Penning Association has recommended ranch horses and those with experience in the working cow horse class. "People also use roping horses, or barrel racing horses, too. Usually you have to choose to show or pen with your horse, because few are so well-trained they can do both." Many penners feel that a cutting horse would need retraining for penning,

A penning horse needs endurance and familiarity with cattle.

because he's been trained to stay back from a cow and keep it in one spot without pushing it to move.

Divisions of Penners

To equalize the contest, penners compete in divisions. AQHA specifies three classes of all-age youth, amateur, and all-age open. Various team penning associations have developed number systems that handicap a team. This matches teams by ability, although the distinctions among pennings can be confusing.

Briefly, the USTPA holds pennings for youth, open, pro-am, and novice. Like team ropers, you earn a classification. The American Team Penning Championships rates riders from 1 to 4, so you compete against penners of equal skill. Beginners are 1, Novices are 2, Intermediates are 3, and Professionals are 4.

You can get your first card free, by completing a Team Penners Criteria Form about your experience and your horse's ability. You must include a reference who can verify you and your horse's abilities. You receive a computerized number, so you

can join with teammates in specific penning. The total ratings of the three penners cannot exceed the penning's designated number. For example, a USTPA Novice #4 penning can include two penners rated 1 and one rated 2. A USTPA Pro-Am #6 penning requires two lower-rated penners to compete with one open (considered professional) penner.

Other categories include the World Championship Team Penning Association's Limited Team Division (LTD), a step above novice, or the Mixed Penning. Here the team has to include both genders and one LTD person. Mixing penner ratings encourages the formation of teams that include riders of greater and lesser abilities.

Team Penning Strategy

When you're new to penning, separating cantankerous cattle, guiding them toward the pen, and getting all three into the pen pose a challenge. Your team may guide two to the pen, and while you try to cut the third, the first two can sneak out to rejoin the herd. Often buddies will join the one cow

Team penning of cantankerous cattle poses a problem. The team may guide two to the pen, but while cutting the third, the first two can sneak out to rejoin the herd.

Penning Variations

In one-on-one, you pen one cow by yourself. Different associations describe variations, but usually officials will plug the alley by setting up panels or moving the pen right up against the arena. You have from one to two minutes, depending on the association's rules, to separate your cow and pen it. Usually one-on-one is run after the conclusion of the usual three-person penning.

Cattle sorting involves a team of three riders separating cattle in numerical order. California penner Pete Loftin describes the event. "I think of it as about half penning and half cutting. It's a fun, competitive event that takes only ten head of cattle at a time, and it's a little easier on the critters, too!"

Your team has 90 seconds to sort cattle and get all ten of them lined up in sequence. You might start at any number, say #3 or #4, and go from there. You drive them across the start line (marked from 65 to 75 feet from the cattle end) in numerical order. The team with the most total cattle and least time wins. Any cow out of order gives you a "no time."

you're trying to cut, and if a total of four (some associations say five) cattle cross the foul line, your team is disqualified.

Team penner Peggy Lewis describes the sport as "sheer skill, and a lot of luck. You can't figure it. Every run is different; you have 30 individual personalities to deal with and your team of three. The biggest challenge is learning to read cattle. It's obvious that most of us don't have that opportunity, so working cowboys do have an advantage."

Whatever your teammates' abilities, you have to work as a team. You might work frequently with the same riders, so you know who works best in what role. Or you might join a team minutes before you enter the arena. Lewis says: "The longer you

work together, the better your team gets. But you can come out and team with perfect strangers."

Time is a factor. Penning started with a two-minute limit, now reduced to 90 seconds in many association rules. The shorter time speeds up the competition and reduces wear on the cattle. Good times can be amazingly fast, such as 38 or even 22 seconds. And a lot of penners end up with a score of no-time, especially with wild cows that run back to the herd at least once or when a bunch decide to run across the foul line. You'll also get a no-time if a wrong-numbered cow ends up in the pen when your team calls for time.

Teams usually agree on a game plan, which varies according to the cattle. Larger, heavier cows can't be chased too hard, or they'll sull up. Wilder cows require a lighter touch, so they don't high-tail it back to the herd or run right over your horse.

Penning includes three segments: herd entry, separating, and penning. All three riders try to spot the prey as you enter the herd, but one rider, called the "cutter," usually enters the herd first. (Cattle wear large numbers on their sides.) The other two herd holders can wait to "catch" steers "passed" to them, turn back the cattle they don't want, and prevent the herd from scattering. With many teams, the first into the herd is the most skilled penner.

Another approach, with quiet cattle, is to "shotgun" the penners into the herd, one after another, to "feather" (spread out) and then peel out the desired cattle. Successful teams have a leader, usually the most aggressive rider on the best cow horse. This person yells commands to the other two penners. You'll probably start out as a herd holder, and you'll need to stay in the right place at the right time. Sometimes you need to block a cow. Other times you drive forward, or let one pass by.

Ideally, your team can send two separated cows down toward the pen, and they'll remain behind you while you get the final one. Then all three of you gallop to the pen to take up positions there. If an escapee happens to bolt toward the herd, block its attempt and turn it back before it crosses the foul line.

The Rodeo Queen

Many rodeos, fairs, breed associations, and community groups sponsor queen contests. To win the title, the aspiring monarch must demonstrate her knowledge of horses and her horsemanship abilities. She gains honor and applause by combining beauty and poise with riding skills. The queen has to enjoy performing before an audience and look good doing it. As an equestrian, an actress, and a spokesperson, her duties include riding in parades, fairs, and rodeos.

In most cases, a queen reigns for a year. The Queen of queens, Miss Rodeo America, acts as rodeo's goodwill ambassador, traveling more than 100,000 miles during her reign to appear at over 100 rodeos and special events. The National Little Britches Rodeo Association chooses a queen in each age division, 8 to 13 years, and 14 to 18 years.

Every queen competition involves three or more phases, where judges evaluate candidates both in and out of the saddle. They rate candidates on horsemanship, personality, and poise.

The queen must be a good rider to bear the American flag in a parade or lead the rodeo's grand entry. Rodeos don't expect her to ride rough stock or perform trick riding, but they don't want her to ride in a sloppy "cowgirl" style either.

The horsemanship phase often requires candidates to perform on the rail (Western Pleasure), a horsemanship pattern, and a two-minute freestyle routine to music. The competition ends with the crowning of the new queen and her attendants. The panel may name Miss Congeniality, Miss Personality, Miss Horsemanship, the first attendant, the second attendant, and finally the Queen herself. She then gallops the arena and salutes the cheering crowd during the traditional "Queen's Run."

Rodeo queens dream of the Miss Rodeo America pageant, held during the National Finals Rodeo every December. Miss Rodeo America performs in the media spotlight across the nation as a representative of the sport.

The pageant includes appearances, photo sessions, speeches, and private interviews, in addition to the horsemanship contest. They're asked questions on horsemanship, rodeo, and current events.

The American Quarter Horse Association (AQHA) sponsors the horsemanship contest by funding a trophy saddle and the Quarter Horses used in the competition. Horsemanship includes two go-rounds, with each pattern chosen from the pageant's rulebook by the reigning Miss Rodeo America. Each contestant draws a horse for each go-round, and she may not ride the same horse twice. She goes in cold, as members of the Miss Rodeo America Horsemanship Committee warm up the horses before the contestants ride. The current Miss Rodeo America demonstrates the chosen pattern.

Every queen performs throughout her reign by presenting awards, doing interviews with the media, and making speeches. As an articulate young equestrian, she represents equestrian sport and the Western lifestyle.

Your leader makes the decision to call for time, which might be at the 30-second warning buzzer. He'll yell, "Pen 'em!" maybe with only two cattle in the pen. Three cattle penned always places over two, and two place higher than one, regardless of time.

If your team isn't one of the first to go, you enjoy a slight advantage. You can note which numbers previous teams have penned, and keep an eye on the leftover (numbers not yet called) cows. After each work, watch the settlers regroup the herd.

Like other timed events, the clock determines the placings. Most pennings follow an award system similar to roping, with different schemes to divide the cash prizes among go-rounds, finals, and average. Even those penners who are out of the money gain satisfaction with a job well done.

Appendices

CYNTHIA MCFARLAND

THE
WESTERN
HORSE

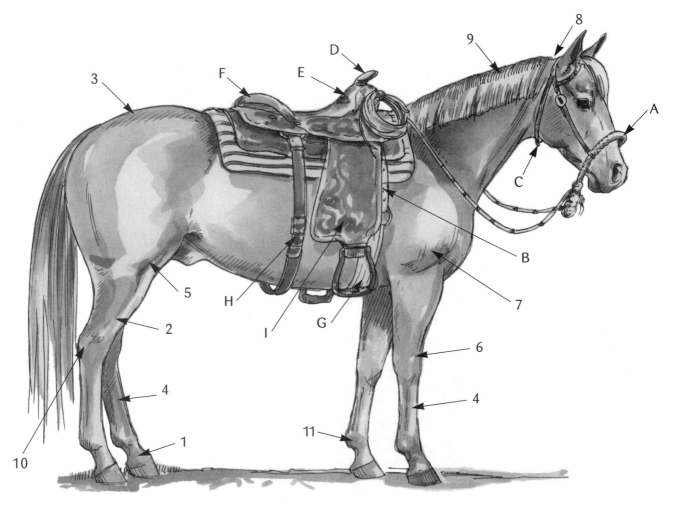

Tack Components

A Bosal
B Billett (also called "latigo")
C Throat latch
D Horn
E Pommel
F Cantle
G Cinch
H Flank billet
I Fender

Anatomy

1 Pastern
2 Gaskin
3 Croup
4 Cannon Bones
5 Stifle
6 Knee

7 Elbow
8 Poll
9 Crest
10 Point of Hock
11 Fetlock

Parts of the Hoof

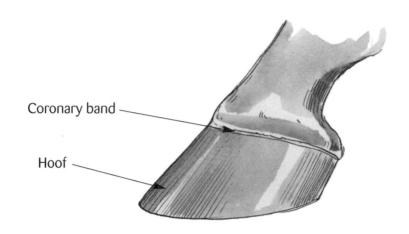

Coronary band

Hoof

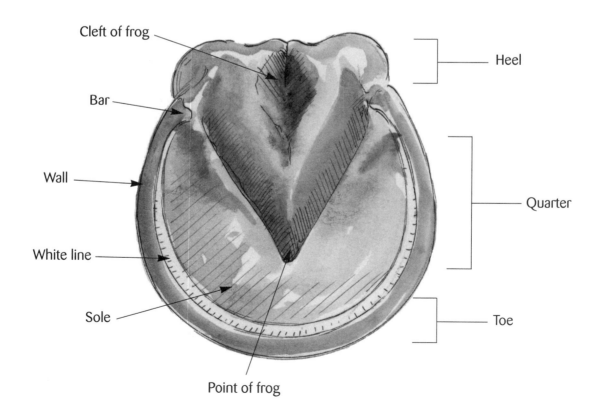

Cleft of frog

Bar

Wall

White line

Sole

Point of frog

Heel

Quarter

Toe

Glossary

Aids. Your signals; how you communicate with the horse.

Bars. Inside the horse's mouth, the gums between the incisors and the molars.

Bosal. A noseband of plaited rawhide, used as the controlling device in the hackamore.

Box. To hold or contain a cow in a certain area. Also, the roper's box.

Bridle. To maintain contact with the reins so the horse moves "in a frame" and "on the bit."

Bridle path. A clipped section of the mane, starting behind the ears.

Brindle dun. A dun body color with darker streaks.

Broke. Trained and reliable.

Bull pen. A training corral, also called a "round" pen.

Bump. To pull and release the reins for a brief contact with the horse's mouth.

Burner. A rawhide section on a rope, covering the eye of the hondo to protect the rope from wear.

Catch rope. A rope for catching cattle.

Chrome. Flashy white markings.

Chouse. To chase cattle, also to exhaust them.

Chute. In cattle events, a fenced lane that contains a single cow behind a gate.

Closed reins. Two reins connected to each other by a long, flexible quirt, the romal.

Coggins certificate. A veterinarian's document that certifies the horse free of the disease, equine infectious anemia.

Collect. To coordinate the horse's moving forward with impulsion while shortening the frame for slow motion.

Cone. A red vinyl traffic cone, used as a marker.

Consignor. The person who consigns a horse for sale or puts it up for auction.

Crupper. A strap that secures the saddle on a mule, running from the back of the saddle and under the mule's tail. Used only in trail riding.

Dally. To wind the rope end around the saddle horn.

Diagonal. At the trot, the movement of the horse's right and left shoulders. The rider posts with either diagonal. Also, a diagonal aid, such as inside rein and outside leg.

Double. To bend the horse sharply.

Drag. To hang back. Also, at the end of a column of riders, to "ride drag" or be a "drag rider."

Drop the shoulder. To shift weight on the forehand and lean too much to the inside during a turn.

Easyboot. A brand name for a vinyl boot that encloses the horse's hoof.

Engage. To shift weight to the hindquarters, to work off the hindquarters and stride forward with the hind legs.

Face. The horse's head. Also, to turn toward a cow.

Flank. In roping, to hold a calf by its flank and leg and place it on its side.

Flex. To bend the horse to the inside. Also, to give in the poll and yield to rein contact.

Flexion. A bend to the inside of a turn.

Flying change. A change of lead at the lope, without slowing to the trot.

Forehand. The horse's shoulders and front legs.

Four-beat. An incorrect lope, where the horse strikes the ground in a broken rhythm.

Futurity. A show class or event open to young horses that owners have nominated.

Go-round. A preliminary round. Some events have two or three go-rounds, and scores are averaged.

Ground tie. To stand in one place, with reins dropped on the ground.

Grulla. A dun body color that ranges from bluish gray to a brownish gray.

Gymkhana. A program of competitive games on horseback, usually timed events.

Hackamore. A bridle that uses a bosal.

Half hitch. A knot, also called a "hooey."

Header. In team roping, this rider ropes the steer's horns.

Headstalls. Another name for bridles.

Heeler. In team roping, this rider ropes the steer's heels.

High lope. A gallop.

Hobbles. Rope, cloth, or leather loops that fasten the forelegs together.

Hogtie. To tie three legs with a narrow rope.

Hondo. The eye on the end of a rope that forms the loop. Also called "honda."

Hooey. A half-hitch knot.

Impulsion. Forward energy.

In the hole. Third in line to enter the pen; after "on deck."

Inside. In a pen, the side of the horse toward the center.

Jerk. To pull or yank a rope or rein.

Junior. A horse four years old or younger; a rider 18 years or younger.

Kiss. A smacking noise made with the lips, to cue the horse to move forward.

Lateral. A sideways movement. Also, lateral aids, such as outside rein and outside leg.

Lead. During the lope, the horse's legs on one side stride forward first. The legs on one side hit the ground before and forward of the legs on the other side.

Legging up. Conditioning a horse's muscle tone by gradually increasing his work.

Long trot. An extended jog; a brisk trot.

Longe. To exercise a horse in a circle on a long lead rope (the longe line).

Loose rein. A slack rein.

Lope. To canter slowly.

Manty. A piece of canvas that encases the load tied on a pack animal.

Mark. To earn a score.

Marker. In reining and horsemanship, a location for the pattern.

Mecate. Braided horsehair reins; knotted to a bosal.

Near side. The horse's left side.

Neck rein. Movement of the rein against the horse's neck cues him to turn. Also called a "brace rein" or "bearing rein."

Neoprene. A synthetic rubber.

Non pro. An amateur, non-professional rider.

Off side. The horse's right side.

On deck. Next to go in the pen.

Outside. In a pen, the side of the horse toward the fence.

Overo. A Paint or Pinto coat pattern of spots that are irregular, scattered, or splashy. The horse usually has a large white facial marking as well.

P.A. The public address system in the arena or show pen.

Pattern. A course you follow in certain classes.

Pen. The show ring. Also to corral cattle, as in team penning.

Picket line. Rope tie rail.

Piggin string. A short, narrow rope used to hogtie a calf or steer.

Pitch. To loosen the reins abruptly and completely, or to toss a rope.

Pocket. A comfortable, secure place in the saddle. In timed events, the area where you collect the horse and start your turn around a barrel or pole.

Post. To rise from the saddle in rhythm with the horse's trot.

Prop. In timed events, a pole or barrel.

Quirt. A riding whip with a short handle and a rawhide lash.

Rail. The fenceline, as in a "rail" class.

Reata. A braided leather rope; coiled and fastened to a Western saddle.

Rigging. On a saddle, straps that connect the cinch and the saddle tree.

Romal. A leather quirt, attached to braided leather or rawhide reins, or "closed" reins.

Rope. A running noose. To catch a cow with the noose.

Rowel. A small wheel with points, attached to the shank of a spur.

Sclera. The area of the eye that encircles the cornea, the colored or pigmented portion.

Score. In roping, to break quickly to overtake the cow.

Scotch. In reining, to anticipate a stop by slowing the gallop.

Senior. A horse at least five years old. A rider at least 50 years old.

Serpentine. A winding pattern of loops or half-circles, in which the horse changes directions through the pattern.

Set. To fix, to establish. In cutting or team penning, a group of competitors that use the same group of cattle.

Settle. To group a bunch of cattle into a quiet, compact herd. Riders act as settlers to get the cattle used to horses moving around them.

Side pass. To move sideways, crossing one leg over another.

Slack. Loose rope or reins, or to loosen. In rodeo, the morning or afternoon performance.

Snatch. To jerk the reins sharply.

Steward. A show official who assists the judge in or out of the show pen.

String out. To move without engaging the hindquarters, so hind end looks "strung out" from the forehand.

Sull. To move slowly, to resist moving forward.

Tapadero. A leather hood fixed to the front of the stirrup.

Tiedown. A strap that connects to the noseband and the cinch or breastcollar; a control device to limit the height of the horse's head.

Tobiano. A Paint and Pinto coat pattern of spots that are regular and distinct.

Tovero. A Paint coat pattern that has markings of both the overo and the tobiano.

Track. A path. Also to follow.

Transition. Upward, the horse moves at a faster pace. Downward, the horse changes to a slower gait.

Two hand. To ride with one rein in each hand.

Two point. To rise from the saddle, so you contact the horse with only your thighs, not your seat.

Two-track. A lateral movement, where the horse's forefeet and hind feet move on separate tracks. Also called the half-pass.

Associations

BREED ASSOCIATIONS

American Buckskin Registry
  Association
PO Box 3850
Redding, CA 96049-3850
916-223-1420

American Paint Horse
  Association
PO Box 961023
Fort Worth, TX 76161
817-439-3400

American Quarter Horse
  Association
PO Box 200
Amarillo, TX 79168
806-376-4888

Appaloosa Horse Club
PO Box 8403
Moscow, ID 83843
208-882-5578

International Buckskin Horse
  Association, Inc.
PO Box 268
Shelby, IN 46377
219-552-1013

National Quarter Pony
  Association, Inc.
PO Box 922
Galion, OH 44833
419-468-6591

Palomino Horse Breeders of
  America, Inc.
15253 E. Skelly Drive
Tulsa, OK 74116-2620
918-438-1234

Pinto Horse Association of
  America, Inc.
1900 Samuels Ave.
Fort Worth, TX 76102-1141
817-336-7842

Pony of the Americas Club, Inc.
5240 Elmwood Ave.
Indianapolis, IN 46203
317-788-0107

Spanish-Barb Breeders
  Association
PO Box 641
Lyons, CO 80540
303-823-0407

Spanish Mustang Registry, Inc.
Route 3, Box 7670
Willcox, AZ 85643
602-384-2886

Show/Contest Associations

American Endurance Ride
  Conference
701 High Street, Suite 203
Auburn, CA 95603
916-823-2260

American Horse Shows
  Association
220 East 42nd Street
New York, NY 10017-5876
212-972-2472

American Team Penning
  Championships
1776 Montano Road NW,
Bldg. #3
Albuquerque, NM 87107
505-344-1776

International Halter-Pleasure
  Quarter Horse Association
256 N. Highway 377
Pilot Point, TX 76258
817-686-9390

National Barrel Horse
  Association
PO Box 1988
Augusta, GA 30903-1988
706-722-7223

National Cutting Horse
  Association
4704 Highway 377 South
Fort Worth, TX 76116
817-244-6188

National Reined Cow Horse
  Association
1318 Jepsen
Corcoran, CA 93212
209-992-9396

National Reining Horse
  Association
448 Main Street, Suite 204
Coshocton, OH 43812
614-623-0055

National Saddle Clubs
  Association
3031 York Road
Helena, MT 59601
406-227-5796

National Snaffle Bit Association
One Indiana Square, Suite 2540
Indianapolis, IN 46204
317-632-NSBA

North American Trail Ride
  Conference
PO Box 20315
El Cajon, CA 92021
619-58TRAIL

U.S. Team Penning
  Association, Inc.
PO Box 161848
Fort Worth, TX 76161-1848
1-800-848-3882
817-439-0010

U.S. Team Roping
  Championships, Inc.
PO Box 7651
Albuquerque, NM 87194
505-899-1870

World Champion Team
  Penning
2460 Cloverdale Road
Escondido, CA 92027
619-743-2377

Youth Show and Contest Associations

Intercollegiate Horse Show
  Association
PO Box 741
Stony Brook, NY 11790-0741
516-751-2803

National 4-H Council
7100 Connecticut Avenue
Chevy Chase, MD 20815-4999
301-961-2959

National Future Farmers of
  America Foundation
PO Box 45205
Madison, WI 53744-5205
608-829-3105

National High School Rodeo
  Association, Inc.
11178 North Huron, Suite 7
Denver, CO 80234
303-452-0820

National Intercollegiate Rodeo
  Association
1815 Portland Avenue, #3
Walla Walla, WA 99362
509-529-4402

National Little Britches Rodeo
  Association
1045 West Rio Grande
Colorado Springs, CO 80906
719-389-0333

Ride and Tie Association
1865 Indian Valley Road
Novato, CA 94947
415-897-1829

References

RULEBOOKS

American Endurance Ride Conference, Endurance Riders Handbook

American Buckskin Registry Association, Official Handbook, 1991

American Endurance Ride Conference, Rules and Regulations for Endurance Riding, 1992

American Horse Shows Association Rule Book, 1994–1995

American Paint Horse Association, Official Rule Book, 1993

American Quarter Horse Association, Official Handbook, 1993

American Team Penning Championships, 1994 Rules

Appaloosa Horse Club, Official Handbook, 1993–1994

International Buckskin Horse Association, Inc., Official Handbook, 1991–1992

National Cutting Horse Association, Rule Book, 1993

National High School Rodeo Association, Rules, Constitution, and By-Laws, 1993–1994

National Little Britches Rodeo Association, Revised Official Rule Book, 1993–1994

National Reining Horse Association, Handbook, 1993

National Saddle Clubs Association, O-Mok-See 1994 Rules and Regulations

National Snaffle Bit Association, Official Handbook, 1993

North American Trail Ride Conference, Rule Book, 1992

Palomino Horse Breeders of America, Inc., Official Handbook, 1994

Pinto Horse Association of America, Inc., Official Handbook, 1992

U.S. Team Roping Championships, Inc., 1994 Rules

Books on Western Riding

General

Foreman, Monte, and Patrick Wyse. *Monte Foreman's Horse-Training Science.* University of Oklahoma, 1983.

Jones, Suzanne Norton. *Art of Western Riding.* Wilshire, 1966.

Kirksmith, Tommie. *Ride Western Style.* Howell, 1991.

Kirksmith, Tommie. *Western Performance: A Guide for Young Riders.* Howell, 1993.

Mayhew, Bob. *Art of Western Riding.* Howell, 1990.

Strickland, Charlene. *Show Grooming: The Look of a Winner,* second edition. Breakthrough, 1994.

Strickland, Charlene. *Tack Buyers Guide.* Breakthrough, 1988.

Tellington-Jones, Linda, and Ursula Bruns. *Introduction to the Tellington-Jones Equine Awareness Method.* Breakthrough, 1988.

Specific Disciplines

Back, Joe. *Horses, Hitches, and Rocky Trails.* Johnson Publishing Company, 1959.

Camarillo, Leo. *Team Roping.* Western Horseman, 1982.

Camarillo, Sharon. *Barrel Racing.* Western Horseman, 1985.

Cooper, Roy. *Calf Roping.* Western Horseman, 1984.

Dunning, Al. *Reining.* Western Horseman, 1983.

Elser, Smoke, and Bill Brown. *Packin' In on Mules and Horses.* Mountain Press, 1980.

Freeman, Bill. *Cutting.* EquiMedia, 1994.

Harrel, Leon. *Cutting.* Western Horseman, 1989.

Harrison, Sally. *Cutting: A Guide for the Non-Pro Competitor.* Howell, 1992.

Loomis, Bob. *Reining: The Art of Performance in Horses.* EquiMedia, 1990.

Paulo, Karen. *America's Long Distance Challenge.* Trafalgar Square, 1990.

Shrake, Richard. *Western Horsemanship.* Western Horseman, 1987.

Index

Page references in *italics* indicate illustrations.

Storey Publishing/Garden Way Publishing Horse Titles

Becoming an Effective Rider: Developing Your Mind and Body for Balance and Unity by Cherry Hill

From the Center of the Ring: An Inside View of Horse Competition by Cherry Hill

Horsekeeping on a Small Acreage: Facilities Design and Management by Cherry Hill

Horse Sense: A Complete Guide to Horse Selection and Care by John J. Mettler, Jr., D.V.M.

The Illustrated Guide to Horse Tack by Susan McBane

101 Arena Exercises: A Ringside Guide for Horse & Rider by Cherry Hill

Safe Horse, Safe Rider: A Young Rider's Guide to Responsible Horsekeeping by Jessie Haas

Your Horse: A Step-by-Step Guide to Horse Ownership by Judy Chapple

Your Pony, Your Horse: A Kid's Guide to Care and Enjoyment by Cherry Hill

These books are available at your bookstore, tack shop, or they may be ordered directly from Storey Communications, Inc., Department WM, Schoolhouse Road, Pownal, Vermont 05261.

To order toll-free by phone, call 800-441-5700.